Hospitality Experience

An introduction to hospitality management

Editors:
Frans Melissen
Jean-Pierre van der Rest
Stan Josephi
Rob Blomme

Authors:
**Rob Blomme, Jeroen Bosman, Hans Breuker, Michael Chibili,
John Hornby, Stan Josephi, Alinda Kokkinou, Annemieke de Korte,
Xander Lub, Frans Melissen, Rob Nierse, Jeroen Oskam,
Monique van Prooijen-Lander, Bert Smit, Lesley Tomaszewski,
Rolf van der Veer, Tjeerd Zandberg**

First edition

Noordhoff Uitgevers Groningen/Houten

Cover design: Rocket Industries, Groningen
Cover illustration: iStock

If you have any comments or queries about this publication, please contact:
Noordhoff Uitgevers bv, Afdeling Hoger Onderwijs, Antwoordnummer 13, 9700VB
Groningen, The Netherlands. E-mail: info@noordhoff.nl

The greatest care has been taken in the preparation of this publication. The authors,
editors and publishers cannot be held liable in case any information has been
published incompletely or incorrectly. If you feel that your rights as a copyright owner
have been infringed, please contact Noordhoff Uitgevers bv. They will be pleased to
receive any adjustments to the contents.

MIX
Papier van
verantwoorde herkomst
FSC
www.fsc.org   FSC® C118189

0 / 14

© 2014 Noordhoff Uitgevers bv, Groningen/Houten, The Netherlands

ISBN 978-90-01-81385-7
NUR 801

Preface

Most textbooks on hospitality management focus on explaining – in detail – the ins and outs of today's hospitality industry. They usually focus on hotels and how the various departments of traditional hotels function and interrelate. For instance, how do the banqueting department and the front office relate to each other, and what responsibilities do their managers have, and so on. As important as the answers may be, they are not the main topic of this book. As the editors and authors of *Hospitality Experience*, we would never claim that we could do a better job of answering these questions than the makers of other textbooks already out there.

However, we do like to think that *Hospitality Experience* will be a valuable addition to the collection of books now available to you to explore and reflect on important aspects of your current or future role as hospitality manager. As its title suggests, this book is about hospitality experiences. In it we answer one main question: **how do you design, stage and manage successful hospitality experiences?**

We discuss why we feel the answer deserves special attention throughout the book. It is what makes this book different. Like other hospitality management texts, it reflects on the now and future hospitality industry and the roles and responsibilities of hospitality managers. However, this book continually links these discussions to the crucial role of experiences in today's highly competitive and ever-changing market. This allows us to predict why some hospitality businesses and managers will likely be more successful than others. It allows us to explain how other perspectives, not just a managerial one, can help in designing, staging and managing hospitality experiences both in and outside the hospitality industry. Finally, it allows us to establish what it all means for hospitality management and define the competencies required to excel in this profession.

Hospitality Experience is the result of collaboration between our publisher, Noordhoff Publishers, and all five hotel management schools in the Netherlands. Please allow me to thank my fellow editors, Jean-Pierre van der Rest, Stan Josephi and Rob Blomme. In turn, the four of us are grateful to Noordhoff's Ageeth Bergsma for making this book happen and our special thanks go to all the authors and reviewers from the Dutch hotel management schools. Without you, *Hospitality Experience* would not exist. Finally, we would like to welcome you – our reader – to our views on hospitality management. We hope you feel a welcome guest in our 'train of thought' and that you enjoy and value the experience!

Frans Melissen
Breda, March 2014

Contents

Effective learning

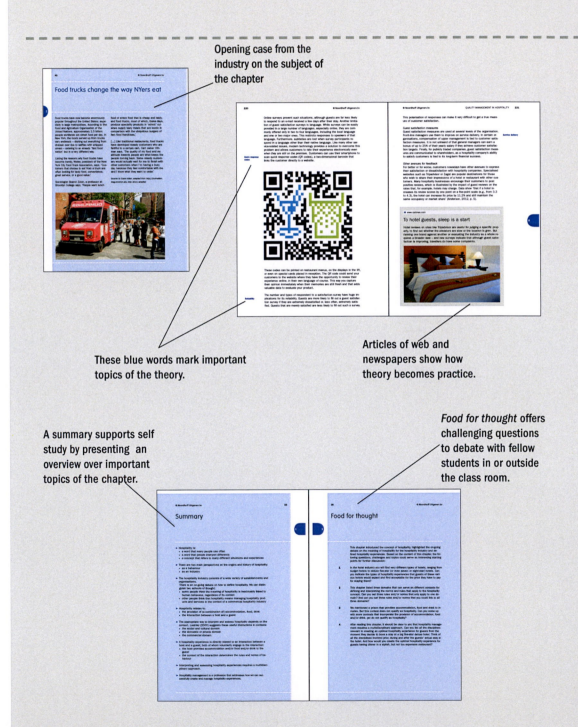

Opening case from the industry on the subject of the chapter

These blue words mark important topics of the theory.

Articles of web and newspapers show how theory becomes practice.

A summary supports self study by presenting an overview over important topics of the chapter.

Food for thought offers challenging questions to debate with fellow students in or outside the class room.

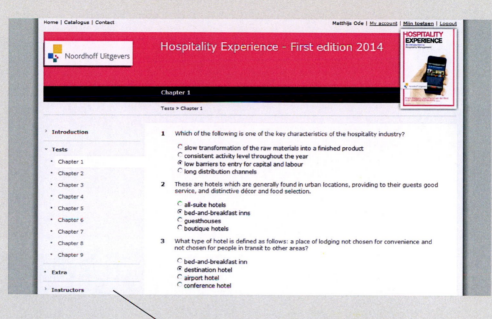

Test questions support comprehension of concepts and definitions. The given feedback and study advice refer to sections in the text book.

1

The concept of hospitality

Frans Melissen

This first chapter introduces you to the origins and history of the concept of hospitality and the on-going debate in academia on the meaning of hospitality. We use the lessons that can be learnt from this to define hospitality experiences and explain our approach towards managing hospitality experiences. Finally, we provide an overview of the contents and explain the links between the remaining chapters of this book.

1

Quotable quotes on hospitality

Here is a selection of quotes on hospitality that you will find if you type in the words *memorable*, *quotes,* and *hospitality* in a Google search:

'Christmas is a season for kindling the fire for hospitality in the hall, the genial flame of charity in the heart.'
— Washington Irving

'The hospitality of the wigwam is only limited by the institution of war.'
— Charles Eastman

'I've got high standards when it comes to boys. As my dad says, all girls should! I'm from the South – Tennessee, to be exact – and down there, we're all about southern hospitality. I know that if I like a guy, he better be nice, and above all, my dad has to approve of him!'
— Miley Cirus

'When hospitality becomes an art it loses its very soul.'
— Max Beerbohm

'No, Sir, you will have much more influence by giving or lending money where it is wanted, than by hospitality.'
— Samuel Johnson

'When I sell liquor, it's called bootlegging; when my patrons serve it on Lake Shore Drive, it's called hospitality.'
— Al Capone

'Hospitality is making your guests feel at home, even though you wish they were.'
— unknown

'In hospitality, the chief thing is the goodwill.'
— Greek proverb

Al Capone: the godfather of hospitality?

1.1 Hospitality?

Hospitality is a fascinating word we all use regularly. We all seem to have some sort of shared understanding of its meaning. Indeed, in our business – the hospitality industry – it is our shared reference point, *the* characteristic that distinguishes us from *others*. Many of us associate hospitality with particular emotions. This is why some quotes that kick off this chapter refer to things like the heart, the soul, and goodwill. If someone comments on a hotel or restaurant, for instance on a customer reviews site on the internet, in terms of 'hospitality seems to be something unknown to them' or 'they lack the basics of hospitality', you would probably think twice before booking a stay or dinner. Interestingly enough, many of us would feel confident we made the right decision not to book, even without information on the quality of the hotel's rooms or the restaurant's food. Somehow, the room and the food are not all that matters. Sometimes they are not the deciding factor for customers' purchasing decisions, even if you could argue that they do represent the actual product on offer.

Shared understanding

Particular emotions

Ultimately, whether you are willing to pay for a room or food is determined by something more than objective facts and figures about that room or food. That something is usually related to what we call hospitality. Many of us feel perfectly comfortable using hospitality as an important consideration in our final decision. The fact that hospitality might be hard to define or to measure does not change that. An engineer would probably not get that. A scientist might accuse you of basing your decision on subjective data. An economist would tell you that your decision makes no sense without a proper cost/benefit analysis. And a hotel manager? He would tell you that you are right. He would have no problem referring to hospitality as the reason why you are willing to book a room in his hotel.

Hospitality

Hospitality is not just a word

The previous section concluded that we all have a sort of shared understanding of what hospitality means. However, you could question whether this really is true. It is difficult to explain the exact meaning of hospitality and provide a definition that we all would agree with. In fact, ask ten people to define hospitality and you would probably get ten explanations. To understand this we need to realise that hospitality is not just a *word*; it also represents a *concept*. A concept is not something that you can point to or touch or take into your hands. A concept is something intangible that exists only in our minds. That is why most dictionaries define it as something conceived in the mind, as an abstract or generalised idea that relates to the characteristics of a particular object of thought. Hospitality is such an object of thought.

Concept

A key element of this explanation of concept is *generalised*. Concepts are not just ideas but *generalised* ideas. They do not describe just one instance of something, but rather what various instances have in common. To illustrate what this means, consider the concept of love. Once again, it is probably clear to most of us what this concept refers to. It is some sort of emotion. Love has something to do with affection and attachment. However, you can use the concept of love in various contexts. For instance, you could say you love your girlfriend or your mother. However, you can also love Christmas or a book or a boy band. You can love the colour green, or love doing nothing on a Sunday morning, or even love reading books on the concept of

Contexts

hospitality. All these examples refer to the same concept, but that same concept is applied in very different contexts. The concept stays the same, but the situations and actions it refers to are different. The same applies to the concept of hospitality.

1

● gulfnews.com

Jumeirah to be hospitality partner for Ladies Masters

Dubai: Dubai-based luxury hospitality company, Jumeirah, has joined hands with 'golf in DUBAi' as the official caterer and hospitality partner for the Omega Dubai Ladies Masters, at the Emirates Golf Club from December 14-17.

'We believe that "golf in DUBAi" plays an important role in the development and promotion of this exhilarating game in our city. We are proud to be associated with them, and the quality of professional golfers and spectator experience that they bring to Dubai,' said Thatcher Brown, Jumeirah's vice president of brand strategy and management.

Mohammad Juma Bu Amim, vice-chairman and CEO of 'golf in DUBAi', said: 'The Omega Dubai Ladies Masters gives a worldwide exposure to the city and the sponsors, creating interest for people to visit Dubai. Thanks to Jumeirah, the players always have a wonderful opportunity to savour the incomparable hospitality standards of the region.'

December 1, 2011

Golf cupcake

Hospitality is a mystifying concept

However, although the concept of love can relate to very different contexts, you could argue that the basic feelings that are linked to love are always similar. Regardless of context, love refers to positive emotions. It refers to the opposite of hate and to liking something or someone instead of disliking them. Therefore, love is a relatively clear and straightforward concept. The same does *not* apply to hospitality.

Indeed, this is exactly why hospitality is such a mystifying concept. Like any other concept, it can be used in various contexts and, somehow, using the concept 'hospitality' to describe what is happening does seem to help us to interpret the situation. However, unlike love, hospitality can refer to highly dissimilar emotions. For example, consider these two types of companies that operate in the hospitality industry:

Mystifying

Emotions

1 The first type is a chain of hotels that goes by the name Historic Hotels of America. These hotels are all about recreating and reliving the atmosphere of times long gone. To be part of this chain, a hotel must be at least 50 years old and must have historic significance. One hotel in this chain is the Wentworth Mansion. A quick tour of the website tells us that it offers 21 guest rooms and suites with antique furnishings, carved marble fireplaces, and oversized whirlpool tubs. Here, hospitality relates to such things as enjoying a book on the secrets of the history of the region you are visiting, sitting in a comfortable leather chair in front of a crackling fire, conveniently located just where the waiters can and will keep an eye on the level of bourbon in your glass.

Interior of the Wentworth Mansion

2 The second type of company relates to the growing number of hotels and restaurants that offer guests the opportunity to experience *dining in the dark*. This concept originated in Switzerland in the early 1990s and has quickly spread over Europe and, more recently, is attracting attention in the USA. Hotels and restaurants offering these dinners usually refer to it as a unique experience. Apparently your taste buds, and senses of smell and hearing are stimulated very differently when your brain does not have to deal with visual stimuli at the same time. Dining in the dark allows guests to taste and experience a meal like they have never done before.

Industry

Experiences

Without going into the details of what exactly is involved in dining in the dark, clearly a dinner like that would be quite different from a stay in the Wentworth Mansion. However, both the Wentworth Mansion and a hotel or restaurant offering dining in the dark are part of the industry dedicated to hospitality. What is more, both will tell you that they offer a unique hospitality experience. And that is where the mystifying, perhaps confusing side of the concept of hospitality comes in. Somehow, the same word can be used in very different contexts to describe very dissimilar experiences and it still makes sense. One and the same concept – hospitality – can refer to an experience based on history, luxury and comfort, supported by artefacts that you appreciate by sight (visual stimuli) and an experience based on surprise and the unexpected, supported by eliminating your sight (visual stimuli) altogether. It is important to note that these situations are just two examples of a much broader collection of very different situations and experiences, in and beyond the hospitality industry. Somehow all are related to the same concept of hospitality. A third example, mentioned earlier in this chapter, is the newsflash on Jumeirah and hospitality at the Dubai Ladies Masters golf tournament. The remainder of this chapter and subsequent chapters provide many more examples of the various ways in which hospitality can be interpreted and applied. Put together, these provide a clear explanation of the rich concept of hospitality, and the diverse situations and interpretations it encompasses. This diversity is why it is so hard to come up with one definition that would fit all situations in which hospitality plays a pivotal role.

● goeurope.about.com

Save yourself some grief, know what the star system means before you go

So you're wandering around Europe and notice stars prominently displayed in front of every hotel. Say you find one that has three stars. What does it mean?

The short answer is: just about anything, but probably not what you're thinking. Let's get one thing straight, there is no unified definition of a three-star hotel across Europe. And another thing: most of the ratings are provided by the government, and will be a quantitative measure used to determine the price range (and sometimes the tax obligation) of a hotel. The ranges will overlap, so don't even look for that much consistency in price; a three star hotel may be more expensive than a four star, even in the same city. It depends.

You can make generalizations about hotel prices and the star ratings. A four star hotel will indeed cost more than a one star in the same city. The four star hotel will have more services and amenities, including meeting space for conferences. The one star will usually be very basic; not all rooms may have bathrooms in them. I usually look for two or three star hotels when I'm traveling in big cities. Today, most offer private baths in the (usually smallish) room and most of the time include television, a phone and occasionally even a mini bar. For a splurge that's often a good bargain, I'll look for a four star hotel in lest touristy areas, especially when it's hot and I want a day with decent air conditioning.

Just remember – the ratings on the outside of the building are based on an objective facilities and services provided assessment and are not in any way related to ambience, charm or other subjective criteria.

By James Martin, adapted

To recognise, understand, and appreciate the various ways of interpreting and assessing hospitality requires a discussion on the origins and history of hospitality. Usually, when people interpret a concept differently, this is a sign that the concept is relatively young and the final description or definition is still open to debate. The latter is certainly true for hospitality. However, this does not mean that hospitality is the new kid on the block. Saying that could not be further from the truth.

1.2 Origins and history

Here we briefly discuss two perspectives on the origins and history of hospitality. The first reviews the origins of hospitality as a type of behaviour, separate from the context in which it takes place. The second looks at the origins and history of the hospitality industry.

Perspectives

Origins of hospitality

1

Hospitality as behaviour (perspective 1)

Hospitality is not a recent trend and, unlike the internet, it is clearly not an invention of our current era. Some people argue that the origins of hospitality can be traced back to our own origins or, more precisely, Homo sapiens (O'Connor, 2005). Hospitality can be seen as a key concept in the way a newcomer tried to claim membership of a group. In offering the food that he has hunted down, a newcomer hopes to establish a relationship with a group so that they will share their food in return. Daniel O'Connor explains in his paper on this topic that similar expressions of hospitality, usually in the form of feasting, can still be found in remote ancient societies, such as those in the New Guinea Highlands and the Amazon rainforest. However, he emphasises that hospitality in these contexts is often closely related to its opposite, hostility. A feast can easily turn into a fight. On the one hand, we can see hospitality and hostility as the extremes of a continuum that represents all possible expressions of a relationship. On the other hand, these two extremes are very closely linked. As the French would put it, *Les extrêmes se touchent*. From the perspective of our 21st century, most of us would probably associate hospitality with pleasant emotions. However, the Charles Eastman quote at the start of this chapter points out that this might be an oversimplification, considering that hospitality can also be linked to the institution of war. All this means that from an historical perspective, hospitality is not just a one-dimensional, happy-go-lucky concept.

**Hostility
Hospitality
Relationship**

Indeed, in medieval times hospitality was a serious topic. To display hospitality was a matter of honour and morality. Julie Kerr (2007) explains in her discussion on hospitality in twelfth-century England that in this era of kings, dukes and knights, people felt greatly concerned with etiquette and outward display. Engaging in hospitality was guided by strict procedures for both hosts and guests. Adhering to these procedures was important, because the act of hospitality was considered a chance for both guest and

**Honour and
morality**

Castle Hotel Adare in Ireland

host to demonstrate their courtliness, improve their relationship, 'and for the host to exhibit his generosity and largesse of spirit' (Kerr 2007, p. 130). The display of generosity is closely related to the central theme of religious parables that tell the story of how one person disguised as poor traveller tests another person's hospitality. In this context, hospitality refers to unselfish commitment and altruism. In other words, it refers to behaviour that shows someone's good intentions and willingness to help others without expecting anything in return. Both Kerr's discussion on medieval times and the religious parables show how, for many centuries, the concept of hospitality was linked to cultural and religious norms for offering a needy stranger a place to stay, and food and drink, without ulterior motive or expecting a reward.

Unselfish commitment and altruism

Cultural and religious norms

'Because you have offered him lodgings he must be protected and safeguarded from capture and death.'

       – Chrétien de Troyes, *The Story of the Grail*,
          in *Arthurian Romances*, translated by
          William W. Kibbler

The cultural or religious norms we referred to above considered hospitality a virtue, or, more precisely, as appropriate behaviour. Clearly, however, these norms 'no longer have the moral force they once had' (Lashley, 2008, p. 83) in today's society. In other words, what people in the past would think of as appropriate behaviour is probably different from how we would assess that behaviour today.

Virtue

● KPI Hospitality Service, 2009

Disguised as a poor traveller, version 2.0?

These two little excerpts from a mystery guest report are a clear example of why many people still consider hospitality a type of behaviour, even in the 21st century hospitality industry. The management of a hotel or restaurant hires mystery guests to visit their sites and provide feedback on their staff's performance, without revealing what they are there to do. After reading these excerpts, ask yourself if this is any different from disguising yourself as a poor traveller, in days long gone, to test your host's hospitality.

'We were having trouble finding the accommodation, so I phoned ahead and asked for directions. A staff member answered with "Good afternoon, X Lodge, *Linda* speaking." When I told *Linda* that we were having trouble finding the right road, she was very understanding and friendly and pointed me in the right direction. She also told me how long it would take me to get there from where we were, which was handy to know. When we drove up to the resort, a staff member noticed our arrival and came out to the car to

1

greet us. She said, "You must be *Mr Smith*?" When I said yes, she shook my hand and introduced herself, "Hello, I'm *Linda*, welcome! You made it okay?" Linda was dressed smartly and looked very presentable. She smiled warmly and was easy to chat to. She was calm and gentle, which made me feel relaxed. She offered to carry our bags and anything else we may have wanted to offload. We chatted casually about the rough drive up to the resort and where the staff resided. *Linda* mentioned that she understood it was our wedding anniversary to which, I said "Yes." She then told us that they had upgraded our room to a spa suite. "It was available tonight, so I put you in there.' We were very grateful.'

'We were served by *Jack*, who was quite helpful. *Jack* directed us to where we would find the bikes and showed us on a map where to go. He advised us on the most suitable ride for that time of day and our level of biking experience. Although *Jack* handled this perfectly, he did not ask if there was anything else he could help us with.'

Adapted

Hospitality behaviour

The first perspective emphasises that hospitality behaviour can be found everywhere and is far from restricted to the hospitality industry. We find it important to study the various situations and learn how hospitality manifests itself. You can then use this knowledge to understand the concept of hospitality and operate successfully in the hospitality industry.

Hospitality as an industry (perspective 2)

In contrast, some people prefer the second perspective, arguing that it is wiser to stick to the hospitality industry in exploring the origins and history of hospitality. They feel it makes no sense to trace the evolution of Homo sapiens or behaviour in the medieval era to assess hospitality in the 21st century. They claim that the history of the actual hospitality industry contains far more important lessons for interpreting, assessing and, especially, managing hospitality in today's world.

In his study on the historical roots of the industry, Kevin O'Gorman (2009) concludes that commercial hospitality has existed for at least 4,000 years. He illustrates this with three examples. The first refers to ancient Mesopotamia, where there were laws governing commercial hospitality as early as 1,800 BC. O'Gorman claims that by 400 BC, commercial hospitality – hostels and inns providing food, drinks, accommodation *and women* to strangers – had evolved into a distinct, separate sector of the economy and a key source of revenue. The second example relates to the Roman city of Pompeii. The fossilised city that remained after Mount Vesuvius' eruption in 79 AD has provided us with clear indications of hospitality industry contours in a Roman-era city. Evidence suggests that various types of hospitality establishments were found in Roman cities, ranging from a *hospitium* (offering rooms for rent, mostly aimed at business guests) and a *popina caupona* (a public eating house) to a *taberna thermopolia ganeae* (a simple counter for selling foods and drinks) and various combinations of these establishments. The commercial motives of these establishments are evident, because even in those days you would find advertisements and a *menu of the day*. The final example O'Gorman discusses is *caravanserais* (hostels for travellers), for instance along the Silk Route (trading routes stretching from Istanbul, through Iran, to China). Once again, it seems that travelling business people created a demand for lodging, food and drinks, which an extensive system of hospitality establishments accommodated.

Commercial hospitality

Lodging, food and drinks

Pompeii

Could both perspectives be true?
Obviously, these are but a few of the establishments and arrangements that could represent *the origins* of today's hospitality industry. Especially the researchers who have studied classical texts will be able to provide us with many more. However, some researchers have suggested that this perspec-

tive on the hospitality industry is rather romantic and might not tell the full story of what actually happened. Clearly, some establishments described above and similar examples from the medieval era bear a close resemblance to today's hotels, restaurants and other accommodations. Most hotels are still about offering rooms for rent to travellers, both business people and tourists. Restaurants still provide food and drink to travellers and local residents. The set up of today's hospitality industry could be argued to be the result of an evolutionary process lasting 4,000 years. It all seems to make perfect sense.

Evolutionary process

The key word in that last sentence, though, is 'perfect'. Maybe it is a bit too perfect to be true. What if the industry is indeed the result of an evolutionary process, but the name chosen to represent it is actually 'an early attempt at spin' (Lashley, 2008, p. 69)? In other words, what if the name *hospitality* industry is actually an attempt at swaying public opinion, much like a spin doctor (the spokesman of a politician) would give us a more positive interpretation of a decision that could damage his boss's reputation. Some people involved in the on-going debate on the origins and interpretation of hospitality certainly seem to think so. They claim that associating the name hospitality to the industry providing food, drink and accommodation in the exchange for money is actually a modern invention. In their view, the choice of this name could be an attempt to 'create a more favourable impression of [the] commercial activities' (Lashley, 2008, p. 69) in this sector of our economy. Earlier, many people concluded that the word hospitality is associated with something like a virtue and, therefore, primarily evokes positive emotions. What better way to market your company than to point out that your primary concern is the well-being of your guests, your customers, instead of making money?

Invention

All this brings us back to a key question that needs answering in a book focused on hospitality management. Does hospitality refer to behaviour, to an industry, or to both? To understand what exactly needs to be managed and how best to do it, we first need to answer this question. Therefore, the following section addresses the on-going debate, especially in academic circles, on the appropriate way to interpret this fascinating, mystifying concept.

1.3 The debate

Section 1.2 pointed out that the word hospitality can be linked to cultural and religious norms, to virtues and morality, and to unselfishness and altruism, but also to an industry that mostly consists of businesses that provide accommodation, food and drink in exchange for money. You could say there are two distinct schools of thought with respect to interpreting and assessing hospitality. On the one hand, we have people interested in discussing the meaning of hospitality in terms of norms that were based on Biblical texts, the world view of the ancient Greeks and the strict behavioural rules for knights in medieval times. This school of thought is primarily interested in understanding hospitality as inextricably linked to human behaviour, regardless of the context in which the behaviour takes place.

Businesses

Schools of thought

Human behaviour

Products and services

On the other hand, we have people who are mostly interested in how best to manage hospitality products and services, such as the provision of accommodation, food and drink, in companies that need to make money to exist. This second school of thought is likely more interested in revenue management to maximise profits based on selling those products and services in a fiercely competitive global market. Given the very different starting points for these two schools of thought, it should come as no surprise that the concept of hospitality is the topic of heated debate among academics, and both academics and practitioners struggle to define it.

Two schools of thought, linked or not?
The next question is whether we should regard these two schools of thought as separate entities that study clearly different unrelated topics, or whether they could actually help and strengthen each other. A central topic of the debate concerns the different answers to that question. What is the relation, if any, between understanding hospitality as a part of human behaviour, and treating hospitality and hospitality management as an industry and profession? Maybe the best way to illustrate the debate content is to highlight the views of two authors mentioned above, Daniel O'Connor and Kevin O'Gorman. Please consider the following four statements:

'Only once an understanding of hospitality's origins and its place in human nature is achieved can one expect to discover what hospitality means today, and more importantly what it will mean to those entering the industry in the future.'
Daniel O'Connor, 2005, p. 267

'However, with the knowledge of such a thin line existing between hospitality and hostility, it is up to the hospitality industry to be wary of it and, if possible, use it to its advantage. In other words, in order to differentiate one's product from the competition, and gain the highly sought competitive advantage, it is essential to eradicate any feelings of paranoia a guest may have.'
Daniel O'Connor, 2005, p. 269

'Hospitality management research should focus on deepening understanding of management practice within the industry, separate from domestic hospitality practices; that is best left to anthropologists and sociologists who have the necessary training and research skills.'
Kevin O'Gorman, 2009, p.788

'There is nothing wrong with providing a commercial hospitality service within particular institutional forms (now called the hospitality industry, but known by an assortment of different names in the past). Hospitality research should focus on deepening understanding of the industry; learning from the past will help to inform the future.'
Kevin O'Gorman, 2009, p.788

At first glance, these statements seem to reflect perspectives that are miles apart with regards to hospitality, the hospitality industry and hospitality management. O'Connor's statements suggest that the hospitality industry can only advance if it focuses on genuine hospitableness, also in recruiting new employees. Here, hospitableness refers to 'service with a smile' and meaning it. Obviously, this perspective is closely related to regarding hospitality as a virtue. Consequently, making your guests feel at home while wishing they were (at home) – the *wise* words often shared with newcomers to the industry by those that have paid their dues – might actually represent *bad*

Genuine hospitableness

advice. Furthermore, this perspective implies that the customers' act of paying for hospitality should be organised and managed such that it minimises the chances of customers feeling *betrayed*.

1

Hospitality management

In contrast, O'Gorman's statements stress that, ultimately, we are dealing with an industry that is mostly made up of *commercial* enterprises. Therefore, it would make perfect sense to consider management the key in the concept of hospitality management. You needn't feel uncomfortable about it being an economic transaction. Goodwill, as the Greek proverb on the first page of this chapter suggests, is all very nice, but, ultimately, we are in it to make money.

Hospitality as a means of making money?

The two views seem at the very least conflicting, and possibly even irreconcilable. If you took O'Connor's and O'Gorman's statements literally, in other words, if you applied *black and white* thinking on them, the heat of the debate on the *true* meaning of the concepts is understandable. However, we had a reason for saying 'at first glance' above. As interesting as the debate may be from a purely intellectual viewpoint, you could say that much of it can be traced back to semantics and simple differences of opinion on the relative importance of various perspectives. This does not necessarily mean that other perspectives are not important or do not deserve further inquiry. Indeed, if we took another look at O'Gorman's first statement, you could say that he is simply suggesting that hospitality researchers and hospitality managers should focus on the things that lie at the core of their discipline, what they have been trained to do. His statement does not imply that researchers from distinct disciplines should not talk to or learn from each other. He does not suggest that hospitality managers could not benefit from the lessons learnt from viewing hospitality as an integral part of human behaviour.

Similarly, O'Connor does not deny that the hospitality industry is a commercial sector. He does not suggest that making a profit from providing hospitality (services or products) is unacceptable. His statements simply acknowledge that the concept of hospitality is closely linked to human nature and to what people feel is acceptable behaviour. Smart hospitality managers realise that these matters are important aspects to consider in the context of the hospitality industry and hospitality management.

Human nature

Acceptable behaviour

1

Context is the key

Maybe the key to reconciling the two perspectives is to realise that the hospitality industry is made up of a vast array of very different types of hospitality establishments and activities. Obviously, you cannot compare a quick meal in a fast food outlet around the corner with a stay in a Hilton or Marriott hotel. Going for the experience of a dinner in the dark is very different from buying food and having a quick shower at a (gas) station along your route through the Australian outback. The feelings and emotions related to various activities are quite different and the reasons why customers engage in them are different. Surely, all establishments can be considered parts of *the hospitality industry*. However, it is just as clear that they are very different and provide hospitality in different ways and circumstances.

So, the hospitality industry consists of various establishments and activities with clearly distinct characteristics. It is reasonable to assume that there is more than one way to interpret and assess hospitality in relation to all these establishments and activities.

Accommodation, food, drink and...

All this means that we need to consider *context* in a final verdict on the appropriate perspective on hospitality. What is more, context plays a vital role in determining whether the provision of any combination of elements in the 'holy trinity' (Brotherton, 1999) of *accommodation, food, and drink* should be regarded as engaging in an act of hospitality or not. Brotherton (1999) uses the example of prisons to clarify this in his discussion on hospitality and hospitality management. A prison provides accommodation, food and drink to inmates. If we define hospitality as simply the provision of any one or a combination of the three elements, as some authors suggest, the prison service would qualify as hospitality. Yet instinctively or intellectually, most of us would probably not agree with this verdict. Consequently, some contributors to the hospitality debate suggest that we need to add another criterion related to the *manner* in which accommodation, food and drink are provided. What if the prison guards and catering personnel happen to be genuinely hospitable people? Would this mean that the cells given to inmates and the catering services provided to them would suddenly qualify this prison as hospitable? Again, for most of us this would not feel right. This seems to be very different from the fascinating, mystifying concept we discussed earlier in this chapter.

Context

Holy trinity

Hosts and guests

Brotherton's (1999) second important point is that the relationship between hosts and guests lies at the core of the concept. No matter the circumstances, hospitality acts cannot exist without the involvement of people. One person or group – the host – offers hospitality to another person or group – the guest. In some situations guests compensate their hosts for hospitality received. For in-

Host

Guest

Host-guest relationships

stance, a hotel guest pays to stay in a room, while a restaurant customer pays to have dinner. You would often find these host-guest relationships in the commercial hospitality industry. However, there are instances of hospitality that do not involve the exchange of money. A clear example is when you offer a friend, or even a stranger, a place to stay or a meal in times of need without expecting financial reward for your act of hospitality. These acts are usually referred to as domestic hospitality.

Three different domains

Based on the discussion so far, we can conclude that

1 hospitality is the provision of (a combination of) accommodation, food, drink *and* involves a host and a guest
2 there are various kinds of hospitality and depending on the context, there are different ways to interpret and assess it.

Domains

It is useful to distinguish between different acts of hospitality, involving different hosts and guests in different contexts. Conrad Lashley (2000) suggested the three domains of hospitality depicted in Figure 1.1. We can use these domains as a framework for interpreting and studying the concept of hospitality. Ever since Lashley put his framework forward, many academics and practitioners have referred to it in debating the meaning and implications of hospitality.

FIGURE 1.1 Three domains of hospitality

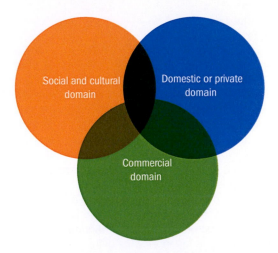

Social and cultural level

The *first domain* relates to the *social and cultural* level. It provides the context for studying and interpreting cultural and religious norms, the rules and obligations connected to eras and societies, and also, for instance, the relationships between a *host* nation and *guests* in the form of asylum seekers and migrants. At this level we could assess the impact of tourists on local residents, the host community in the tourism context. Obviously, this could have interesting implications for hospitality management, because many of these tourist establishments are part of the hospitality industry, and many employees working in them are members of the host community.

The *second domain* is the *domestic or private* level and deals with hospitality in home settings. Offering a free bed to a friend in need is a clear example of hospitality in this domain. This domain is also linked to hospitality management and the hospitality industry. For instance, home-owners offering students a room for rent, or people who turn their homes into a small bed and breakfast establishment.

Domestic or private level

1

● newsfeed.time.com

NYC judge rules Airbnb rental is an 'illegal hotel'

Airbnb, a site that lets people around the world find short-term housing accommodations, suffered a major setback this month when a judge ruled that one of its users broke an 'illegal hotel' law in New York City.

The trouble began last September, when Nigel Warren rented out his bedroom in his East Village apartment on Airbnb for three days. Even though his roommate was home and there was no reported misbehavior, New York City's special enforcement officers slapped fines of more than $40,000 on Warren's landlord for violating illegal transient hotel rules, according to the New York Times. New York City law restricts residents from renting out apartments, or rooms in them, for fewer than 30 days, unless they are also living in the home during the guests' stay.

May 21, 2013

This takes us to the *third domain,* the *commercial* level. This last domain is the topic of this book. It is important to realise that industrialised hospitality and mass tourism cannot be interpreted and assessed in complete isolation from the other two domains. Some of our examples have already clearly illustrated this and we will discuss many more examples and links later on. For now, let us note that hospitality cannot be discussed sensibly without addressing its context and the behaviour and traits of the hosts and guests involved. So, our study of the third domain would benefit if we also addressed the other two domains.

Commercial level

Does this mean the end of the debate on what hospitality and hospitality management constitute? Have we reached consensus? No, unfortunately, that is not the case. Indeed, the above gives only a glimpse into the on-going discussions between practitioners and academics from many fields of study. However, the debaters acknowledge that you can interpret and assess the concept of hospitality from various perspectives and doing so actually helps us understand it better and improve the way we manage it. Therefore, slowly but surely, the study of hospitality has become multidisciplinary.

Perspectives

Defining the hospitality industry is not easy

1

The distinction into three domains of hospitality has contributed constructively to the structure of the debate on hospitality. However, it does not mean the debate is now over, especially not with respect to the follow-up question, How can we define the hospitality industry? In Chapter 3, we try to answer this question pragmatically. To illustrate both the complications and emotions related to trying to define such a heterogeneous (dissimilar) industry, consider the following excerpts from a paper dedicated to the topic:

> 'The hospitality industry is represented in every country in the world and is diverse and complex. It encompasses a range of free-standing hospitality businesses and is also a component of a wide range of venues whose primary function is not hospitality. [...]

> As hospitality venues develop in size and complexity they include commonplace activities that do not fit with the three-domainers' conception of hospitality. For example, most mid-market, up-market and luxury ho-

tels have facilities to meet demand for conferences and health clubs. Similarly, cruise ships, theme parks, motorway service areas and multi-leisure centres have integral components that fall outside the scope of the three-domainers' definition. A vivid example is from Las Vegas where there are 29 venues, each with more than 1,000 rooms. Each venue also includes a major casino, a restaurant campus, at least one theatre, a conference and exhibition centre, a shopping mall, a health club, one has an aquarium, one has a circus and Bellagio and the Venetian each incorporate an art gallery. [...]

This range of activities is legitimate and complementary for the companies and it is nonsense to imagine that only the parts of these companies that fit with the three-domainers' definition can be considered to be hospitality. It would be even worse to exclude these businesses from the definition of the hospitality industry and place them outside the scope of hospitality management teaching and research.'

Paul Slattery, 2002, pp. 23-24

1.4 **Managing hospitality experiences**

Hospitality
Hospitality management

The title of this book is *Hospitality Experience* and its subtitle is '*An introduction to hospitality management*'. The title represents the choice we made with respect to the focus of this textbook and the perspective we chose with respect to interpreting and assessing hospitality and hospitality management. In this section we refer to the lessons that can be learnt from all the above to explain our choices and perspective. They serve as the main reference points in the rest of this chapter, and those that follow.

Hospitality management and the experience economy

Interaction

In today's society, simply delivering a service or selling a product is usually not enough to lure the customers needed to survive in a highly competitive and fluctuating market. Somehow, as customers we value not just the service or product but also the way in which it comes our way. The way in which we *experience* a service or product influences the value we attach to it. It even affects how much money we are willing to spend on it. A critical element of this experience relates to our interaction with the service or product providers. A mobile phone named after a fruit cannot be compared to one that may be just as good from a functional point of view, but bears a logo we do not know. A cup of coffee served with a smile does not taste the same as one that must have been too hot when it was poured and so has hurt the waiter's hands to the extent he is sulking when he hands you your coffee. Experience has become a key concept in today's society and economy (Pine & Gilmore, 1999), and the hospitality industry is no exception to that rule.

Pine and Gilmore's book bears the telling name *The Experience Economy: Work Is Theatre & Every Business a Stage*

As the name suggests, the type of experiences at the core of this sector of our economy, the hospitality industry, are hospitality experiences. Like most other experiences, they relate to personal interactions. However, personal interactions can be differentiated from other forms of interaction (see also Brotherton & Wood, 2000). As we said earlier, hospitality interactions involve a relationship between a host and a guest in a specific context and entail the provision of accommodation and/or food and/or drink.

If you are familiar with *Hospitality: A Social Lens* (2007), edited by Conrad Lashley, Paul Lynch and Alison Morrison, you will notice that our reference point closely resembles the train of thought these authors present in their book and, especially, two definitions of hospitality they quote to set the stage in their first chapter. The first of those quotes is:

> 'A contemporaneous human exchange, which is voluntarily entered into, and designed to enhance the mutual well-being of the parties concerned though the provision of accommodation, and/or food and/or drink.'
> Bob Brotherton, 1999, p. 168

The second quote is:

> 'It represents a host's cordial reception, welcome and entertainment of guests or strangers of diverse social backgrounds and cultures charitably, socially or commercially with kind and generous liberality, into one's space to dine and/or lodge temporarily. Dependent on circumstance and context the degree to which the hospitality offering is conditional or unconditional may vary.'
> Allison Morrison and Kevin O'Gorman, 2006, p. 3

Our definition of hospitality experiences

These two definitions clearly highlight the key elements of the perspective we apply in this book for interpreting and assessing hospitality experiences. First, a hospitality experience is related to the interaction between a host and a guest. Second, it is crucial that these two parties engage voluntarily in the interaction for an experience to qualify as hospitality. Otherwise, situations like the prison case would qualify as hospitality as well. Third, the interaction needs to involve the host providing either one or a combination of accommodation, food or drink to the guest to qualify as a hospitality experience. And finally, the interaction context determines the rules and norms of appropriate behaviour for the parties involved.

Interaction between host/ guest

Voluntarily

Hospitality experiences

So, now we are ready to define *hospitality experiences*:

> A hospitality experience is a voluntary interaction between host and guest, in which the host provides accommodation and/or food and/ or drink to the guest and the context determines the applicable rules and norms for the behaviour of both parties.

A multidisciplinary approach

It should now also be clear that interpreting and assessing hospitality experiences in all its many and varied contexts requires a multidisciplinary approach firstly because the context determines the rules and norms that apply to the interaction. Once again, Lashley's three domains (2000), the social and cultural, the private and domestic, and the commercial, really help to explain this. For instance, understanding the impact of tourists on local residents – including damage to the natural environment and benefits such as new jobs and stimulus to the micro-economy – clearly requires a different approach than understanding the impact of dining in the dark would. Setting up a bed and breakfast is not the same as giving a friend in need a place to stay. All these interactions between hosts and guests are hospitality experiences, but truly understanding them requires insights from various disciplines, such as sociology, psychology, anthropology, biology, economics and management.

Multidisciplinary approach

Context

Interaction

The second reason why a multidisciplinary approach is crucial here relates directly to the subtitle of this book, an introduction to hospitality management. This suggests a focus on management issues. And yes, one of our objectives is certainly to provide insights for future hospitality managers to help prepare them for the hospitality industry. However, in trying to reach this objective, it would be a mistake to ignore non-management issues and insights from other fields and professions. Hospitality management is not just a combination of two words. We cannot fully comprehend the meaning

Management issues

of hospitality management without understanding the two concepts – management *and* hospitality – that lie at its core.

Managing something that you do not understand is 'Mission impossible'. Even if we limit our scope to experiences in the commercial hospitality industry, managing hospitality experiences still requires insight into the types of hospitality experiences that are financially successful. Once we know which experiences lead to success, the next question is how to stage these experiences. What resources do we need to make sure that guests will experience our service or product so that they will come back for more and tell their friends and family about it? Given the fact that hospitality experiences involve customers' interaction with your employees, what does this mean for their behaviour? What is the optimal combination of accommodation, food and drink for a particular interaction? These are but a few of many key questions we need to answer to successfully manage hospitality experiences. Again, the answers require insights from other fields than just management science.

The optimal combination of accommodation, food, drink and interaction?

Although guests may expect and be willing to pay for hospitality experiences in the commercial hospitality industry, this does not mean that we can simply ignore all the rules and norms related to hospitality in other domains. As we discussed earlier, there may be three separate domains of hospitality, but that does not mean that they exist in isolation. Some hospitality experiences might be linked to two or even three domains. Sometimes they are even set up that way on purpose. For example, the bed and breakfast located in the same building as where the owner lives. The idea behind this concept is usually to make you feel as if you are staying with a

1

family, someone you like and can talk to, instead of a room in impersonal mass tourism accommodation. However, even if a hospitality experience is set up strictly as a commercial transaction, and nothing more, this does not automatically mean that the way the guest experiences it will relate only to the rules and norms of the commercial domain.

This chapter started out by stating that hospitality is both a word and a concept that means *something* to most of us. Simultaneously, *what* it means to one person or group is not necessarily the same as *what* it means to someone else or another group. We have all been taught different things. We have all grown up in different circumstances and communities, in the very different societies that together shape our world. Hospitality means something different to all of us. Whether or not a hospitality experience has been set up from a strictly commercial perspective does not change this, nor does it stop us from taking our own perspective and following our own rules and norms in the final verdict. Hospitality managers can use all the help they can get in managing all this. Thus a multidisciplinary approach to managing hospitality experiences is a must.

Hospitality management

To conclude this section, maybe it is wise to refer again to Brotherton's (1999, p. 165) attempt to 'create a clearer view of what hospitality and hospitality management are.' He concludes that it is vital to realise that 'hospitality management is not the combination of management and hospitality but the existence of a hospitality management profession, and all this implies' (Brotherton, 1999, p. 171). This book acknowledges and agrees with his conclusion. That does not mean our book merely repeats what has already been said at length in the debate we summarised in the previous section. Our focus on the hospitality management profession means we address how to create successful hospitality experiences. That means we have to discuss the best ways of managing hospitality experiences in and beyond the hospitality industry context. Such a focus needs to take on board the lessons learnt in other fields and discussions, without losing track of the fact that, ultimately, a management perspective is the main reference point of this book.

⬤1.5 The remainder of this book

Commercial domain

In line with our management perspective, the rest of this book focuses primarily on how to manage hospitality experiences in the commercial domain. However, this does not mean that our examples are limited to (one part of) the hospitality industry, or that the management principles and tools we discuss can only be applied in the commercial domain of the hospitality industry. The perspective we have chosen for interpreting and assessing hospitality focuses on the key elements involved in the profession of managing hospitality experiences. Ultimately, the particular context you, as a (future) hospitality manager, decide to pursue a career in will determine the rules and norms that apply to your day-to-day operations.

Profession

To conclude this first chapter, here is a brief overview of all remaining chapters and, especially, the links between them.

Adding value

Chapter 2 (Adding value to the hospitality experience) focuses on a key question related to the management perspective. Now that we have defined hospitality experiences and discussed the various ways they can be interpreted and assessed, how can we use this knowledge to make a profit? Companies need to understand how staging hospitality experiences create added value for their customers and how this ties in with their overall value chain. Obviously, a key element is assessing what clients are willing to pay for and how much. The answers are clearly context dependent. For instance, the value chain of a snack bar is very different from the value chain of a luxury five-star resort, and the tangible and intangible aspects involved in staging hospitality experiences are quite different as well. Simultaneously, all of these aspects need to be linked to the costs and appropriate pricing of hospitality experiences offered to customers, because for most companies staging experiences, the objective is to make a profit. All of this highlights, once again, that in particular contexts, such as the commercial domain, hospitality experiences are linked to the exchange of money. A guest pays for experiencing hospitality the host offers. However, given the broad nature of hospitality experiences, this does not necessarily mean that only economic rules and norms apply. Consequently, companies need to account for this in the way they price, market and sell the hospitality experiences. They need to be aware of how all this affects important aspects such as customer loyalty and how they can apply methods such as revenue management.

The industry that evolved from exchanging money in return for hospitality experiences is the topic of Chapter 3 (The hospitality industry). Here we discuss the various types of companies that together shape this industry today, and show how the industry and its companies evolved over time. Some examples relate to independent versus chain hotels and the roles of various restaurants and other establishments that focus on the provision of food and drinks. However, we also address the position of other types of hospitality experience providers, such as theme parks, theatres, and so on. We highlight the key attributes of companies and establishments at the core of the industry, that is, hotels and restaurants. We explain their relation to (changing) customer segments and preferences and discuss various ways to rate and classify them. Finally, we establish that companies in today's hospitality industry depend highly on external parties and organisations for marketing and selling their products and services. We discuss the roles of the parties in the hospitality value chain and the implications for day-to-day operations in this industry.

Industry

Chapter 4 (Hospitality beyond the industry's borders) explicitly focuses on how hospitality experiences can and are applied in contexts outside the hospitality industry. Sometimes these experiences could constitute or be closely linked to the core product of companies that are not *formally* part of this industry. For these companies, hospitality principles might not directly relate to their ultimate core product, but applying hospitality principles can help to create added value for customers and employees and establish competitive advantage. Here we show how staging hospitality experiences by applying the lessons learnt in the hospitality industry can help firms create a better functioning internal organisation, gain more satisfied customers and employees, and establish beneficial relationships with people and organisations in today's network-based society.

Beyond

Then Chapter 5 (The future of hospitality) explores how current and future trends and developments might shape the hospitality industry in years to

Future

come. The topics include sustainable development and corporate social responsibility, political and economic developments, as well as the role of technology, social media and e-business in relation to the practices, principles and business models behind staging hospitality experiences. We pay special attention to generational differences and their effects on the ever-changing needs and wants of customers, and new ways of interacting with them. Finally, we highlight some first indications of what it all means for future hospitality managers and business. We demonstrate the importance of being able to scan, interpret and adapt to changing environments. Since this is a key competence of successful hospitality managers we elaborate on this last point in Chapter 9.

Daily operations

But before we get to the final part, Chapters 6, 7 and 8 address the daily operations related to managing hospitality experiences in more detail.

Designing

Building on the reference points made in previous chapters, Chapter 6 (Designing hospitality experiences) focuses on how to design and create hospitality experiences that live up to the context-applicable rules and norms that will generate the added value we are aiming for. We further address key aspects such as satisfaction, loyalty, branding and expectations and how to account for these in setting up hospitality experiences. Applying 'touchpoint design', we explain how we can shape the supporting 'servicescape'.

Delivering

A crucial part of any hospitality experience is the interaction between host and guest. This means that the behaviour of hospitality employees is key to staging experiences as they were designed to be staged. Chapter 7 (Delivering hospitality) focuses on what you need to guarantee that hospitality experiences are more than standard, friendly service. We explore various interactions between hosts and guests and answer questions like, What does a particular hospitality experience design imply for hospitality employees trying to stage the experience in a particular context? Related questions involve issues such as timing and location, and the associated organisational and managerial support needed to stage experiences. We then translate all of this into specific requirements with respect to employee training and support, including appropriate feedback and leadership.

Quality

All the above should make it clear that it takes careful planning and management to successfully execute hospitality experiences. Chapter 8 (Quality management in hospitality) explores three criteria that enable you to consistently stage successful hospitality experiences, providing the right *quality* at the right *time*, at the right *cost*. Here we discuss the processes and resources needed to meet those criteria and give examples of the pitfalls you need to avoid. This automatically leads us back to the role of the hospitality manager. You must make sure that processes and resources are managed so that hospitality experiences add actual value for customers and contribute as planned to the value chain of your company.

Leadership

Indeed, Chapter 9 (Competencies and leadership) focuses on the leadership skills hospitality managers should possess to fulfil their role in staging hospitality experiences, in and beyond the hospitality industry, now and in the future. What are the key management implications of what we discussed in the first eight chapters? Finally, and crucially for any aspiring hospitality manager, what competencies do you need to master to be able to 'take the lead' in staging successful hospitality experiences?

Competencies

Summary

- ▶ Hospitality is:
  - a word that many people use often
  - a word that people interpret differently
  - a concept that refers to many different situations and experiences

- ▶ There are two main perspectives on the origins and history of hospitality:
  - as a behaviour
  - as an industry

- ▶ The hospitality industry consists of a wide variety of establishments and organisations.
  There is an on-going debate on how to define hospitality. We can distinguish two schools of thought:
  - some people think the meaning of hospitality is inextricably linked to human behaviour, regardless of its context
  - other people think that hospitality means managing hospitality products and services in the context of a commercial hospitality industry

- ▶ Hospitality relates to:
  - the provision of (a combination of) accommodation, food, drink
  - the interaction between a host and a guest

- ▶ The appropriate way to interpret and assess hospitality depends on the context. Lashley (2000) suggests these useful distinctions in contexts:
  - the social and cultural domain
  - the domestic or private domain
  - the commercial domain

- ▶ A hospitality experience is directly related to an interaction between a host and a guest, both of whom voluntarily engage in the interaction:
  - the host provides accommodation and/or food and/or drink to the guest
  - the context of the interaction determines the rules and norms of behaviour

- ▶ Interpreting and assessing hospitality experiences requires a multidisciplinary approach.

- ▶ Hospitality management is a profession that addresses how we can successfully create and manage hospitality experiences.

Food for thought

This chapter introduced the concept of hospitality, highlighted the on-going debate on the meaning of hospitality for the hospitality industry and defined hospitality experiences. Based on the content of this chapter, the following questions, challenges and topics could serve as interesting starting points for further discussion:

1 In the hotel industry you will find very different types of hotels, ranging from budget hotels to deluxe five-star (or even seven- or eight-star) hotels. Can you indicate the types of hospitality experiences that guests of these various hotels would expect and find acceptable for the price they have to pay for staying there?

2 This chapter listed three domains that can serve as different contexts for defining and interpreting the norms and rules that apply to the hospitality concept. Can you set three rules and/or norms that only apply to one domain? And can you set three rules and/or norms that you could link to all three domains?

3 We mentioned a prison that provides accommodation, food and drink to inmates. But this context does not qualify as hospitality. Can you come up with more contexts that incorporate the provision of accommodation, food and/or drink, yet do not qualify as hospitality?

4 After reading this chapter, it should be clear to you that hospitality management requires a multidisciplinary approach. Can you list all the disciplines relevant to creating an optimal hospitality experience for guests from the moment they decide to book a stay at a big five-star deluxe hotel. Think of all the disciplines involved prior, during and after the guests' actual stay in the hotel. And how would you create the optimal hospitality experience for guests having dinner in a stylish, but not too expensive restaurant?

2

Adding value to the hospitality experience

Stan Josephi

From a commercial point of view, the high fixed costs commonly associated with producing hospitality experiences and the perishability of the product on sale directly influence the value chain of hospitality experiences. The combination of tangible and intangible parts of the hospitality product determines the value that customers attach or associate with the hospitality experience and, therefore, both parts must be incorporated in a company's pricing strategy. Here we discuss all these aspects, as well as the roles and functions involved in marketing the product and generating optimum revenue.

Food trucks change the way NYers eat

Food trucks have now become enormously popular throughout the United States, especially in large metropolises. According to the Food and Agriculture Organisation of the United Nations, approximately 2.5 billion people worldwide eat street food per day. In New York, the foods served up from trucks vary endlessly – dishing out everything from chicken over rice to waffles with whipped cream – catering to an already 'fast food nation' but in a very different way.

Listing the reasons why food trucks have become trendy, Weber, president of the New York City Food Truck Association, says, 'Customers that choose to eat from a truck are often looking for tasty food, convenience, great service, or a good value.'

Sociologist Sharon Zukin, a professor at Brooklyn College says, 'People want lunch food or snack food that is cheap and tasty, and food trucks, most of which, these days, produce speciality products in 'ethnic' cuisines supply tasty meals that are exotic in comparison with the ubiquitous burgers of fast food franchises.'

[...] Like traditional restaurants, food trucks have developed steady customers who are faithful to a certain cart. Cart owner Othman says, 'The quality of my food and my attitude towards people are what keeps the people coming back. Some steady customers would actually wait for me to finish with other customers when I'm having a busy day, because they feel comfortable with me and I know what they want to order.'

Source: by Sarah Allam, adapted from http://journalism.blog.brooklyn.edu, May 2013, adapted

2.1 The value chain of hospitality experiences

The opening case confirms what you learnt from Chapter 1, that is, a hospitality experience is more than a room or a plate of food that a customer pays for. For some customers of food trucks, simply the food might serve their need to satisfy their appetite, but for others it could be a combination of food quality, the interaction with the person preparing and selling it, the convenience, and price. In other words, the total *experience* makes a customer decide to buy from a particular food truck.

In this chapter, we elaborate on some key elements defining the hospitality experience, including the (voluntary) interaction between host and guest, whereby the host provides accommodation and/or food and/or drink to the guest with the objective of making a profit. When we place this definition in a commercial setting, it implies that clients pay for more than the actual, tangible product. The interaction between host and guest is an intangible component of the product, which is very difficult to measure or even define. The hospitality experience includes more than just the *tangible* product, such as a room or the food served in the restaurant. It also incorporates *intangible* features, such as the receptionist's welcoming smile, the flexibility you have, booking your accommodation when it suits you, the exquisite service you received when the concierge changed your flight, or even the sommelier's great personal story when he recommends the best wine to go with your dinner. The intangible component is the cement that holds the product together and adds value which customers are willing to spend extra money on.

Intangible

Tangible

Let's take the example of a tin of tomato purée. In essence it is nothing more than mashed tomatoes. If you bought it in the supermarket, you would not want to spend more than 30 cents and you will see that the price does not vary much in supermarkets across Europe. However, if we took the same tin of tomato purée as an ingredient in a dinner at the Wentworth Mansion or to flavour the main course of your dining in the dark experience, what would happen to its value? It would become a small part of a larger whole, and although its face value might still be the purchase price (30 cents), its sales value increases. The value of the meal is more than just the sum of its ingredients, since the experience also incorporates intangible product features such as the restaurant's ambience, speed of service, or even the impact of other guests.

We see a hospitality experience as the sum of individual experiences that are staged throughout the customer's journey in selecting, purchasing, consuming and reviewing a product. At each stage, hospitality businesses have the opportunity to add value for the customer. For instance, the tomato purée became a part of the *value chain* of an organisation. A value chain of an organisation is 'a collection of activities that are performed to design, produce, market, deliver, and support its product' (Porter, 1985, p. 36).

Value chain

Obviously, adding value is more than just adding tangible components to your product that allow you to charge a higher price. Organisations that create, stage or deliver a hospitality experience seek to add value through both tangible and intangible products. And although you can present hospitality in many different shapes and forms, in the commercial hospitality industry, the tangible and intangible products that go into the experience

Create, stage or deliver

2

● Gilmore & Pine, 2002

Shuttle-bus service

To illustrate that point, let's turn our attention to another neglected lodging dimension, shuttle-bus service. (As with wake-up calls, there's no special significance to choosing this dimension, we're simply using it to demonstrate how any hotel service or space can be viewed as a place for staging engaging experiences.) Most vehicles used in transporting guests between hotels and the airport come equipped with small signs inside that read, 'Your driver is…,' and a slide-in name placard typically completes the boilerplate sign. ('Your driver is Bob' on one trip; 'Your driver is Ted' the next; and possibly even 'Your driver is [blank]'.) Such posted information represents futile functionality. Seldom, if ever, does an arriving or departing guest actually use the posted information to greet a driver by name. If anything, the sign simply serves to permit the driver (often the first hotel representative making an impression on arriving guests) to avoid eye contact or greeting guests personally.

What if the sign were instead to read, say, 'Your driver has left the building'? Now that might help create a memorable experience. Imagine shuttle-bus drivers for a Graceland Airport Hotel sporting big sideburns and wearing large, white bellbottoms, singing 'Love Me Tender' as guests step on and off. One need not resort to fictitious hotel venues, of course, to see how the concept might work; perhaps a Memphis Marriott or Tupelo Sheraton could take the idea and drive with it.

Using a theme in this manner provides a direct means for hotels to upgrade their offerings from ordinary services (e.g., wake-up calls, shuttle-bus rides) to extraordinary experiences. To do otherwise risks a hotel's offerings becoming further commoditised and undifferentiated in customers' minds. The question, then, is not whether to embrace new experience-staging techniques, but rather what techniques to use and where to employ them for maximum effect.

Adapted

Profit

Price
Buying decision

almost always need to be translated into a monetary value, so that you can make a healthy profit. Pricing and selling the intangible is complex, and this complexity is further aggravated by the fact that you often need to do it in a fiercely competitive market. Usually several organisations compete for the same customers with similar product offers. Especially in market situations fuelled by economic downturn and uncertainty, price is frequently *the* most important tool used to influence the customers' buying decision. However, when companies only use price to attract customers, they will have no other alternative than to compete on price, putting (long-term) profits under pressure and even jeopardising the financial stability of their hospitality business. Therefore, it is crucial for companies creating and delivering hospitality experiences to distinguish themselves from competitors not just by price, but by offering a product with unique features and benefits.

As Pine and Gilmore (1999) state, customers are no longer taking standardised and commoditised products for granted. Instead, companies that offer tailor-made products that keep up with the wishes and needs of the customer gain the opportunity to promote the uniqueness of the experience. Even when people think twice before spending their money, it is easier to convince customers of the value of the product or experience than emphasise price discounts. It is an old and well-known saying, customers buy benefits, not features. In other words, you need to tell your customers what your product *does* for them, instead of what it simply *is*.

Defining value

Before we continue analysing hospitality experiences, searching for value adding opportunities, we first need to define what value is. People from different backgrounds will give you different views and definitions of 'value'. If you asked an economist, he would tell you that value is 'the maximum price a customer is willing to pay for a product'. However, if you asked a management consultant with a background in organisational theory, he would tell you that values are the 'core beliefs and expectations that people have in relation to their company'. Other keywords frequently used to define value, include 'willingness to pay [...], benefits received [...], performance of the product [...], usefulness [...] higher quality [...]' (Ng, 2008, p. 24). If we link this to our hospitality experience definition provided in Chapter 1, value is 'the economic sacrifice customers are willing to make in exchange for a hospitality experience'. With the stress on *economic sacrifice*, value means more than price and money. Although a full analysis of this definition goes beyond the scope of this book, it does illustrate how important it is to understand all the customers' needs, including the sacrifices they are willing to make in exchange for buying your product. The sacrifices may refer to money, but also to such aspects as time and effort. To illustrate the relevance of these types of sacrifices, consider the world-famous Michelin Guide that awards stars to exceptional restaurants, and links its ranking system to the diner's time (and, by implication, effort). A restaurant with one Michelin star is a great place to stop, two stars are worth making a detour for, and you really should consider planning an entire trip to establishments awarded three stars.

As the Michelin example shows, the sacrifice of time is an important consideration in the hospitality experience from a customer's point of view. But from a producer's point of view, time is an essential factor in the quest to earn money by staging hospitality experiences. Since substantial parts of the product are produced and consumed simultaneously and on the spot, such as the host-guest interaction, the hospitality experience is a good example of a product that cannot be *stored*. The moment can pass, or the product can age, and this is known as the perishability factor (Weatherford & Bodily, 1992). In addition, most hospitality experiences have restricted capacity, which means for example, that you cannot increase the number of products on sale simply by adding extra hotel rooms. Put together, this means that organisations need to think carefully how to price and sell their hospitality experience, to achieve optimum profit.

Competitors

Value

Economic sacrifice

Needs

2

Restaurant Noma, Copenhagen, with two Michelin stars, is regarded as one of the best restaurants in the world

Another unique characteristic of the hospitality experience becomes clear when you define a hospitality product as 'anything that can be offered to a market for attention, acquisition, use or consumption that might satisfy a want or need, [including] physical objects, [but also] services, places, organisations, and ideas' (Kotler, Bowen, & Makens, 2003, p. 302). This definition stresses the importance of both *physical* and *non-physical* parts of the product. Clearly it makes sense to divide the hospitality product into levels that include the different *tangible* and *intangible* parts in a coherent whole.

2.2 Product levels

Here, we look at the hospitality experience as a product, meaning that we will use the terms experience and product interchangeably. We can divide a product into levels. Let's go back to the Wentworth Mansion for a closer look at the different levels of the hospitality product. The glass of bourbon served in the library is obviously a tangible product. But what about the fireplace, the bar, the waiters keeping an eye on you and your glass, the background music, or the dimmed light? How would you include them in your product? According to Grönroos (1987), we can divide a hospitality product or experience into four levels:
1 The core product
2 The facilitating product
3 The supporting product
4 The augmented product

We also call the facilitating and the supporting products the peripheral parts (Norman, 1984) that together with the core product become the augmented product, as illustrated in Figure 2.1.

FIGURE 2.1   Product levels

Source: Grönroos (1987)

Core product

The basic level of the core product fulfils the customer's primary need and describes what he or she is actually buying. For customers needing a place to sleep, the core product is a room or a bed. For hungry customers, restaurants provide food in the form of starters, main courses and desserts. Other examples of core products include entertainment for a theatre, or transport for a railway or airline. The hospitality experience often combines products, activities and interactions. Even so, its core product is still the part that most likely satisfies the customer's most important need. Note however, that this might not be why the customer bought it from *your* organisation.

Primary need

Facilitating product

When a guest arrives at your hotel for an overnight stay, he or she cannot walk straight to their room. Although there are self-service hotels where your credit card literally opens doors, in most hotels the receptionist will take down the guests' registration details and payment guarantee before handing over the key to their room. So the front desk is a good example of a facilitating product, since you cannot provide the core product without it. This vital part of your service facilitates or enables customers to use the

Facilitating

core product and thus gain the hospitality experience. Other examples of facilitating products include the hotel restaurant, the business centre in a corporate hotel, or the transfer desk of an airline at an international airport. A key element of the facilitating product is **accessibility**. In the case of a delayed flight, obviously the transfer desk should stay open to help passengers with their connecting flights. Hospitality providers need to have a clear understanding of not just the customers' primary needs that their core product will satisfy, but also the additional facilitating services customers need in order to consume the product.

Accessibility

Supporting product

Supporting products are different. Whereas a facilitating product is essential for customers to enjoy the hospitality experience, you can create the experience without a supporting product. Customers do not need supporting products to consume the core product. However, we use supporting products to **add value** to the product and, if they are unique and difficult to imitate, they can give you **competitive advantage**. Some examples in a hospitality context are the hotel's health spa, or a theatre tickets desk in the lobby, 24-hour room service, the ability to pre-order drinks for the theatre intervals, or even room cancellation insurance hotels offer when you book a room. The dividing line between facilitating and supporting products is often blurred in the eyes of customers. Some may see it as a facilitating product, whereas another target group may regard it as a supporting product (Kotler et al., 2003). Take for example the availability of Wi-Fi in a hotel. For a business guest who needs to e-mail his colleagues about the meeting he attended that day, it would be an indispensable service, whereas the family that stays in your hotel for sightseeing purposes might not require it at all.

Add value
Competitive advantage

Augmented product

As you can see from Grönroos' model, the augmented (literally, 'greater than before') product serves as the final layer of the core product and its **peripheral components**. The customer and the environment play important roles in the augmented product. As we said before, a hospitality experience requires an interaction between the host and the guest. The three other product levels can all be delivered *without* customer interaction. But this final level describes not just *what* the product is, but more importantly, the *how* and *where* (the 'environment') of the interaction that adds so much to the core product. A key element is the **atmosphere** of your surroundings. To illustrate this, picture yourself on a dark winter's day in the library of a traditional English country hotel. You sit in an old Chesterfield, the lights are dimmed, a wood fire is burning in the fireplace, and the walls are full of paintings of English aristocrats. Other guests, all dressed stylishly, greet you politely as they are seated, and quietly converse with each other. Someone plays classical music on a grand piano in the background. The butler, immaculate in his uniform, silently serves you and your partner your favourite aperitif.

Peripheral components

Atmosphere

The size, layout, and colour scheme of the library, as well as the furniture, lighting, volume of music and conversation, plus the scent of the fireplace have a significant impact on the atmosphere. The added value is a clear message, we serve you with grandeur, class and style in this setting. Contrast these surroundings with a fast food restaurant in the city centre, filled with loud music and bright colours that create a dynamic atmosphere.

The next component of the augmented product is the customer's interaction with the product delivery system. When we place that on the hospitality experience timeline, we distinguish three phases:

1 Prior to the experience
2 During the experience
3 After the experience

Timeline

Although we make a distinction between these stages, keep in mind that together they create the *overall* hospitality experience that the customer will remember your organisation for. The 'prior' and 'after' phases contain supporting and facilitating products, whereas the 'during' phase is most associated with the core product. In the before phase, the customer physically arrives at your hotel, restaurant or other hospitality business. Broad flexibility and accessibility are vitally important here. Today's technology permits instant responses to enquiries about prices and availability so organisations should supply product information on the spot. With unlimited online information and booking options available to prospective customers, an organisation cannot afford to delay a customer's purchase decision with a slow flow of information. Consider the state of mind of a guest who has been trying to get to your hotel for over two hours, but cannot reach it because construction works have turned the city centre into a building site. Even worse, what if he were delayed because of a faulty map he downloaded from your website? As you can imagine, it will take immense effort to turn this negative experience into a positive one. You only get one chance to make a first impression, so make sure it is a good one! Realise, too, that this first impression is often created before the customer arrives at your premises and consumes the core product.

First impression

The process of the actual experience must be designed so that it allows you to deliver the product efficiently, putting the customers' demands and expectations at the forefront. Organisations can align the tangible and intangible elements and deliver customised products to different target groups by making on-going improvements to the physical product, and ensuring that staff are trained regularly and appropriately.

Finally, the hospitality experience is not complete without proper closure. This can vary from the banquet manager's aftersales call to the contact person of a group, a couple of days after their meeting took place, to a hotel providing clean and safe parking. Or it could range from the accounts department dealing quickly and efficiently with an invoice inquiry, to the receptionist handling the checkout procedure inviting a customer to book ahead for his or her next stay. Next to the first impression, the last impression is equally important. It is a vital ingredient in forming loyalty relationships with potential customers to generate repeat business in the future.

Closure

The customer's own interaction with other customers also takes place prior, during and after the hospitality experience. Nowadays there is an increasing emphasis on virtual interaction between customers. When prospective customers are planning their business or leisure trip to a certain city, or looking for a restaurant for a romantic diner, nowadays they often turn to social media and increasingly rely on the experience of other customers who have shared their views on sites such as Tripadvisor, or Zagat. This user-generated content, known as electronic word of mouth (eWOM) or *word of mouse*,

Virtual interaction

Word of mouth

is ranked one of the most important sources of information that customers base their purchase decision upon.

This stresses the importance for hospitality companies to get their product right, as negative opinions of experiences tend to travel faster and a lot further than good ones. Another aspect that organisations need to manage are the inter-customer interactions during their stay. A well-known example is the business hotel in a central but remote location that focuses on the training and meeting market from Monday to Friday, and attracts families during the weekend. As you can imagine, business guests in the final stages of an important meeting or training session do not appreciate the disruptive noise of excited children playing in the corridors. Nor does the couple celebrating their first wedding anniversary appreciate the loud speeches and singing from the bachelor group sitting next to them. This forces the hotel or restaurant to make choices that could potentially be harmful to revenue and profit levels in the short run, but will most likely optimise returns in the long run due to better (online) reviews and ratings.

"The Amsterdam Gem!"

⊚⊚⊚⊚⊚ Reviewed 26 May 2013

We stayed at Mauro following a Rhine River Cruise and found the place to be an oasis of calm in the midst of an active city center! Berry and Marcel are perfect hosts, pleasant, knowledgeable and respectful. Service quality is excellent and all delivered with a terrific sense of humour.
This is the place to stay if you want to experience the best of Amsterdam. Everything is a short (under 30 mins) walk, including the Rijksmuseum, Anne Frank House and the Marine Museum. If you need a ride, they can give you numerous options from canal to bus!
Breakfasts were fantastic with a treat made by Berry each morning! And the bread, oh the great breads!!
Stay here! You will have a real Amsterdam experience. It is a comfortable and safe base from which to explore!
We loved the Barber Chair in Room 21!!

Room Tip: Take a Canal Room! A little noisy at certain times of the night but it is worth having the view of...
See more room tips

Stayed May 2013, travelled as a couple

⊚⊚⊚⊚⊚ Value   ⊚⊚⊚⊚⊚ Rooms
⊚⊚⊚⊚⊚ Location   ⊚⊚⊚⊚⊚ Cleanliness
⊚⊚⊚⊚⊚ Sleep Quality   ⊚⊚⊚⊚⊚ Service

Source: www.tripadvisor.com, May 26, 2013

Involvement

The final component of the augmented product describes the customer's involvement in hospitality experience delivery. Returning to our Chapter 1 definition, the interaction between host and guest plays a central role in staging the hospitality experience. And as we said earlier, production and consumption of the product mostly take place at the same time – often called inseparability. The customer's involvement is a crucial component in staging the hospitality experience. Yet it is also an aspect that is beyond the control of the host (organisation).

Inseparability

A customer's active participation in staging the hospitality experience is called co-creation (Prahalad & Ramaswamy, 2004), and comes in many forms and shapes. Higher involvement in product delivery can help companies reduce costs, and more importantly, lead to increased guest satisfaction (Kotler, et al., 2003). Some typical examples of guest involvement vary from restaurant buffet service, or the resort's option to self-clean accommodation, to terminals abroad that allow customers to print their favourite national newspaper. And think of a company like Starwood that involved customers in the innovation process of Aloft, by launching a prototype of the hotel concept on Second Life. Using the feedback they received, they made many changes before launching the hotel in real life (Kohler, Matzler, & Füller, 2009). When hospitality organisations design their product, as we will discuss in Chapter 6, it is essential that they consider the host-guest interaction in the delivery and staging of the experience.

Co-creation

Guest satisfaction

Now that we have defined the various levels of our product, the hospitality experience, we can identify the costs associated with the tangible and intangible components. Due to the high involvement of people, as well as the high fixed costs that are commonly associated with adding an additional core product, clearly the complex cost structure of hospitality experiences has significant implications for potential profit levels. This is why, it is imperative that hospitality organisations have a solid understanding of their cost structure, as this enables them to control their fixed and variable costs and make adjustments if necessary.

2.3 Operating leverage

Traditionally, the hospitality industry has high fixed costs, and relatively low variable costs. Just consider a Sunday night in an average hotel, with a typically low occupancy, since both business and leisure guests often prefer not to travel on that night. Since many rooms remain unsold, the hotel faces lower variable costs on that night, such as for cleaning, or breakfast food. However, the fixed costs of sales and marketing and staff wages still have to be paid, even when rooms are unsold. This is closely related to the principle of perishability we discussed before. After all, in this industry employees form a significant part of the product, which ex-plains the high labour costs that sometimes take up more than 35% of the total costs. The high capital expenditure commonly associated with the hospitality industry (adding an extra room to a five-star deluxe hotel might cost tens of thousands of euros), adds to the high fixed costs in re-lation to variable costs. As a result of these high fixed costs, hospitality organisations are traditionally very vulnerable during a period of low demand, especially if it lasts for a long time, as in economic downturns.
To analyse the cost structure of a hospitality organisation, the fixed costs are expressed in relation to variable costs, which results in the operating leverage ratio of a company. Figure 2.2 demonstrates the effect of the operating leverage ratio.

Fixed costs

Variable costs

FIGURE 2.2 Operating leverage

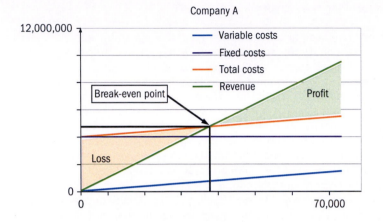

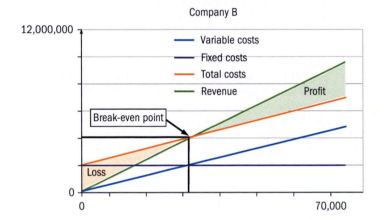

Financial risk

The operating leverage ratio is a strong indicator of the level of financial risk a company faces under different market conditions and varying demand.

Consider the example in Table 2.1.

TABLE 2.1 The impact of operating leverage

	Company A	Company B
Revenue	€ 6 m	€ 6 m
Fixed Costs	€ 4 m	€ 2 m
Variable Costs	€ 1 m	€ 3 m
Profit	**€ 1 m**	**€ 1 m**

Financial performance

Both companies sell 50,000 products for €120. The variable cost per unit for Company A come in at €20 per unit, and for Company B at €60 per unit. Although both companies achieve equal profits, a drop in sold products will clearly have a much more severe impact on the financial performance of company A. If demand drops by 20%, and both companies sell 40,000 units at €120, profit is affected as shown in Table 2.2.

TABLE 2.2 The impact of operating leverage due to a drop in sold products

	Company A	Company B
Revenue	€ 4.8 m	€ 4.8 m
Fixed Costs	€ 4 m	€ 2 m
Variable Costs	€ 0.8 m	€ 2.4 m
Profit	**€ 0**	**€ 0.4 m**

As you can see, Company A has a higher operating leverage, meaning they will be more at risk in periods of slow demand, whereas Company B will have more stable profits, also in times of economic uncertainty and decreasing demand. This emphasises that the financial success of a hospitality organisation first depends on a suitable cost structure that limits risk in troublesome economic times. This is why a recent trend shows many hotel chains selling off their buildings, trying to reduce fixed costs and return to their core business, managing hotels, instead of also operating as real-estate investors. To formalise the sale of the property and retain the right to manage the hotel, real-estate owners and hotel operators can agree on contracts in many shapes and forms.

Risk

Contracts

● www.reuters.com

Casinos consider asset-light model

Los Angeles (Reuters) – Casino companies with expensive properties in Las Vegas are considering following some major hotel operators in shedding their real estate to focus solely on operating the properties, industry leaders said.

The so-called 'asset-light' model has become increasingly popular among hotel companies, but casino owners are approaching the concept cautiously.

'Maybe for us it wouldn't be as meaningful because we have more high-end properties,' Terrence Lanni, chief executive of MGM Mirage Inc. [...], said on Tuesday at the 2007 Reuters Hotels and Casinos Summit in Los Angeles.

When a company adopts an asset-light model, it typically sells its property and retains the right to manage it. For Las Vegas casinos, in particular, the model could be lucrative as real estate prices in gambling meccas have skyrocketed in recent years, quintupling in some cases.

'It has increased the efficiency of the hotel industry,' said Matthew Jacob, an analyst at Majestic Research, noting that casinos face a different set of risks.

The topic gained prominence last week when Harrah's Entertainment Inc. [...] said it plans to divide its real-estate assets into separate subsidiaries as part of its acquisition by two private equity firms.

Lanni said an asset-light model makes sense for some casinos. But he said it may be especially risky to split ownership and operation for high-end properties like the Mirage or the MGM Grand because owners and managers may disagree on the investments needed to keep particular operations up to the standards demanded by guests.

The model is popular among companies like Hilton Hotels Corp. [...], which derives less than 40 percent of its income from the hotels it owns, down from 90 percent 10 years ago. The company now owns about 60 hotels, but would like to shed most of them.

February 14, 2007

MGM Grand, Las Vegas

Pricing

Still, cost control is only one consideration in staging a hospitality experience in a commercial context. Looking for other ways to influence the price of your products is another route to profitability. A unique product will allow for higher rates, and put the organisation in a stronger competitive position to achieve its objective of generating revenues and making a healthy profit. Therefore, an effective pricing approach also contributes to profit optimisation. If you manage the costs effectively, but do not sell the product at the right price, your organisation is in danger of leaving a healthy profit lying on the table. An effective pricing process is divided into distinct stages, separated in *strategic* and *operational* pricing decisions. This allows an organisation to add profit in the process of selling and delivering its product.

2.4   Pricing

Once an organisation has decided on the kind of hospitality experience it wants to stage, it needs to decide how to price the product and subsequently position it in the market in relation to its competitors. The pricing and selling process involves people from various departments. The sales and marketing manager can explain what customers would most likely want to pay for the product, while the financial manager can provide insight into the cost structure and calculate profit levels. We elaborate on the roles and responsibilities of important actors in the pricing process later in this chapter.

Product design and delivery are among the determining factors of price. If your product is a five-star deluxe hotel in the middle of Paris, your location will of course have a major impact on your rates. And the opposite would apply to the cosy countryside bed & breakfast with only five rooms. We will deal with product design and delivery of various levels of hospitality experiences in Chapter 6. But for now, let us focus on the process of establishing the right price level for the hospitality experience, regardless of design and delivery.

The pricing process of a hospitality experience includes two main stages:
1   Strategic pricing
2   Operational pricing

Ad 1 Strategic pricing
Hospitality organisations, like any other organisation, have to determine how they will distinguish themselves from their competition. Michael Porter's work on strategy (1985) teaches us that three generic strategies allow an organisation to create both competitive advantage and an above-average performance in relation to its competitors:

1   *Cost leadership*: The organisation aims to produce and deliver its products, in a standardised market, as cheaply and efficiently as possible, below the cost price of its rivals. The organisation's prices are below the industry average, aimed at increasing market share. A good example of cost leadership strategy are the budget hotels you find close to the motorway, that successfully fulfil the essentials for an overnight stay, without any frills that people would have to pay extra for.   **Cost leadership**

2   *Differentiation*: The organisation pursues uniqueness by developing and positioning the product favourably against the competition on attributes that customers perceive as important. Customers reward the successful companies with either an increased market share, or the willingness to pay higher prices. A good example of a differentiated hospitality experience is the Icehotel in Jukkasjärvi, the world's first hotel built from ice every year and open from December until April.   **Differentiation**

3   *Focus*: This strategy stands out from differentiation and cost leadership, mainly because it selects a 'narrow competitive scope within an industry' (Porter, 1985, p. 15). Companies that follow this strategy first decide which niche market segment to focus on. They then decide how they can best serve this group of customers, either with a differentiated product or through low-cost production or a combination of both. Because of the small scope and size of the market segment, the strategy will initially yield low sales volume, but once the number of customers grows, it might   **Focus**

2

Differentiated hospitality experience: Icehotel in Jukkasjärvi, Sweden

develop into a cost leadership or differentiation strategy. This is for example the case with the Burj Al Arab in Dubai. When it opened, the niche market segment they wanted to serve was the world's rich and famous. Although the rooms are still beyond many people's budgets, nowadays it attracts a large clientele from diverse market segments. A more recent example of focus strategy is the rise of eco-tourism, with resorts, such as the Kingfisher Bay Resort on World Heritage-listed Fraser Island aiming to offer a unique hospitality experience to a select group of travellers.

The choice of generic strategy has a significant influence on the operating leverage of an organisation. If an organisation pursues the cost leadership strategy, it would be mission impossible if it had high fixed costs caused by a high number of staff. Alternatively, if an organisation is unwilling to reserve substantial sums of money for the research and development of new products, it is not likely to create a competitive advantage by following a differentiation strategy.

Each of these generic strategies needs to be linked to a pricing strategy that will enable the organisation to price its products effectively and turn its competitive advantage into actual profit. The three most commonly used approaches are defined as follows (Collins & Parsa, 2006):

Cost-based pricing

1 *Cost-based pricing*: uses the total fixed and variable costs connected to the base of product production and delivery, adding a profit margin on top to generate a positive financial return

Competitive pricing

2 *Competitive pricing*: used to protect or grow a companies' market share. Price is based on what the competition is charging

Customer-driven pricing

3 *Customer-driven pricing*: uses a measure of the customers' willingness to pay to establish the price charged for a product

Each pricing strategy has its pros and cons, partially due to its inability to incorporate all the dynamics of today's fast-moving hospitality landscape. Just imagine a customer-driven approach that warrants prices below cost price. This would make it virtually impossible for most organisations to be financially viable. Similarly, hotel operators widely practice competitive pricing in the fiercely competitive environment, but often in the wrong way. Hotels want to protect their market share, so many operators follow their competitors' lead and base their prices on what the competition is charging. What they often overlook, however, is that a competitor's prices are determined by factors that should not affect the price levels of another hotel. The competitor might have received a cancellation for a large piece of business, or their online guest rating has worsened considerably. Or they might lack effective pricing knowledge and skills and simply follow your rates, which ultimately could lead to a vicious downward spiral that sees rates plummeting and signals the start of a price war with profits vaporising market wide. And although short-term organisations may achieve profits by price-cutting, they must keep in mind how the market perceives their pricing, since in the long-term it could have substantial implications on the customer's perception of the price-value relationship of hospitality experiences.

Customer-driven pricing, also called value-based pricing has emerged to help change 'strategic thinking about price from seller concerns regarding costs, to critical buyer concerns with value' (Piercy, Cravens, & Lane, 2010, p. 39). In other words, it is considered the opposite of cost-based pricing and effectively sets prices based on the (potential) customers' perception of the value of the hospitality experience. This forces an organisation to stay up-to-date on the expectations and demands of their clients (Shoemaker & Mattila). In a manufacturing context, value-based pricing sets prices before the product is manufactured, incorporating a 'cost-performance target that is set by customers' (Collins & Parsa, 2006, p. 94). In a service sector context, companies often use the value-based approach when they do not want to offer deeply discounted rates for their products to stimulate sales. A typical example of value-based pricing of a hospitality product is the introduction of Courtyard in the 1980s. Marriott positioned the new product as a medium-priced hotel, below their high-end hotels, and aimed at another market segment. The research conducted to develop this brand involved examining guests' preferences and willingness to pay for particular attributes of their hospitality product and service. As this example illustrates, organisations make strategic long-term decisions on pricing and positioning. However, it is important to note that these choices need to be supported by a consistent day-to-day approach to pricing.

Ad 2 Operational pricing
Once the organisation has made all the strategic pricing decisions, depending on the anticipated demand for the product at a particular time, they now need to decide on the price levels and booking conditions for their product at that period. After all, the hospitality industry commonly practices dynamic pricing, whereby different customers pay a different price for the same product, for example a room. We call this operational pricing.   **Dynamic pricing**

Earlier we defined value as the economic sacrifice that customers are willing to make, with a substantial part closely associated with the money paid in exchange for the hospitality experience. Yet, the price charged for the product is not always the same, and can vary per day, and for some industries

Revenue management

even change multiple times in one day. We call this process revenue management (or yield management), which is defined as (Cross, 1997, p. 33):

> the application of disciplined tactics that predict consumer behaviour at the micro-market level and that optimise product availability and price to maximise revenue growth.

In short, organisations charge different prices to different customers for the same product to generate the best possible financial return from selling their inventory of products. The decision-making process that makes variable prices available under variable conditions is based on an extensive analysis of past and expected future demand including seasonality patterns, events, and macro-economic trends. Companies have to gain a solid insight into the booking behaviour of their guests, including the moment of booking, the likelihood of booking cancellations or no-shows, and the reservation source. The revenue manager procures this information, and based on the findings, decides which price level in the strategic price structure will be made available on a particular date, in combination with the terms and restrictions that might apply to discounted rates.

Booking behaviour

Because a hospitality product meets the vast number of criteria traditionally associated with products suitable for applying revenue management techniques and principles, many hospitality organisations have a dedicated department responsible for operational pricing decisions. This aspect is enhanced by the fact that *production* and *consumption* of the hospitality experience take place simultaneously (inseparability) and that contributes to the often short-term focus of many hospitality organisations.

The number of available units or products (e.g. chairs or rooms) is fixed and cannot be increased without a serious time lag. In the case of high demand, you cannot achieve revenue maximisation by temporarily increasing product supply. Instead, you should use price optimisation to ensure the right rates and booking conditions are available. Customers are segmented according to their price sensitivity and/or other buying behaviour traits. Price-sensitive customers generally buy well in advance, so you can link booking restrictions to the *time* of purchase. An example could be a discounted rate that needs to be prepaid and cannot be cancelled, and can only be booked up to three weeks before the day of arrival.

Price sensitivity

Next, demand for hospitality products is subject to fluctuation, with a varying number of customers wanting to purchase the product per day. This can be a reason for offering different rates on different days. Finally, while the costs of selling one additional product are low, production costs are high. This means that hospitality organisations first need to cover their variable costs, the costs incurred only when a product is sold. They will use the additional revenue to cover the fixed costs incurred even if the product is not sold.

In summary, the combination of fixed capacity and inability to store the hospitality product creates the conditions for a high probability of product spoilage of unsold rooms or seats. With high fixed costs for adding an extra product, utilisation of all available rooms or seats becomes crucial (Brotherton & Mooney, 1992). Obviously, a revenue manager has a complex task. He or she needs to match the variable demand for the hospitality product under competitive market situations, with an inflexible and fixed supply of products.

● www.hotelmarketingcoach.com

Revenue management for dummies… (like me)

Smaller Hotels Should Reap the Benefits Too

[…]

The airlines were the first, in travel, to realise that the principle of 'supply and demand' could be used to maximise revenue. They realised that selling all their seats at high prices was nearly impossible most of the time. They needed some way to fill enough seats to cover expenses; yet have the ability to raise prices after that base is obtained. Thus, the magic 7-day fare was born. Anyone making a reservation more than seven days in advance of a flight got a real deal; after that your reservation is profit and it has worked for them for many years.

The principle is the same for hotels as well. As occupancy demand increases and supply (room availability) decreases, lower rates are closed to sale and only higher rates are available. Hotels today need a base of business in order to cover operational expenses. Selling all one's rooms at the same rate rarely produces good occupancy or a good average rate.

Let's examine how hotel rates are determined. Contrary to what some hotel owners may believe, setting rates has little to do with the hotel's furnishings or design. Hotel room rates are determined by what people will pay for those rooms. I've seen many hotel rooms that sell for $150 per night in Florida, which would sell for $500 per night in New York City, for the same room. Occupancy demand is the major difference. Higher demand allows for higher rates, plain and simple.

[…]

For many years, hoteliers have realised that various market segments tolerate different rate levels. Most well-operated hotels set rates by market segment all the way up and down the scale. All rates flow from your highest rack rates down to lower deeply discounted rates. Once your scale of rates is determined, it's time to begin setting up revenue management parameters.

[…]

Once rates are set for each segment of business, […] the next step is to set desired occupancy levels needed to close each discount level; what is needed to establish a base of business. This example is for a 100 room property.

0 to 50 rooms sold – all rates are available
51 to 70 rooms sold – close Deep Discount rates
71 to 85 rooms sold – close all rates except Walk-in Corporate and Rack Rates

[…]

Adding restrictions

For high demand periods, many hotels add restrictions to increase revenue yield. Some common restrictions, such as minimum stays, closed to arrival, etc. are excellent tools for experienced yield managers. Restrictions should be applied with some caution because they do limit demand.

By Neil Salerno, adapted

Price-elasticity of demand

Adding further complexity to the decision-making process on price levels is the price-elasticity of demand. This ratio expresses a change in demand, because of a change in price. Although experts differ in their opinion on how far the demand for hospitality products, such as hotel rooms, is influenced by a price change, the rise of low-cost carriers in the airline industry shows that customers are willing to sacrifice higher service levels and flexibility in exchange for a better price. On the other hand, sensitivity to price might differ significantly per market segment. A businessman needing a hotel room or meeting facility is less likely to be influenced by a price change than a leisure guest who might be willing to spend more time and effort in the hunt for a good deal for a city trip.

Competitive pricing the smart way

Competitive pricing

Earlier in this chapter we discussed how many organisations use competitive pricing as an important, and sometimes even sole pricing tool. We said that price, together with location, past experiences and online customer reviews form the deciding criteria for guests to select where to book their hotel room (Barsky, 2013). This applies to many other hospitality products as well. Considering the customers' criteria, using competitive prices as your only source of data for deciding on your own pricing approach might be risky. However, getting your prices right, also in relation to the competition, can make a huge difference in occupancy levels or usage of hotels, restaurants, or other hospitality experiences. This justifies competitive pricing as an important pricing mechanism for hospitality experiences.

Competitive set

In addition, whereas product quality always used to create lively but subjective debate in management meetings, quality has now become much more objective and transparent, due to the popular review sites customers use to grade their experience with your product. This information is available for your own property, and is obtainable for your competitive set, which includes organisations that compete for the same customer, and offer products of similar quality and in the same price range. When hospitality organisations combine price and customers' ranking from online reviews they can position themselves in relation to their competitive set on these two axes, as illustrated in Figure 2.3.

Its position in the middle is our organisation's starting point to determine its closest rivals. Organisations to the left of the green dotted line offer a product rated as inferior and/or more expensive, whereas the companies to the right of the line are rated to have a better price-value proposition.

Based on the organisation's position relative to its competitive set, price levels can be opened and closed. Figure 2.4 illustrates how this works for a hotel with two room types (standard rooms and suites):

Skimming

- *Skimming*: the organisation outranks its entire competitive set, with a superior product that allows them to attract higher rate business by restricting availability at low rate levels, thus increasing the average spend per customer

Penetration

- *Penetration*: customers' perceive the product as inferior to the competitive set, forcing the organisation to make lower rate levels available to gain market share

Surrounding

- *Surrounding*: if the hotel suites are rated significantly higher than the competition, the organisation can communicate higher price levels to the

FIGURE 2.3 Market positioning

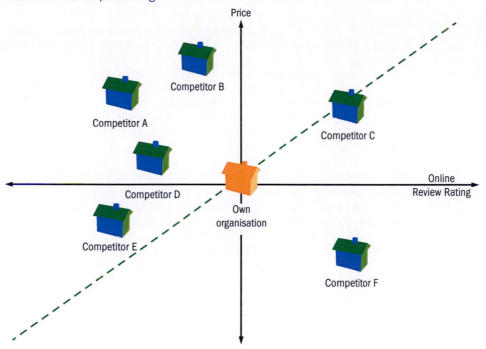

FIGURE 2.4 Pricing approaches

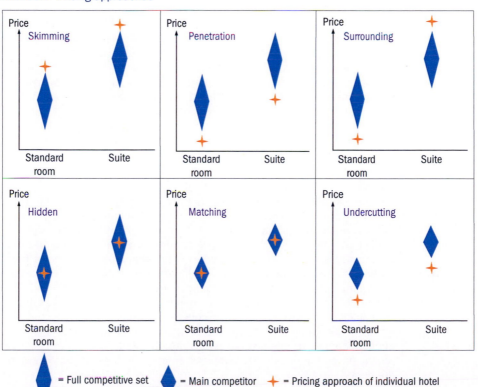

market. If the standard product is considered inferior, the organisation can make discounted rates available to drive volume

Hidden

- *Hidden*: when an organisation lacks a clear vision (according to Porter, they are 'stuck in the middle') and simply follows its competitors' pricing approach

Matching

- *Matching*: a competitor's rating matches your own organisation's rating and jointly you outrank the competition. This allows you to follow them in your aim to attract higher spending guests

Undercutting

- *Undercutting*: a competitor demands your full attention because it has superior customer reviews and ratings. You want to gain market share and offer slightly lower rates

It is important to note at this point that owners and shareholders often demand quick returns on their investment, especially in times of increased economic uncertainty. This means that in today's hospitality industry, the planning and pricing horizons of many organisations are limited, and focus on producing profitable results in the short term, often with competing by discounting. All this means that many ideas we discuss in this chapter do not get applied to their fullest potential. In practice many organisations leave an unknown amount of profit on the table. Maybe you, the future hospitality manager, can take on this challenge and help the industry fulfil its potential in this area!

2.5 Roles and functions

As you know, deciding on the monetary value and availability of price levels is a complex process that involves gathering information from many sources and viewpoints. This process needs to address all the stages that add value in satisfying the customers' needs, the actual staging costs, the required financial returns, and the competitive market in which the organisation operates. Due to the high complexity of pricing, the decisions involve many people from different departments in a hospitality organisation. Figure 2.5 shows an example of a basic organisational chart, which we will use to explain the role of each hotel department in the pricing process.

Organisational chart

Price structure

Once a year, the hotel reviews price levels and adjusts them accordingly for the upcoming year. Sales managers can use these new price levels to renegotiate contracts with corporate clients, and draw new budgets based on the new rates. In normal circumstances, the price structure remains fixed for the whole year. That makes it of utmost importance to ensure that the price levels allow the hotel to remain competitive in changing market situations. It explains why we use macro-economic data on trends affecting long-term demand, as well as micro-economic data on the hotel's particular market, such as a possible increase in competition. The executive team, including the general manager, the heads of the financial department and the sales & marketing departments typically establish the price levels. The revenue manager contributes crucial data to support the decision-making process as he or she can make reasonable predictions about upcoming trends and developments for the demand in the next period, based on the booking behaviour of potential groups of customers in the past.

Executive team

Demand

FIGURE 2.5   Standard organisational chart

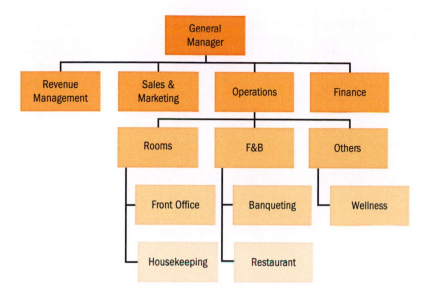

Once the executive team has agreed on the price levels, and head office has approved them if necessary, the revenue manager can start to apply detailed forecasts to decide which prices, and against which conditions, will be made available for particular days (operational pricing). Ideally, the revenue manager will chair a regular revenue meeting held, for instance, weekly to discuss and evaluate these decisions with the sales & marketing manager, the operations manager and the general manager. Each manager has their own role and brings their own data to the meeting table.

Revenue manager

The revenue manager has accurate information on expected demand, and recent data on the number of reservations made for the (near) future. They can identify critical days well in advance, when anticipated demand is either extremely low or extremely high. Armed with this data the hotel can find ways to stimulate demand, for example, selectively making rooms available only to guests who will generate the highest revenue. The revenue manager closely monitors the actual booking patterns and number of reservations against the forecast. As long as the business on the books (the number of reservations made for a particular day in the future) stay inside the accepted boundaries of the anticipated booking curve, no further action is needed. However, when the actual booking pace is significantly slower or faster than the forecast, the hotel needs to take action to cover these *unusual days*. The actions can vary from easing booking restrictions when demand is slow, to closing down the lower price levels in the case of excessive demand. Obviously, the revenue manager considers any upcoming events that might stimulate demand or have a possible negative effect.

Booking patterns

The sales & marketing manager is responsible for developing the hotel's share of (potential) corporate clients. They network daily with major clients, so the sales & marketing team should be able to provide an accurate

Sales & marketing manager

estimate of the value of clients, and generate new business leads. This is in contrast to the revenue manager, who knows what is selling, and what is not. Due to their often conflicting objectives, revenue managers and sales & marketing managers can have opposing viewpoints on which price levels should be opened or closed. A sales manager is traditionally rewarded for the number of contracts or the sales volume he or she generates and might therefore opt for a discounting approach that generates volume. The revenue manager is commonly assessed on revenue per available room (RevPAR) targets, and thus keeps a close eye on the average spend per room or customer, in combination with the number of units sold. The general manager usually rules on any unresolved disputes between the two managers.

RevPAR

What came first, the chicken or the egg? It is a long-standing debate and the same can be said about sales & marketing and revenue management. At the end of the day, a revenue manager relies on information from the sales manager, who in turn depends on accurate forecast information from the revenue manager to sell the product.

Operations manager

The final player in the decision-making triangle is the operations manager. Although this role might not be obvious at first glance, the operation manager's involvement can be crucial in guaranteeing the profitability of certain pricing decisions. The value of a particular group or meeting might be too good to be true, because if the event turns out to overstretch operational capacity, the unforeseen extra cost will have a negative impact on the profitability of that piece of business. Operational staff have direct regular contact with guests and can discover valuable information about future business that might contribute to better decisions.

To avoid conflicts arising from opposing departmental views, a sensible hospitality business will make the *entire* team responsible for the overall financial performance of the organisation, with each department valued for its contribution to success. For example, sales and marketing follow-up on leads and bring in new clients and the revenue manager makes sure guests can book the product at the right rates. Meanwhile the operational departments deliver outstanding service and create good customer reviews and the maintenance department keeps the physical product up-to-date in a cost-efficient manner.

Online travel agents

In addition to these internal parties, a number of external parties are involved in pricing decisions, such as online travel agents (OTAs) that play an important role in the distribution of the hospitality product. More on that in the next chapter!

In summary, hospitality is all about creating meaningful experiences. From the host's perspective it comprises the provision of accommodation, food and/or beverage. For a guest it represents the consumption of a service that has a value. This value, however, is not limited to the core benefit but involves all four levels of the hospitality service product. Therefore, a whole collection of value-adding activities (i.e. the value chain) is needed to stage, market and deliver the hospitality experience. A room is not 'just a space with a bed', but 'a rejuvenating experience in a delightful atmosphere of luxury which treats the guest like a royal'. Traditionally, value-adding hospitality activities were staged in a hotel, restaurant, or café/bar setting. However, the traditional hospitality industry has expanded its boundaries to, for example, include entertainment and event organisations. Moreover, the channels through which hospitality is sold and distrib- **Channels** uted (e.g. booking a room via an app) have also changed drastically. The one thing these companies have in common is that they are all in the business of making make money from selling (aspects of) hospitality experiences!

2

Summary

▶ Hospitality experiences are a combination of:
- tangible products
- intangible features

▶ According to Grönroos (1987), a product can be divided into four value-adding levels that each form an integral part of staging hospitality experiences:
- the core product
- the facilitating product
- the supporting product
- the augmented product

▶ The operating leverage ratio is an indicator of the financial risk a company faces under different market situations. It considers the fixed costs in relation to the overall costs.

▶ Hospitality companies are primarily in the business to make money. Next to managing costs, an effective pricing process contains two distinct stages:
- strategic pricing
- operational pricing

▶ Strategic pricing decisions are preceded and strongly impacted by the manner in which a company wants to distinguish itself from competitors to create a competitive advantage. According to Porter (1985), an organisation can pursue this by following one of three generic strategies:
- Cost leadership
- Differentiation
- Focus

▶ The revenue manager is a key decision maker in the operational pricing phase.

Food for thought

In this chapter, we explained the process of adding value to create and deliver a profitable hospitality experience. Based on the content of this chapter, the following questions and statements could serve as an interesting starting point for further discussion:

1   The hospitality experience can be categorised according to Grönroos' product levels. Can you explain which of the four levels a hospitality organisation could use to differentiate its hospitality experience from competitors? And can you provide an example of such a product level?

2   To stage profitable hospitality experiences, you must monitor and manage both costs and revenues. Because of the precarious balance between fixed and variable costs, companies with a high operating leverage face higher financial risks in periods of slow demand. Besides selling off their properties, can you think of other ways that hospitality organisations could reduce their fixed costs, without jeopardising experience quality?

3   The pricing process has two distinct phases, strategic and operational pricing. Can you come up with some real-life examples of pricing decisions that are typically associated with the strategic pricing phase? And do the same for the operational phase?

4   All the departments we described in this chapter are involved in the process of adding value to hospitality experiences. Can you draw the value chain of a hospitality organisation and explain who or which department is responsible for each stage of the whole process?

3
The hospitality industry

Jeroen Oskam and Tjeerd Zandberg

This chapter portrays the contours of the hospitality industry. We discuss the various types of businesses in the industry and explain how they evolved over time. We utilise a common framework to delineate the industry, including lodging, food services and drinking places, entertainment and recreation, travel service providers, and assembly and event management. The chapter also addresses contemporary changes that define the way the international hotel industry operates, such as the internet, social media, and booking and distribution channels.

Carry in? Hotels deliver fast food for guests

Fast food has gone glam at hotel restaurants Hotels are moving away from traditional, sit-down restaurants and serving comfort food with an upscale twist.

Some examples:

- The Hudson Hotel in New York, a Morgans Hotel Group property, recently opened Hudson Common, 'a modern-day beer hall and burger joint.' Customers order burgers on brioche buns, sandwiches such as the French toast grilled cheese, or duck-fat fries from a counter. A text lets them know when they can pick up their food to eat, in a dark lounge with leather couches, or elsewhere.
- Taco stands are in vogue. IHG's Holiday Inn Resort Los Cabos has turned its La Terraza restaurant into a taco stand between noon to 5 p.m. with a rotating menu of tacos and freshly made drinks. Back in the States, the Hudson Hotel has opened an outdoor taco stand, Tequila Park.
- Kimpton's Eventi Hotel in New York has Brighton, made to look like Brooklyn's Brighton Beach boardwalk. Diners order from GoBurger, Fish Shack or a Tiki Bar. Lobsters rolls, BLTs, shakes and beer can be consumed indoors or outside on the Eventi Plaza.
- All Hotel Indigos have casual, fast-dining options with locally inspired dishes. At Hotel Indigo Alamo in San Antonio, for instance, guests can dine on fresh tacos from 1909 Bar & Bistro.

Source: adapted from http://www.usatoday.com, May 3, 2013

3.1   The nature and scope of the hospitality industry

The hospitality industry is a multi-billion Euro industry in the service sector. It is an umbrella term for a wide range of industries, such as the hotel industry, and the restaurant industry. To delineate a clear industry boundary for commercial hospitality is a challenging task. For example, do hospitals belong in the hospitality industry? What about breweries or tour operators? While all three involve or relate to the provision of hospitality, they are generally classified in the health care industry, beverage manufacturing industry, and tourism industry, respectively.

Hospitality industry

De Wit and Meyer (2010, p. 238) define industries as groups of firms 'making a similar type of product or employing a similar set of value-adding processes or resources'. In other words, they define industries based on a particular supply-side similarity. For example, we speak of the airline industry (i.e. product similarity), the consulting industry (activity similarity, not necessarily product similarity), and the cotton industry (resource similarity). Defining the hospitality industry thus involves personal choice.

Supply-side similarity

Product similarity

Activity similarity

Resource similarity

3

● De Wit & Meyer, 2010

Defining industries

Census bureaus – that provide data about a nation's people and economy – prefer industry definitions based on economic activity (e.g. NACE Rev. 2). Strategists tend to favour regrouping existing industry classifications according to underlying value-adding activities and resources. They place Swatch in the fashion industry, for instance, as opposed to the watch industry.

Using our definition of hospitality (see Chapter 1) you could say that supply-side similarities in the hospitality industry generally relate to:
- a voluntary interaction between a host and a guest involving a cordial reception, welcome and entertainment aimed at enhancing the well-being of a guest through the provision of accommodation and/or food and/or drink
- the context, and the rules and norms that determine the appropriate behaviour

The hotel and restaurant industries are thus certainly part of the hospitality industry. Broadly speaking, hotels are considered part of the 'lodging industry', while restaurants fall under the subsector 'food services and drinking places'. Table 3.1 provides an overview of these two and all the other subsectors that put together are generally regarded as the ones that shape the hospitality industry.

TABLE 3.1 Main groupings of firms in the hospitality industry

Subsector	Sub-division
Lodging	Hotels and resorts
	Motels
	Holiday centres and villages
	Youth hostels
	Other holiday and other short stay accommodation
	Camping grounds and recreational vehicle parks
Food services and drinking places	(Un)licensed restaurants
	Take away food shops and mobile food stands
	Event catering activities
	Managed and other food service activities
	Licensed clubs
	Public houses and bars
Entertainment and recreation	Amusement, attraction and theme parks
	Gambling and betting activities
	Creative, arts and entertainment activities
Travel service provider	Deep sea cruising
	Short-term cruising and other scenic and sightseeing transport
Assembly and event management	Convention and trade show organisers
	Exhibition and fair organisers
	Live event organisers

Subsector

First, as Table 3.1 illustrates, the lodging industry includes hotels, resorts, motels, holiday villages, hostels, and camping grounds, etc. Industries in the lodging subsector provide short-term accommodation and complementary services for travellers or vacationers. Secondly, the subsector food services and drinking places consists of restaurants, event catering, managed food services, clubs, and bars. These firms prepare meals, snacks, and beverages for immediate consumption. Of course, lodging firms may also offer food and beverage (F&B) services on their premises. Yet, these will only be considered 'food services and drinking places' if a separate food or drinking place is primarily involved in providing F&B (NAICS, 2012). Thirdly, the entertainment and recreation subsector contains amusement, gambling/gaming, creative arts, and other entertainment activities. For example, it includes water parks, bingo halls, theatres, but also pinball arcades and gambling cruises. Fourthly, travel service providers are broadly categorised as deep sea cruising, and short-term cruising and other scenic and sightseeing transport. Think of cruise lines, stream train excursions, fishing charters or whale watching excursions. Finally, the assembly and event management subsector consists of convention and trade show organisers as well as exhibition and fair organisers, such as trade fair promoters or festival managers.

Together these five subsectors form what we traditionally regard as the 'hospitality industry'; the businesses that first come to mind when asked to define the hospitality industry. But, as new business models create new types of commercial hospitality, the industry scope is constantly broadening. Today it is quite common to include medical spas and care hotels within the scope of hospitality management education and research. Similarly, the business model extensions of the Las Vegas Bellagio or the Venetian still qualify them as 'hospitality business', even though the range of complementary services nowadays includes theatres, aquaria, and art galleries (Slattery, 2002). However, as a full discussion of all businesses that could possibly fit the hospitality industry definition is beyond the scope of this chapter, in the following sections we discuss only the most common types of hospitality business in more detail.

3.2 **Hotels and other lodging services**

Lodging services have existed ever since people began travelling. The medieval inn became more refined in pre-industrial Britain and subsequently flourished in North America. Some mythical inns, such as the Hoshi Ryokan in Komatsu, Japan, a spa hotel open since 718, or the Hospital de los Reyes Católicos, a shelter and recovery accommodation for Saint Jacob's pilgrims in Santiago de Compostela, Spain, that opened in 1511, are still operated today as hotels. The modern hotel has evolved from historical inns and guesthouses by developing elements that have become critical to the modern traveller, especially, privacy, luxury, the range of services offered and branding.

Hotel

In the 19th century, hotels became important meeting places in North American cities. Whereas inns used to be ordinary houses prepared to accommodate travellers, these hotels were, at the time, gigantic structures – the New York City Hotel (1794) had 73 rooms! – built especially for the purpose. In 1829, the Tremont House in Boston introduced the novelty of private rooms, each equipped with a bowl, a pitcher and free soap; a revolution compared to the dormitories in inns, where guests usually had to share beds. As 19th century technological innovations led to increased mobility, lodging services had to adapt to the demand of growing business travel. The Buffalo Statler Hotel (1908) is considered the first modern commercial hotel, with private bathrooms among many other innovations. The hotel advertised itself with the slogan 'A Room and a Bath for a Dollar and a Half' (Lattin, 2005; Rushmore, 2004).

Business travel

In the meantime, Europe saw hotel developments in such holiday resorts as the French Côte d'Azur and Switzerland. In major cities, Grand Hotels offered extreme luxury to visitors and the local upper class. An important representative of this luxury segment was the Swiss hotelier César Ritz who, around the turn of the 19th century, opened the Ritz Hotels in London, Paris, and Madrid and thus created the first international hotel brand.

Holiday resorts

The first actual hotel chains were formed during the first half of the 20th century in the United States. Statler built new hotels in north-eastern US cities.

Two other chains, Hilton and Sheraton, could expand more rapidly by a strategy of purchasing existing hotels. In 1919, Conrad Hilton bought his first hotel in Cisco, Texas. His company suffered severely from the 1929 depression, but would profit later from the depressed hotel market, buying hotels at low prices. Ernest Henderson bought his first hotel in Springfield, Massachusetts, in 1937, and his hotel company, later to become Sheraton, grew like the Hilton chain. Statler was eventually taken over by Hilton in 1954.

Today's biggest hotel brands

Hotel chains

Although there are exceptions like Germany, where independent, family-owned hotels still lead, hotel chains – with different organisation models and structures – now tend to dominate the industry economically. There are several reasons behind the success of chains. Probably the most important is the guests' recognition. Once you enter a Hilton, for example, you are assured of a certain service level.

● Accor, 2007

Accor's early years

After the Second World War, French hotel guests had to choose between luxury five-star hotels in city centres or low-quality inns. There was a large gap in the market for a standard quality room aiming to meet the demand of a growing number of middle class travellers. Gérard Pelisson and Paul Dubrule filled this gap with the creation of the Novotel brand. Offering standardised rooms, Novotel hotels were located near traveller's destinations like airports and holiday sites, with good parking facilities at reasonable prices. The format proved to be very attractive and when its first hotel opened near Lille in 1967, many other hotels opened soon after.

Only six years later, Accor planned a second hotel chain, Ibis. Ibis was a two-star no-frills budget chain and just like Novotel, designed on the drawing board of Pelisson and Dubrule. In 1975, Accor acquired the Mercure hotel chain, which owned many city hotels aimed at business guests. With the acquisition of Sofitel, the Accor group established itself in the luxury hotel market, offering brands from basic to luxurious hotels.

Adapted

Global coverage

Until the end of the 20th century, hotel chains remained largely an American phenomenon, with branches in related markets, such as Europe, the Caribbean, and South America. This panorama changed with the end of the Cold War and the emergence of 'new' economies, especially in Eastern Asia, which has become the major growth market for hotel companies. Now the trend for hotel chains is to pursue global coverage, both geographically and in terms of market segments. Globalisation has become manifest in the appearance of luxury hotel chains originating in these new markets, such as Shangri-La and Jumeirah. However, the outcome of this process is that today the global hotel market is still dominated by a relatively low number of very large companies. Table 3.2 demonstrates the size of these companies.

TABLE 3.2 Top ten ranking of hotel groups as of 1 January 2013

		Rooms	Properties
IHG	UK	675,982	4,602
Hilton Worldwide	USA	652,378	3,992
Marriott International	USA	638,793	3,672
Wyndham Hotel Group	USA	627,437	7,342
Choice Hotels International	USA	497,023	6,198
Accor	FR	450,199	3,515
Starwood Hotels & Resorts	USA	328,055	1,121
Best Western	USA	311,611	4,024
Home Inns	CHI	214,070	1,772
Carlson Rezidor Hotel Group	USA	166,245	1,077
Total		**4,561,793**	**37,315**

IHG = International Hotels Group

Source: adapted from www.hospitalitynet.org

Table 3.2 clearly shows the dominance of the USA with seven positions in the top ten. IHG and Accor are European groups, and new in the top ten since 2012 is Home Inns, a Chinese hotel group with brands like Home Inn, Yitel, and Motel 168. Some names like Hilton or Best Western are very familiar while others like IHG or Starwood are less well-known to the general public. Hotel groups use brands for different markets to be clear and identifiable for their guests. For example IHG operates brands like Holiday Inn or Crowne Plaza.

Dominance of the USA

Brands

The aim of most of the major players is to attain global coverage in all relevant market segments. Several reasons explain the success of chains. First, this type of hotel is a business partner of global corporate companies like Shell or IBM. When board members travel to Beijing, for example, they want to stay in luxury hotels. But, when junior engineers are sent abroad, they may stay in midscale hotels. So, to serve the various market segments, hotel companies offer different brands across the world. The number one (IHG) has several upscale brands like Intercontinental and Crowne Plaza, but also Holiday Inns and Holiday Inn Express hotels. Similarly, a chain like Accor now also encompasses a number of distinct brands, as Figure 3.1 illustrates.

Market segments

Recently, we have seen some interesting new developments in corporate brand strategy of some of the main players in this market. For example, Starwood, traditionally more active in the upscale market with brands like W, Westin, St. Regis, and Le Méridien, introduced the Aloft brand in 2008. Aloft offers modern rooms with sassy design and good technological facilities to attract hip business travellers and tourists.

A second reason behind the success of most of these chains is the high level of professionalism in management. Most chains pay serious attention

FIGURE 3.1 Accor brand portfolio

Source: http://www.accorhotels.com

to training and developing their management, resulting in high standards on average. A third reason is the sales operation at headquarters. An average chain hotel gets at least 20% or 30% of its reservations through the central reservation system of the chain, putting independent competitors at a substantial distance. Indeed, an important activity of hotel chains nowadays is to drive demand with revenue management systems, central reservation systems and loyalty programmes.

Central reservation system

Standard hotel classification systems

Classification systems

Hotels carry classifications of usually one to five stars to show potential guests what level of luxury they may expect. The classification systems often differ in each country and are managed by a government body or by hotel or tourism associations. National ratings criteria may also differ. The US uses an entirely different system with one to four diamonds. There is no internationally unified system, which means we cannot compare the classifications of different countries and the number of stars or diamonds may raise the wrong expectation in international visitors.

In general, hotel classification schemes list the formal requirements that a hotel must comply with to deserve one or more stars. For examples, in the Netherlands, a one-star hotel must offer one bathroom per ten hotel rooms, a two-star hotel per 50% of the rooms, and in a three-star hotel all rooms must have private bathrooms. Then four-star rooms must have extra pillows and light-blocking curtains, while five-star hotels must have a minimum of two suites, turn-down service, and 24-hour meal service. For one and two stars, there is no minimum room size. The minimum for three stars is 17 m^2 and for five stars, 26 m^2.

But do hotel guests really choose their hotel because of strictly tangible assets, or do they look at intangible characteristics as well? Rigid formal specifications may conflict with creativity and innovation, especially in the luxury segment. Château St. Gerlach, for example, is a Dutch luxury resort where George Bush, then American president, stayed in his 2004 visit to the Netherlands. The hotel does not use the star rating because its classification would not correspond with its luxury level. One of its 'shortcomings' is that the hotel offers two-storey suites with staircases, not elevators.

It seems logical that five-star hotels seek to differentiate themselves by service excellence. Nevertheless, this differentiation will not show in a higher star classification. This has led some hotels to use fantasy ratings. The Burj al Arab in Dubai and the Galleria in Milan, Italy, claim seven stars. Since there is no seven-star scale, this probably simply means: 'We think we are better than other hotels'. But hotels may also opt for voluntary downgrading for commercial reasons. Internal company regulations or guidelines by professional organisations may rule against the use of five-star hotels for their employees or for congresses. In that case, it can be interesting for hotels to drop their fifth star.

Differentiate

3

Burj Al Arab in Dubai claims seven stars

Finally, to what extent are star classifications still relevant to hotel guests? In recent years, travellers exchanging detailed information on social media and on sites like Tripadvisor have fully made up for the lack of systematic information on the intangible qualities of hotels. Hotel guests consider these sites a reliable source of information for their choices (Hensens, 2010). The trend is that social ratings are gaining importance against traditional star classifications, and you could expect the latter to become obsolete in the near future, unless the classification schemes manage to successfully adapt to these developments.

Social media

Business hotels

When we look at different types of services for travellers, the most important distinction is their *reason to travel*. Business travellers and leisure travellers are the two largest travel segments. The successful growth of large
international hotel brands since the 1950s is due to the increasing demand from the business segment. For example, in 2010 the American Hotel and Lodging Association reported that 40% of total travel was for business purposes. Business hotel bookings are normally made under the
framework of a corporate contract. As business travel starts to enter new
parts of the world, this is why hotel companies seek to expand their geographical coverage. The business travel segment is stable and predictable
in both volume and guest expectations – business people are often frequent and experienced travellers – and this makes it an important market
for the hotel industry.

A location close to the place of work is essential for business hotels which
is why most business hotels are in city centres. But we may find examples
on special sites, such as the Ritz-Carlton Wolfsburg, which mainly caters to
the business guests of Volkswagen. As reservations are made through
business channels, this type of guest is usually not the most price sensitive, although recently many companies have been obliged to review their
travel policies. The typical business stay is short, two-to-three days on average (Rushmore, 2004), and obviously concentrated on week days, with little
activity in the summer season or in December.

We could say that the typical business accommodation is a city hotel that
offers its guests an elegant professional ambience focused on sleeping
and meetings. Cleanliness and comfort are the most important criteria for
business guests (Rushmore, 2004). The range of services offered is also
of interest. Firstly, work-related amenities – such as a desk, work space
and internet connection – (Lattin, 2005), but also other living-away-from-
home amenities, such as adjustable room temperature, an ironing board or
a fitness centre. It is important for these hotels to offer meeting rooms or
dedicated business centres where guests can print, make photocopies and
use communication services and obtain assistance with travel or meeting
arrangements. Possibly though, technological advances may change the offer of these centres in the near future.

Standardisation used to be considered a benefit during the growth peek of
hotel chains. The idea was that a business guest could travel from Mexico
City to Cairo and find the light switch in his (or, far more rarely, her) hotel
room on the same spot as the night before. Nowadays this idea is under
discussion. Two socio-cultural trends may have contributed to the changing
guest experience in business hotels. First, the divide between work and leisure in today's society is not as sharp as before. People check their work
e-mail on Saturday night or at the beach, and expect a pleasant environment when they travel for work. Second, globalisation has broadened business travel from something engaged in by a few professional 'road tigers'
to larger groups of employees. One reaction to this trend is that business
hotels are trying to create a 'home away from home'. This was the idea behind the NH hotel chain's *Nhube* concept, launched in 2002. Another example of de-standardisation and exclusivity is the Puerta América Hotel in Madrid, with rooms and spaces designed by 19 different architects.

Margin terms:

- Business travellers
- Business segment
- Location
- Cleanliness
- Comfort
- Standardisation
- Globalisation

A third reason for the changes in the concept and design of city hotels is the sustained growth of the leisure segment. Maybe the best thing about the two major hotel markets from a hotel's perspective is that they are complementary. Leisure guests start coming when the business market slows down, and vice versa. To maximise its occupancy through all seasons, a hotel must therefore address two challenges. Its concept should attract both groups, and the different uses both groups make of a hotel should be compatible. It is a complicated balance to maintain. Leisure guests expect more frivolous decoration in their hotel, and business people frown upon children playing in the corridor during their meetings. Barcelona and Amsterdam are good examples of city destinations with low seasonality in business hotels thanks to leisure guest occupancy at weekends and in summer.

Leisure segment

Leisure or resort hotels

Dedicated leisure hotels are a different category. We find these hotels in seaside or mountain resorts, close to theme parks or in other leisure-oriented locations such as, for instance, Las Vegas. Leisure travellers are more seasonal, they stay longer on average than business travellers, and they want to be accommodated, in general, with friends or relatives. Nowadays most leisure guests no longer book through tour operators, which is leading the big travel companies to rethink their business models. If purchasing and reselling travel packages becomes too risky, these companies will have to seek other sources of revenue. As a result, today we sometimes see holiday hotels and resorts integrating with tour operating companies. For example, TUI now operates brands like Riu, Robinson Club, or Club Magic Life through vertical integration.

Leisure travellers

Obviously, resort hotels cater to holiday goers. The layout and comfort of hotel rooms tend to be more important to leisure guests than to business guests, which may have to do with the length of stay and time spent in the rooms. In-room facilities may include items as sofa beds, kitchenettes, or balcony furniture. Depending on their location, these resorts usually offer outdoor swimming pools and other entertainment services. Themed resorts are in a special category that reflects a relatively recent trend. Famous examples are The Venetian or Luxor in Las Vegas, or the Disney hotels. More recent examples can be found on the Turkish coast, where tourists stay at the Kremlin Resort or the Amsterdam canal-styled Orange County Resort.

An important mainstream development in international holiday resorts is the all-inclusive concept. Here, meals, drinks (except alcohol, sometimes) and service are included in the room price. Club Med created the concept in the 1950s as a 'no worries' service to guests, and its popularity is partly explained by its appeal to certain tourist markets. On the other hand, the concept brings important benefits to the hotel company. For example, it simplifies operations, such as purchasing and logistics. It also is a means for price maximisation. Bundled services are sold at a fair total price, in the guest's opinion, regardless of their intention to buy individual services if they were offered separately. Working with the all-inclusive concept is especially profitable in countries with a low living standard where the marginal cost of meals and drinks – the cost incurred by serving each additional meal or drink – is low because of inexpensive labour and low product costs.

All-inclusive concept

The downside is that all-inclusive resorts are far less beneficial to local economies, since tourists stay on the resort's premises and spend their money inside the hotel. While these resorts may bring business to less developed regions, not all local communities benefit from it, making some wonder if all-inclusive truly is a sustainable and responsible form of tourism. The question is, who profits, the local community or the resort owners. All-inclusive can of course be sustainable, for example if it contributes to reducing energy cost and waste, sourcing fresh local produce, and offering employment and training to the local population.

In general, leisure stays and guests demand different management approaches than in business hotels. Length of stay and simultaneous arrival and departure patterns change the planning and logistics. The background and holiday disposition of guests make for another sort of interaction with staff and other guests. Communication between guests combined with their heightened price sensitivity often determines pricing policies. A holiday resort will not risk dissatisfaction in guests discovering that they are paying more for the same service than their hotel neighbour.

Club Med's latest advertising slogan is: And what is your idea of happiness?

In the leisure segment, we also find other types of operations. Instead of presenting itself as a hotel, a hotel-like resort may consist of separate units sold to individual owners. The big advantage is that the initial investment is recovered with a profit right at the start, so that the hotel company can concentrate on what it does best, managing the property. These resorts can either consist of fully owned units which owners can use for

Condominiums
Time-share

themselves or rent to others (*condominiums*). Alternatively, the *time-share* is a later development of the same concept, where multiple owners possess a single unit and each has the right to use it for a limited time, say two weeks a year. Since the early 2000s, most international hotel companies offer time-shares. The concept has also crossed over to city properties in cities like Boston and New York (Lattin, 2005).

Mid-range and low-cost hotels
Low-cost and mid-range hotels are a relatively recent phenomenon. The 1960s roadside motels in the US are the forerunners of what is currently one of the most interesting trends. Hotel chains like Accor identified the low-cost segment as having the most promising growth opportunities. Note that this implies an important shift in commercial strategy. Rather than luring away customers from competitors, as providers in a saturated market must do, these inexpensive hotels attract entirely new customers, people who, if it had not been for budget hotels, would not travel or would have chosen a different type of accommodation.

Europe saw the introduction of no-frills accommodation in the budget hotel boom around French motorway crossings. Ibis (est. 1974) was Accor's first two-star budget brand, and it was followed by even 'simpler' concepts such as Formule 1 (est. 1985). Standardisation and prefab hotel construction, staff reduction through multifunctionality – receptionists who double as bartenders – and automated check-ins and bathroom cleaning operations are cost-reducing innovations in these hotels.

The evolution of the demand side is of course driving the success of mid-range and low-cost hotels. The continuous growth of leisure travel is an important factor, especially true for travellers using low-cost airlines, also a relatively new phenomenon. At the same time, 'unpackaging' and online booking means that cost conscious travellers can be more selective and find their optimal price-quality combination. Finally, we have to consider the fluidity of consumer behaviour. Rather than identifying with a single kind of offer –upper class and luxury, or under 30 and adventurous – today's consumer has a wider range of preferences for different occasions. A company executive may stay at a five-star brand on business trips, but choose a less sophisticated hotel for personal travel. The consequence is that economy hotels have to offer a basic level of comfort acceptable to the experienced traveller, a need detected and covered by budget chains.

If the above is true for the old markets, it is even more the case for the emerging economies. International companies and new local chains are investing in budget hotels in China and India, where the upcoming middle **Budget hotels** classes represent an impressive volume of travellers, but with an average daily spend still below that of the traditional four- and five-star guest. Modern budget hotels compete with outdated guesthouses and traditional accommodation, on the one hand, or staying with friends and family, on the other, including B&Bs and more recently 'couch surfing'. Especially in regions where a hotel industry is still to be developed, we can expect investments to focus on the economy rather than the luxury segment. As an Indian hotelier explains, 'The returns are faster, and even the break-even is quicker' (Bhaduri, Sayoni, 2012).

The organisational structure of hotels
So far, we have discussed different hotel types as if they were variations of a single business. The reality is more complex. Many people unknowingly

assume that hotel property is commonly owned and managed by the same company or person. However, the company behind the front door is often a network of interwoven organisations. Not only non-core activities like maintenance are outsourced, F&B and management can be outsourced too. For example IHG, the world's largest hotel group, owns only ten of its 4,573 hotels. All the other IHG hotels are either managed or franchised.

Franchising

Franchising means that a hotel operates under the name of an existing brand (e.g. IHG), but in reality is not owned by the brand. The hotel owner pays the brand a fee to use the brand name, concept and for example the distribution or reservation system. Franchising is successful because it reduces risks and allows hotel companies to focus on their core business – managing hotels – rather than on real-estate investment. This becomes especially relevant if we have a high growth rate in hotel chains, often in new destinations. Another reason is that in many markets around the world, foreign companies are only allowed to operate under the condition that they cooperate with a national company. For example in China, one of the fastest growing markets for the hotel industry, foreign countries are not allowed to own property. Therefore, they are obliged to cooperate with local partners that own the properties. A third reason is that in order to finance rapid growth, chains relied on local investors and business people, who were willing to invest their money in hotel properties.

Franchisor

Franchisees

The first benefit for the franchisor (the chain) is that granting franchises reduces investment to a fraction of the cost of actually constructing or buying a property. In some restaurant cases, such as McDonald's, local franchisees (or franchise holders, the restaurant or hotel owners) have to pay a substantial entrance fee to the corporate organisation to be accepted. Besides limited investment, the franchisor gains the commitment and market knowledge of local entrepreneurs. These advantages enable a hotel or restaurant chain to roll out a franchise format over a new area at high speed and low cost. The franchisee has several benefits. Using a tried franchise format reduces the risk of starting up a company and having access to central reservation systems and sales operations help to sell rooms.

Collaborations can be found throughout the hospitality industry

Besides franchising, many hotels are under a management contract. More and more, hotel properties are owned by investment companies or REITs (Real-Estate Investment Trust). An investment company manages money on behalf of its shareholders and a REIT is an investment company that specialises in real estate. Some investment companies are listed on the stock exchange, while others are private investment funds.

Management contract

Shareholders

If a hotel is owned by an investment company, or by wealthy individuals who see it as an investment, the owners usually do not want to be involved in operations. That is why they often join a franchise chain and hire a management company to operate the hotel. A dedicated management company is specialised in managing hotels. They can work for several franchise brands, as well as investment companies.

Apart from franchising and management, many other network relations are possible. For example, a spa or a luxury resort hotel is often operated by a well-known spa brand. Operating a spa demands specialist qualified knowledge. Dedicated spa companies have developed strong brands, and are attractive collaboration partners for hotels. In cases like this, the spa is not outsourced, but it is run in a clearly visible partnership. Sometimes, certain activities are outsourced. This means that activities are carried out under the name and responsibility of the hotel company, but sub-contracted. Well-known examples of outsourcing are housekeeping and security. Nearly all activities can be outsourced. Some hotels outsource their restaurant, effectively handing over the operation of their F&B department to a catering company. This is because many budget or midscale hotels primarily compete on price and costs, and hiring a caterer for a limited number of hours a day is often much cheaper than employing their own staff. And if a guest asks for a meal outside regular kitchen hours, a front-office manager can always put a readymade meal in the microwave.

Network relations

Outsourcing

It is interesting to have a brief look at the geographical distribution of different business structures in the hotel industry. In Table 3.3, you can see the numbers of hotels IHG has franchised, managed, and owns or leases.

TABLE 3.3 Hotel count IHG per area and type, as of 30 September 2012

	Franchised	Managed	Owned/leased	Total
Americas	3.339	199	5	3.543
Europe	520	100	2	622
AMEA	48	177	2	227
Greater China	4	176	1	181
Total	3.911	652	10	4.573

AMEA = Africa and Middle East

Source: adapted from http://www.ihgplc.com

Table 3.3 shows that franchising is especially popular in the Americas and to a lesser extent in Europe, but managing hotels is more common in AMEA and Greater China. The background of this skewed distribution lies in the fact that many owners or investors in AMEA and Greater China lack the knowledge and experience to manage a hotel. IHG needs to ensure that a property under their brand is operated according to international hospitality standards and quality levels, and so they will want to manage it. Often the management involvement is restricted to two or three people, for example the general manager, financial director and the F&B or Rooms division director.

Product-life cycles

Just as with any other commercial product, the lifetime of a specific hotel concept is limited. Products go through a *life cycle*, as Figure 3.2 depicts. Hotels introduce a new product when they detect a market need. Initially the product appeals to trendsetters or 'early adopters'. When they become popular, other companies start producing the same product, until every potential customer has it and the market is saturated. Finally, someone develops an improvement or creates an innovation, which solves a problem the initial product had for the market. The 'old' product is now obsolete and the newly developed product starts its own cycle.

FIGURE 3.2 The product-life cycle

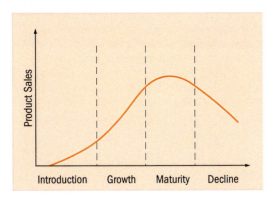

Source: QuickMBA.com

Hotel rooms wear out not only physically, but also functionally and aesthetically. New items are introduced and require adaptations. Bathrooms have evolved over the years, and more recently communication – first cable, then wireless – and flat screen TVs have changed hotel rooms. The colour schemes that impressed guests in the 1990s are now old fashioned. Generally speaking, hotel rooms need to be renovated about every five to seven years.

Location

When we know that location is normally a hotel's most important asset, it makes sense that hotel companies often prefer to renovate and upgrade a run-down hotel at the end of its life cycle rather than build a new hotel on another spot (Rushmore, 2004). This is not always feasible. In 1964, the Rossiya Hotel in Moscow was built close to Red Square, across from the Kremlin, as a flagship Soviet hotel. With 3,200 rooms and 245 half-suites it was the largest hotel in the world until the 1990s. The average room size was 11 square metres, well below western standards. In the last decade, we have seen a rapid modernisation of Moscow's hotel industry. The Rossiya was torn down in 2006, and a year later, a Ritz-Carlton opened at the other end of Red Square. But the fate of a hotel may be due to entirely different reasons. The Hong Kong Hilton was built in 1963 and held an excellent reputation until its closure and demolition in 1995. Rocketing soil prices made it simply more profitable to build an office complex on the same spot. In the US, the average life span of a hotel before demolition is 33 years.

The Rossiya Hotel in Moscow

Awareness of product-life cycles is also important when we look at the services hotels offer. Telephone charges used to be an important source of revenue. After mobile telephones became current, hotel companies tried to make up for lost revenue by charging for internet use. Radisson SAS started offering free Wi-Fi in 2002. While this was ground-breaking back then, nowadays it has become a required amenity for many hotel guests.

3.3 Food and drink services

The modern restaurant origins go back to 18th century Paris although, obviously, commercial food and beverage services existed well before then. Previously, aristocrats would enjoy meals prepared and served by professional cooks and servants, whereas ordinary (*third estate*) travellers could enjoy 'family style' meals served at common tables in inns. The societal changes at the roots of the French Revolution also contributed to the birth of the restaurant. These included, most importantly, the modern view that personalised elegant food services should also be available to non-aristocrats (Spang, 2000). Another factor was the elimination of guild rules that prescribed for instance that bakers were not allowed to slice meat for sandwiches and

Restaurant

Food and beverage

butchers could not sell bread. This made it possible to integrate these formerly separate trades. Finally, professional cooks formerly employed by aristocratic families entered the labour market and spurred the restaurant boom.

Types of restaurants

Restaurants can be arranged in 'quick service', 'midscale' and 'upscale' categories. Even if the type of service in these categories is entirely different, we may consider Michelin star restaurants as the high end of the range. Michelin ratings – up to three stars – come from the travel guide published since 1900 by the tyre maker, and have become the most prestigious qualification for restaurants. Michelin does not use an explicit set of standards, to allow for creativity and originality, but it values high quality staff, facilities, ingredients and wines as well as service consistency and tradition. The Michelin stars are a definitive reference in the world of haute cuisine, and gaining or losing a star has a big impact on business.

Michelin star

At this end of the market, running a restaurant is close to a vocation that demands a 'sacred obsession' from its chef. This is not usually the most efficient business model, and it is not rare to see gastronomically successful restaurants not performing well otherwise. The most famous example is Ferran Adrià's 'El Bulli' (Roses, Spain), voted 'best restaurant in the world' for five years by the prestigious *Restaurant Magazine*. Despite being fully booked for months ahead, it had to announce its closure in 2010.

Ferran Adrià

If we look at independent restaurants in all categories in general, a crucial characteristic is that they are small, often family enterprises, relying heavily on family both socially and financially, often fully dependent on private investments and family savings. Consequently, we see extreme variations in the levels of professionalism in this sector, including lack of professional knowledge and management skills as reasons for the high failure rate. Considering its fiercely competitive market, this makes the restaurant business highly vulnerable when circumstances or events combine to produce an economic crisis.

The basic principle underlying independent restaurant business models is simple. Sell meals for roughly three times the food cost – traditional rule of thumb – to cover fixed overheads such as rent, wages, and to generate profit. A restaurant can either focus on volume, producing simple meals, or on exclusivity with a more expensive range on offer. Establishments specialising in food with low-cost ingredients – pizzerias, pancake houses – can increase their relative profitability. A restaurant's ability to compete then mainly depends on its location and distinctiveness in quality, concept, and price. It is vitally important for an independent restaurant to make people aware of its unique selling points, an endeavour ever more difficult in the light of a dominant trend, the rise of the branded restaurant.

The rise of restaurant chains

Branded or 'multi-unit' restaurants started their spectacular success with the rise of fast food chains in the USA in the middle of last century. McDonald's is the largest fast food company and one of the world's most valuable brands. Several innovations have determined its growth:

'Multi-unit' restaurants

Fast food chains

- The introduction of standardisation and automation. An industrial, conveyor-belt style operation has eliminated the need for skilled labour ('deskilled'). Unskilled workers prepare and serve meals in fast food restaurants, leading to a substantial reduction of wages
- Focus on children. Fast food used to be aimed at young adults. McDonald's started targeting children, anticipating the rise of general consumer trend in the last decades of the 20th century with children deciding certain family purchases
- Standardised architecture. McDonald's restaurants are designed to enhance their visibility and recognisability from nearby roads, like gigantic billboards
- An aggressive franchise policy. Although the fast food industry did not invent franchising, chains like McDonald's applied the formula most successfully. Their expansion set the trend and 'turned franchising into a business model soon emulated by retail chains throughout the United States' (Schlosser, 2001)

With retail companies like Gap or Hallmark adopting franchising, this business model is now also becoming mainstream in midscale restaurants, where brands like Olive Garden, Applebee's or Red Lobster flourish. Not long ago, it would have been hard to imagine midscale restaurants being able to produce complex meals with consistent quality at different locations, as customers expect at chain restaurants. But the evolution of food engineering, artificial and natural flavourings, as well as the practice of making products available to the mass market and concentrating supply in the agro food industry all help explain the standardisation required to enable this consistency across the chain. Their large scale gives restaurant chains a big advantage over independent restaurants in market intelligence. Monitoring their multi-unit operations means they can efficiently fine-tune menu offerings to customer demand.

Franchising

Business model

Standardisation

3

A typical McDonald's outlet

Fine dining chains 'Fine dining chains' such as Landry's Seafood House or Longhorn Steakhouses have also appeared recently in the higher end of the market. You could say that the standardisation of restaurant chains is incompatible with upscale restaurants. The question is whether customers in this segment **Gastronomy** choose a restaurant because of its distinct gastronomy and service, or if they are following the trend in branded restaurants. A countertrend is the **Slow Food** *Slow Food* movement, which emphasises locally and sustainably food produced and served by independent businesses.

In this discussion, it is important to consider the concept of 'experience'. The theory of the 'Experience Economy' (Pine & Gilmore, 1999) states that customers no longer look for mere products to purchase but for enriching experiences. Thus, businesses should add value to their products by staging experiences. Such staged experiences are sometimes associated with themed brands. Curiously, one famous example is the coffee house chain Starbucks, where for a customer, drinking a *latte* is deemed an experience as opposed to the customer simply buying a coffee 'product' at a traditional café. Although the marketing power of chains allows them to develop the experience component of their offer, there is no reason why non-branded establishments cannot stage an experience. On the contrary, the distinctive concept and service of independent restaurants could be their main appeal in a market increasingly dominated by standardised outlets.

Event catering and managed food services

A catering company prepares food that will be served somewhere else. A restaurant can offer catering services, for instance when both food and ser- **Event Catering** vice are delivered at a wedding venue. 'Function' or 'Event Catering' is an attractive business for restaurants or dedicated companies. Meals are sold in advance and margins are higher than in regular restaurant operations due to larger volumes and lower fixed costs.

Managed food services Managed food services also fall into this subcategory. These are catering companies specialising in large-scale food production, in part because of the trend towards outsourcing of non-core activities in many organisations. Nowadays it is usual for hospitals, schools or corporate restaurants, sometimes even hotels, to contract food services from an external company. A large player in this field is Sodexo, originally Société d'Exploitation Hotelière. Besides food, Sodexo now offers the full range of facility management services to other companies. At large caterers we find industrial processes which, thanks to food production innovations, always seek to improve the balance between volume and quality.

3.4 Entertainment and recreation

There is a wide array of businesses, all with their own organisational characteristics, in the field of entertainment and recreation, also known as commercial leisure activities. If we look beyond the differences, these businesses share a market with the hotel industry – the leisure market– and thus the ways to approach this market. Entertainment businesses and hotels are often interdependent. Hotels host entertainment visitors, and entertainment businesses can sell more services when visitors stay longer, which is possible if there are hotels. Their common feature is that they approach guests with hospitality, which is why hospitality graduates often find employment in the entertainment industry.

Commercial leisure activities

The entertainment industry has undergone explosive growth because of the simultaneous increase of wealth and leisure time in the Western world since the 1950s. The variety is unlimited, from large spectacles – sports, music – to small-scale activities with more active visitor engagement, such as clubs, spas, or fitness centres. In this section, we discuss two types of large-scale entertainment businesses with highly distinct operations, casinos and theme parks.

Casinos
Casinos constitute a controversial part of the entertainment industry, for two reasons. The ethical implications of gambling – not allowed by some religions and the risk of addiction – and, sometimes, its connections with organised crime. Many countries regulate casinos and gambling (or *gaming*, the more neutral term) by law. Regulations determine the size and shape of this industry in most countries. Macau, and various Caribbean islands, are famous gambling paradises. In the US, where commercial casino revenues total 35 billion dollars, Las Vegas and Atlantic City are national tourist destinations thanks to casinos. In recent years, they annually attracted close to 50 and 35 million visitors, respectively, while New York City drew 47 million visitors, the same number as the four Disney World parks.

Ethical implications of gambling

Gaming

The business model of casinos obeys a simple principle. They retain a certain percentage of the money that is played. A 'payout ratio' of 97% means that out of every €100, €97 are paid out to game winners, and €3 is casino revenue. Payout ratios differ per game and are normally higher at the table games – where stakes are higher – and lower at slot machines. A higher payout ratio encourages guest to play more and thus add to volume. Since revenues depend on numbers of visitors playing, casinos often offer complimentary (free) food and beverage and even hotel rooms.

Las Vegas Strip

Theme parks

Amusement parks

Although Disneyland was not the first theme park, in 1955 it renovated the layout by creating a themed world completely apart from the outside environment. This has become the model for modern amusement parks. Their business model is based on park entrance fees in combination with F&B sales on their premises, as well as souvenirs and merchandising. Though their original offer focuses on families with children, they have gradually incorporated other attractions like roller coasters aimed at other age ranges. Due to the short life cycle of attractions, theme parks have to reinvest large sums of money periodically, since the new attractions generate repeat visits.

The high costs of investment and the entertainment business's sensitivity to an adverse economic climate explains why so many parks are in difficulties. It seems that labour intensive parks – actor-based concepts, such as the Dutch *Land van Ooit* (Everland) that went bankrupt in 2007, the English Camelot Theme Park that shut down in 2012, and zoos in general – are under pressure because their concept makes both cost reductions and the renewal of attractions problematic. But also Disneyland Paris, Europe's most famous theme park and number one tourist destination with 16 million visits a year, today combines record attendance with increasing losses and a debt of € 1.9 billion.

3.5 Travel service providers

Hospitality is not limited to fixed destinations. Moving destinations have always appealed to tourists. A journey with the Trans-Siberia Express has always been a holiday in itself, and several companies are expected to offer excursions into space in the near future. However, the largest number of tourists can be found travelling by sea. The present cruise industry has its origins in the 1960s when due to the growth of airline traffic, shipping companies shifted from passenger transport to holiday services.

Cruise industry

In the beginning almost all of these cruises aimed at upscale and luxury holidays, but although luxury cruising is still an interesting market, nowadays cruising has become a destination for mass tourism, and the majority of cruises are in the premium and contemporary segment. Still, one attractive feature of the cruise industry is the high service level. For example, Disney cruises has organised the departure of guests so that a family's individual luggage pieces are kept together on disembarkment, giving guests one last good impression of a well-organised cruise. A reason behind the success of the cruise industry is that they manage to keep the perception of high quality and service intact, and at the same time make cruises attractive to the large midscale and contemporary market segment. They achieve this by offering many activities targeted at families and younger groups.

The cruise industry is split into river cruises and sea cruises, but usually we focus on developments in sea cruises. The sea cruise industry is one of the fastest growing segments in the tourism industry with a growth from 7 million passengers in 2000 to over 16 million passengers in 2011. In the same period, the North American market share declined from 91% to 69%. This reflects the growth of popularity in other markets, particularly in Europe. And there is much more space for growth as the percentage of the population that has taken a cruise is on average only 2% in Western markets.

To attract guests, the choice of appealing destinations is crucial. The majority of cruises have the Caribbean as their destination, but other destinations like northern Europe, Alaska, and especially the Mediterranean are growing in popularity. The format for many cruises is to arrive in a port in the morning, allowing passengers onshore to explore during the day, and setting sail in the evening to the next destination. The economic and environmental impact of the cruise industry is huge, especially for smaller islands where sometimes several ships embark on the same day. The industry has created jobs in the harbours, in organising excursions, and in the retail industry. But despite the efforts of the cruise industry to become more sustainable, its negative impact on the environment is substantial.

Destinations

One remarkable characteristic of the cruise industry is that companies often operate at 103 or 104% capacity. They do this by placing extra beds in family cabins. The first sales objective of a cruise company is to fill all the capacity. Many cruise companies are willing to sacrifice on price and accept large discounts in times of economic downturn, with the sole objective of filling their ships. Additional on-board sales can only be achieved if cabins are filled. Although cruises are all-inclusive, passengers must pay for extras or special drinks and some on-board services. The importance of on-board revenues can be seen from the fact it is sometimes as large as 60% of total ticket sales. On-board revenues also signal a shift in cruise company policy.

Sales objective

In the early days of cruising, the attraction of cruising was visiting unknown destinations while being pampered in a luxury environment. Nowadays most cruise ships are often called marine destinations because the ship itself

Marine destinations

has become the main destination. They achieve this by offering high standards of luxury and comfort, with many on-board facilities like spas, wall climbing, casinos, golf courses and other forms of entertainment. These activities have contributed to a change in the market perception of cruises. In the beginning, cruises were thought to be very expensive and luxurious, but since then cruises have become contemporary, which is reflected in the large numbers of families and younger people taking a cruise.

In contrast to land-based hospitality, suppliers in the cruise industry are rather stable. Due to the complexity of the cruise industry, and the high investment in ships, there are large thresholds for new competitors in this industry. The largest company, Carnival Corporation has a market share of almost 50% while numbers two and three, Royal Caribbean Cruise Lines and Star/Norwegian Cruise Lines account for another 40% of the market share (UNWTO, 2012). These companies offer several brands to serve distinct markets. For example, Carnival Corporation exploits a number of brands like Carnival Cruise Lines that serves lower segments with large (up to 4,000 beds) ships in the Caribbean. Aida caters especially to the German market but also operates the high-end Seabourn cruise line that operates smaller upscale ships with 100-200 suites.

Distribution channel

Land-based hotels have strongly reduced the role of traditional travel agents in their sales, but travel agents are still the number one distribution channel in the cruise industry, despite an average commission of 14%. In the US, the homeland of the cruise industry, still over 80% of cruises are sold through this channel (UNWTO, 2012). One reason is that a cruise is mostly sold as a part of a package, consisting of the cruise itself, excursions, transport to and from the port of call, and hotel stays.

3.6 Assembly and event management

Globalisation

Events are a particularly booming part of the hospitality industry. The main explanation for its explosive growth is globalisation (Ferdinand & Wesner, 2012). For tourists, events have become a reason to travel and get to know countries or cities. For destinations, they are a means to step into the spotlight and attract visitors. In business travel, globalisation - the international expansion of companies and rise of international organisations - have made it necessary to arrange international meetings.

Both the Beijing and London Olympics (2008 and 2012) are examples of major international events meant to strengthen the visibility and attractiveness of city destinations. The effects are always highly controversial. While such an event generates a high volume of international visits, the side effects may keep other tourists from travelling to the destination, resulting in a net loss of visitors. Normally major events are preceded by towering investments in infrastructure, hotels, and event-specific facilities, which the investors claim will have a lasting effect on the economy of a city. Whether or not this is the case is the subject of the 'event legacy' discussion. Will it lead to an oversupply of hotels and other facilities, or will all these benefit from sustained growth obtained from the event? Qatar is already anticipating a temporary spike by making the football stadiums for the 2022 World Cup partly transportable to other places in the world.

The acronym MICE stands for the business of organising meetings, incentives, conferences and exhibitions. The worldwide MICE market was estimated at $US 65 billion in 2010 (Reic, 2012). The size of the market – e.g. in the Dutch market, 15% of corporate travel is categorised as MICE – and much higher spending levels for MICE travellers make it interesting for destinations as well as individual hotels to offer appropriate venues and related services to attract corporate events. Currently, the top three cities for association meetings are European locations, Vienna, Paris, and Barcelona, with London ranking number seven, and Amsterdam, number eight.   **MICE**

A wide range of businesses are in the events industry, such as trade fairs, exhibition centres, conference facilities, as well as event organisers. Hotels with large capacity meeting rooms target the MICE market. Dolce Hotels and Resorts is a specialised chain that in addition to meeting rooms offers quiet locations close to large business centres, and technical and logistical meeting support. In general, the events industry is woven into the hospitality business because of its impact and shared markets. Unsurprisingly, many hospitality graduates find employment in the events industry.   **Events industry**

3.7 Industry developments in marketing and distribution

No matter of how excellent or attractive a hospitality service product is, it will not sell if it is not understood or unknown. As travellers and vacationers come from all over the world, marketing, sales, and distribution are crucial functions in the competition with other hospitality businesses.

Travel agent

Traditionally the most important distribution channels have been tour operators and travel agents. Though often used interchangeably, they are different. A travel agent is a travel broker. The moment a customer inquires about a journey, they start searching and make an offer. Their main source of income is a commission paid by their supplier, for example the hotel or car rental company.

Tour operator

A tour operator buys capacity, like room nights or airline seats and tries to resell this to consumers. Often the operator combines this capacity in holiday packages containing hotel stay, airline tickets, and transfers. The tour operator's incomes come from their ability to negotiate large discounts with suppliers, and reselling at higher prices. Most tour operators focus on holidays, while travel agents are also active in the business market. Many activities by travel agents and tour operators have shifted to the internet, home of many internet-only companies like Expedia.com and Booking.com and this has resulted in a gradual decline of traditional agents and operators. Yet important market segments are still attracted to the traditional approach, for example, the market for corporate travel agents, large companies who use the services of a travel agent to organise their travel.

Online travel agents

The growth of internet bookings has also generated a new threat to many hotels. At first hotels were very happy with OTAs, online travel agents, because hotels could use this new distribution channel to find new customers to fill empty rooms. But soon the success of many OTAs turned them into opponents in the battle for online distribution channels. In 2010, OTAs generated over 40% of online bookings. Their growth has led to two problems for hotels. First, they are afraid of losing contact with their loyal customers. This is a serious marketing issue because gaining new customers is harder than retaining existing customers. Then hotels must struggle to lure guests to their own websites, but this is hard given the aggressive price strategies of OTAs.

Commission

A second problem is the impact OTAs have on hotel profits. Through their high market share, the four or five largest OTAs have gained a near-monopoly position and are often able to dictate their prices and other conditions to hotels desperate to fill their rooms. As a result, OTA can charge high commission rates of 25% on average. For example the size of gross bookings through Expedia.com was $US 11.8 billion in 2009, of which $US 2.7 billion was commission. When we realise that on average hotels achieve gross operating profits of between 30% and 40%, paying 25% commission destroys profit. This is a second reason why hotels attempt to attract guests to their own websites.

Besides the impact on profits, OTAs also reflect a fundamental shift in the hospitality industry. Chapter 1 discussed the core issue of the hospitality industry. Is the core goal providing hospitality or generating profits? The rise of OTAs signifies a shift away from providing hospitality to profit-oriented goals. The bulk of employment and labour is still in operations, investments are mainly in hardware, but added value and profits are shifting towards distribution and marketing. And especially parties in control of the information streams are at an advantage.

Control of information will become even more important as the distribution channels become more diverse and volatile. This is also due to the growth of interaction on the internet. Established companies are no longer the only providers of information on the internet. Users also contribute, on either blogs or review sites, or on social media like Facebook. This not only forms a new influence on the decision-making process of customers, it also provides new opportunities for hotels to communicate directly to their customers. People can make reservations through Facebook, and same-day booking apps attract the modern walk-in guest.

Information

3

Summary

3

▶ We distinguish five subsectors in the hospitality industry:
1 Lodging
2 Food services and drinking places
3 Entertainment and recreation
4 Travel service providers and assembly
5 Event management

▶ In the lodging subsector
- hotels have been offering rising levels of luxury and privacy since the late 19th century
- the growth of business travel in the US led to standardisation at accessible prices and to the first hotel chains
- globalisation caused hotel brands to spread to all corners of the world.

▶ There used to be a clear distinction between hotel types according to the market in which they operated. Today this distinction is not as strict. Leisure travel has become more important, and guests are now more flexible in that they may be business or leisure travellers at different times, even during the same trip.

▶ People are travelling more than ever, creating opportunities for the contemporary and comfortable budget hotels segment.

▶ The level of services and luxury of hotels is often expressed in terms of (star or diamond) classification systems. These classifications are limited, since they only consider the tangible assets of a hotel, and they are not comparable in different parts of the world.
Guest reviews sites and social media are increasingly taking the place of star ratings in helping people choose hotels.

▶ Hotel companies are rarely the owners of hotel buildings. More commonly they:
- just manage a property, under contract by a different owner or company
- let another company manage the hotel according to the established standards, using the chain's brand and distribution channels (franchise).

▶ The food and drink subsector has seen a similar development from individual independent establishments towards standardisation and the creation of chains.

► In the three other subsectors, we have looked briefly at specific business models:
  - in *Entertainment*, gaming is a financially important industry, especially in places where legal circumstances have allowed it to flourish. Amusement parks can be of strategic importance for tourist destinations, but the examples show that there is no universally valid business model, as some parks are in serious difficulty
  - in *Travel*, the cruise industry is especially popular among holiday goers
  - in the *Assembly and event* subsector, we see explosive growth in a wide range of businesses. This growth is connected to globalisation and has made capturing events a focus for destinations worldwide

► Today's society and business world is undergoing thorough changes because of developments in information and communication technologies. It would be absurd to think that this transition is complete, which means that hospitality entrepreneurs should keep their eyes open for new technologies and new opportunities.

3

Food for thought

3

This chapter discussed today's hospitality industry. Based on the content of this chapter, the following questions, challenges and topics could serve as interesting starting points for further discussion:

1   We see examples of hotels where personal interaction between supplier and guest is reduced to a minimum, such as the automated Formule 1 Hotels. If we look at health spas and care hotels, is hospitality the core service on offer, or is it health care? In theme parks, new virtual experiences may be more exciting for future visitors than what we have seen until now. Are these still hospitality businesses, or are they something new?

2   Hotel industry growth in past decennia has resulted in large international hotel groups. When they develop new properties or refurbish existing ones, they hire international designers to develop interior designs suited to the global market. To run their hotels efficiently, hotel companies appoint their own (non-local) staff in top management positions and rely on corporate manuals and standard operating procedures. This often results in high standardisation and lack of attention for local influences. What would you suggest these companies do to deal with these challenges? Do you think the approach described above is the best?

3   Emotion plays a large role in the hospitality industry. Appreciating a room interior, enjoying food or friendly service are not just rational responses but feelings too. The casino, for instance, hones in on emotion by ensuring we hear an exciting jangling sound when a slot machines pays out. But hotel companies are tuning more in to profit, and yield management is gaining importance. Managers need to develop a rational, calculation-based strategy. One of the modern hotel manager's important challenges is to combine the rational and the emotional, two seemingly incomparable entities. How would you tackle this challenge?

4   In terms of the guest's emotional satisfaction, hospitality professionals often draw on creativity. Hoteliers try to create the perfect environment, chefs experiment with new textures, tastes and combinations. The trend is towards standardisation, especially in multinational chains, which can limit creativity to a small part of the organisation and impact on the attractiveness of the work of 'hospitality operators' on the floor. How should hotel management education deal with this situation in preparing future professionals tor entering this industry?

4

Hospitality beyond the industry's borders

Michael Chibili and John Hornby

Over the course of the last few decades, we have witnessed dramatic changes in the way people view the world and the way in which they choose to interact socially, economically and politically. In turn, these changes are related to wider developments, such as a growing concern for the environment, the impact of the internet and, more recently, dramatic shifts in the economy and financial markets. These developments have not only resulted in a changed role of principles inside the hospitality industry, but also beyond its borders. This chapter demonstrates how more and more companies, organisations and managers have realised that hospitality is an essential element to address in adapting to the changing needs and wants of customers and employees in non-hospitality contexts.

The shop assistant

A salesman in a large department store was breaking all kinds of records. Let's call him Pierre. One of the managers decided to study Pierre for a day. He caught sight of Pierre talking to a man in the sporting goods department.

Pierre asked, 'Do you have a good rod?'
'I do not know about good,' said the man.
'Probably not.'
'Let me show you something,' Pierre said and the man followed.
The man tried the one Pierre handed him.
'This is definitely nice. I'll take it.'
'What about a life preserver, have you got one?' asked Pierre.
'No,' said the man.
'I think you should, if nothing else then to set a good example,' said Pierre.
Together, they walked over to the life pre-servers. The man tried on a few and chose a yellow one with a green belt.
On their way back to the cash register Pierre asked, 'Are you planning to fish from land or a boat?'
'From land,' said the man.
'Do you have a boat?'
'No I don't.'

'Come let me show you something,' said Pierre.
'This one is really nice, I think,' said Pierre.
'It's perfect for rowing out and fishing.'
The man checked out the boat, touched the rail, looked up at Pierre and said, 'Well, why not. Let's go for it.'
Pierre nodded and asked, 'Do you have a hitch on your car?'
'Yes, I do.'
'Then, you'll need a trailer. You have to be able to take the boat out of water for winter. I'll show you.'

Pierre made sure that the trailer and the boat were rolled out and hooked onto the man's car in the parking lot. When Pierre was back inside, the manager said, 'That was the most amazing thing I've ever seen. A guy comes in for some fishing lures and you manage to sell him a boat, trailer and everything to go with it. That's fantastic.'
'That's not completely true. He came in to buy vacuum bags and didn't really want to go home.'

Source: adapted from Gunnarsson, J., Blohm, O., 2003, pp. 33-34.

4.1 Hospitality revisited?

The previous chapter showed that the hospitality industry broadly consists of a wide variety of establishments, organisations and companies. The final section of Chapter 3 indicated that today's society is rapidly changing due to, for instance, constantly evolving information and communication technology. These changes not only affect the hospitality industry, but other industries as well. Indeed, these changes are causing boundaries between industries to fade and be replaced with newly emerging, often cross-sector business models.

Cross-sector

This chapter looks at those new business models and the concept of hospitality in this changing society. Indeed, hospitality is a dynamic concept that is already a component of many businesses not traditionally associated with the mainstream hospitality industry. Many hospitality and hotel school graduates find employment in sectors as varied as banking, retail, diplomacy and politics, to name but a few.

Chapter 1 has already discussed an important explanation for this. It highlighted how experiences have become a key concept in today's society and economy (Pine & Gilmore, 1999). This important role of experiences is certainly not limited to the hospitality industry. With the reality of today's society and business world, and especially with the emergence of the 'experience economy', many different types of businesses have realised that hospitality is an essential element of successfully dealing with people, both employees and customers. Regardless of the industry, companies will pay large sums of money to ensure that hospitality functions properly in their business models.

This chapter seeks to explore hospitality in its non-industry guises. It shows that viewed from afar the concept of hospitality usually leads us to associate it solely with the hospitality industry. However, from closer up, and in more recent times, it is more and more seen as an essential management competency that is found in business models far beyond the borders of the hospitality industry.

Management competency

We explore this 'new and extended' role and meaning of hospitality in two ways. First, this chapter contains several cases and examples illustrating the various ways in which hospitality can play a crucial role in businesses, organisations and situations in other industries and circumstances. Secondly, the main text revisits the concept of hospitality, as it was first introduced in Chapter 1, and links the characteristics of this concept to developments in other industries and our society as a whole.

However, before doing so, it is important to end this introductory section with a warning or, to be more precise, with a request. To better understand the role that hospitality can play beyond the industry borders, we not only need to deepen our understanding of the concept of hospitality, we also need to understand the evolution of the macro environment and business models in and outside the industry. This chapter does so by re-addressing the phenomenon of accommodation, the physical versus the virtual, role versus position, and the fluidity of location.

Macro environment

All these interdependent aspects set the context for the new and extended interpretation of hospitality and the role it can play in today's society. Given the complexity, it is not easy to portray and interpret this context. As we indicated above, **boundaries** between industries are fading and new business models are emerging, all in a rapidly changing society. The developments and concepts we address in this chapter are not black and white. They cannot be explained on the basis of simple formulas and definitions. Therefore, bear with us as we cross our industry's borders and explore the role of hospitality in other parts of our business world to arrive at a new, extended interpretation of 'hospitality'.

FIGURE 4.1 Hospitality; where and when

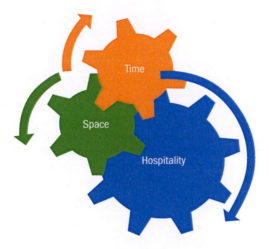

4.2 Our society is changing

Before crossing any borders, however, let us start our exploration by going back in time. As we said in Chapter 1, hospitality has been around for many years. References to hospitality can be found in numerous classical stories, tales and legends. The Odyssey story (see box) is a classical text that contains many references to hospitality.

● Mandelbaum, 1990

An example from classical literature:
The Odyssey

Throughout *The Odyssey* guests are treated to wine and food before their host asks for explanations and introduction. Nestor welcomes Telémachus and his crew amid a feast in honor of Poseidon. Nestor ensures that his guests have enjoyed a magnificent banquet before he asks for Teléma-chus's story. Guests and hosts tell their life stories in an atmosphere of friendship. They share their own stories as well as regional legends retold by bards. The presence of bards entertains guests while exhibiting the wealth of the household. Rich homes like those of Meneláus and King Alcínoüs retain the most talented of poets and musicians. Their performances are emotionally moving and both Telémachus and Odysseus are brought to tears by the powerful stories. Telémachus and Odysseus also receive opulent gifts from their hosts. The Phaeácians ensure that Odysseus leaves their shores as a man satisfied and grateful for their extravagant hospitality. His ship is laden with gifts that announce the wealth and power of both the men who gave the gifts and the man who received them.

The luxuries that the guest experiences are meant not only to bring him pleasure now but also to ensure that the good reputation of the host will be spread across the region, establishing friendships and fortifying positive interpersonal relationships, very similar to modern-day networking. So early literature regards this 'storytelling' as the most prominent way that reputations are communicated between people. There are many stories around the acquisition of gifts and their history.

All the lavish gifts and regal treatment impress upon the guest the great wealth and power of their charitable host. Thus a host can ensure that his reputation of generosity and greatness is spread throughout the region. These good relations and the spread of a good reputation can lead to positive trade relations and allies in times of war. The effects of good hospitality reach beyond the individual and forges bonds between families and cities. In stories people are often named along with their father and occasionally their mother or grandparents. Children are thus able to benefit from the good reputation of their family.

In some respects the situation today is similar to the time of *The Odyssey*. Today's guest at a hospitality establishment still requires much that earlier travellers did. The ancient Greeks believed hospitality served several purposes, such as pleasing the gods, satisfying guests, developing a good reputation and establishing bonds with other families and cities. Hospitality was linked to the pleasure of guests and providing them with luxury and a special experience. In summary, hospitality was and still is about people, facilities and locations.

Hospitality establishment

From The Odyssey extracts, we can clearly see many similarities with the concept of hospitality and hospitality experiences as we know them today (see Chapter 1). Although modern hospitality seldom involves protection and survival, as in earlier times, you could argue that it is still omnipresent in our world today.

But our world has changed dramatically over the last 2000 years. It is a different place, and now it is defined by different types of hosts, luxury and experiences. These differences influence the way hospitality is provided and embedded in the hospitality industry and in our society.

Some key developments

Globalisation Recent history (the past 50 years) can broadly be represented by globalisation, a growing concern for man's continued existence (sustainable development issues), the rise of the internet and, more recently, the dramatic shift in financial markets. These changes have significantly altered peoples' view of the world, and have and will continue to alter the way people choose to interact socially, economically and politically. Just think what an impact the

Internet emergence of the internet has had on our daily lives.

Are hosts mirrors of their guests?

The internet can be seen as a reflection of human evolution. Many elements of the internet are very similar to the roles and positions of human beings in society. Many people support this view, including Vinton Cerf (Google VP), a founding father of the internet who believes that 'the internet is a mirror of the people that use it.' With particular reference to hospitality, in our own industry we would be very familiar with the element of the 'host'. Hosts play a crucial role in interactions between people in both the physical world and the virtual world. Indeed, without hosts, there would be no internet. Hosts have become vital to the connectivity of the world we know today. The host is a link between the physical and the virtual, and between time, space and people.

Roy Posner, President of Growth Online, believes that the internet is characteristic of a mental stage of evolution in which the 'blossoming of individual freedom and initiative, the universal aspirations of education, and the empowerment of the individual' are coming together. This is happening because of the internet's ability to organise the flow of information in and between societies. The internet is a communication medium that supports individual expression and creativity on a mass scale.

If we consider the internet to be an integral mirror of our society, we should consider the structure and elements that allow it to operate so effectively. As we said above, in this context we have a single element of particular interest to us, hosts. Again, without hosts the internet would not exist. Someone and something needs to provide the location and facilities (websites, apps, forums, and so on) to host the interactions between people through the internet. Obviously, this is much the same in the non-virtual world. The voluntary interaction between people that forms the core topic of this book, that is, hospitality experiences, cannot exist without hosts (see Chapter 1). The virtual reality mirrors the physical reality and in turn, with more hosts and guests in and beyond the borders of the hospitality industry relying on virtual means to interact, the physical is shaped by the evolution of the virtual capacity of individuals and organisations. However, in this evolution we always recognise that the host is an essential element. The host provides the resources and facilities that permit the flow of information to occur.

Tectonic shifts Obviously, as an industry sector hospitality has been greatly influenced by macro environmental factors. In our wider society, the role and meaning of concepts such as the host and hospitality are undergoing tectonic shifts. Besides the internet, maybe the best example of this is how we as the human race view our relationship with the planet we live on. Planet Earth has been a host to life for around 3.5 billion years, but we know that change must occur for this symbiotic relationship to continue. The way we humans or guests have treated our planet or host is no longer sustainable. Climate change is a most obvious indicator why our relationship with our host needs to change. And this is only the Planet side of the equation. People and Profit show similar signs of decline from a sustainable development perspective.

Planet
People
Profit

This could clearly indicate the end of the notion of hospitality as a 'one-sided relationship' between host and guest. An unsustainable relationship always puts the guest first. From a sustainable development perspective, true hospitality needs to be an exchange process that benefits all parties, without harming each other or the environment supporting the transaction process. We can thus expand our definition of hospitality to include this aspect. Combined with the knowledge from Chapter 1, this basic guideline could serve as the background for exploring the 'new and extended' role and meaning of hospitality in today's and tomorrow's world.

4

Evolutionary vs. revolutionary developments

All the above also influences the types of products and services that companies offer and customers want. We can distinguish two types of change when it comes to products and services. Simply put, if the appearance of a product or service changes, but it essentially continues to perform the same function, this is evolutionary change. However, when the definition or the functionality of a product or service changes, then we are dealing with what is called a revolutionary change. The hospitality industry is experiencing both.

Evolutionary change

Revolutionary change

Evolution is a gradual process in which something changes into a different and usually more complex or better form. With respect to the concept of hospitality, this can be seen as the slow process in which hospitality organisations' competitive advantage and customer retention get more and more linked to their service delivery quality and the overall hospitality experience that they can stage.

Evolution

The second type of change – revolution – is marked by or results in radical change. With respect to hospitality, this type of change is primarily linked to new and faster flows of information (the internet) and the what is called fluidity of location. Revolutionary change in this context is best illustrated by the 'new and extended' role and meaning of hospitality in today's society. Hospitality no longer only deals with goods and service provision in a specific industry, but is found in and linked to a wider societal context. In this wider context, we find all kinds of new interpretations of who the end consumer is, who pays or should pay for services, and new choices in service providers.

Revolution

4.3 The 'new and extended' role of hospitality

All the changes described in the previous section contribute to the 'new and extended' role of hospitality in our society. As Table 4.1 illustrates, the concept of hospitality now plays a crucial role in industries that we may not readily associate with this term and beyond the ones already addressed in Chapter 3. There has been revolutionary change in what we define as hospitality, and how we (could) use hospitality across society in all these different types of organisations.

TABLE 4.1 Hospitality and hosts in different environments

The Hospitality Business		Hospitality in Leisure	Hospitality in Travel	Hospitality as Competitive Advantage	Hospitality as Experience
Traditional (often symbiotic services)				Evolutionary	Revolutionary
Hotels	Casinos	Airports		Workplaces	Internet
Holiday centre	Night Clubs	Rail Station		Health Care	Role
Quasi Hotels	Cinemas	Ferry Terminals		Education	Position
Cruise ships	Theatres	Aeroplanes		Military	Emotion
Time – Share	Sports	Trains		Custodial	
Bars	Attractions	Ferries		Retailers	
Restaurants	Spa and Health				

Source: adapted from Slattery, 2002, p. 24.

4

Hospitality across society

In Table 4.1 we see that hospitality has taken on an increasingly large role in all our lives. In the past 12 hours, every reader of this book has probably interacted with at least a few of the industries listed in this table. For example, if you are studying this book, you are engaged in learning about an industry that uses hospitality to improve services. If you are a student, you are probably reading this as part of your education. The education 'industry' is increasingly about engagement and interactions between students and teachers, teachers and teachers, and students and students. Teachers no longer preach from the front of a classroom. Students are encouraged to interact and exchange ideas and intellectual goods and services, for the benefit of all concerned. Increasingly, the role of a school is to provide a hospitable environment in which these exchanges of goods and services can occur.

Society

You could say that the increased use and importance of hospitality in different sectors is brought about by the changing social fabric of society. The catalyst of change has been the changing nature of the customer, and thus the various industries interacting with these customers. Over time, customers – whether they are students, employees, buyers, guests or travellers – have been empowered both in and outside the hospitality industry with two great 'gifts'. These are (1) readily available free flowing information, and (2) choice. Often, these two elements are hosted on a single medium, the internet. In the hotel industry the impact of these two aspects is reflected by the evolution of the search engine or more specifically by bookings sites such as Expedia and Booking.com, and review sites such as Tripadvisor.

Market space

The modern customer has become more discerning, knows more about products, prices and previous user experiences from other customers. If you combine this with choice, which is the underlying principle in free market economic systems, and a free flow of information about these choices, the market space in which companies compete in any sector has become extremely difficult to manage. Companies trying to deal with this are resorting to hospitality as a crucial element of success. Hotels, retailers or

● www.guestcentric.com

Booking.com's success for independent hotels

Booking.com has taken Europe by storm, and is now making inroads into the US. Studies show that over 50% of all hotel nights booked in Europe are booked through booking.com.

This level of market consolidation has been a bonanza for independent hotels. Without any brand recognition, Booking.com has become the ideal digital marketplace to promote and sell their rooms to guests from all over the world.

Booking.com has been able to create a formidable inventory (many consumers consider that 'all hotels are on Booking.com, at least all that matter'), it takes no payments up front, and its increased focus on user reviews provides a one-stop-shop for consumers.

> Booking.com now claims to be the number one online hotel reservation service in the world. From our experience with hoteliers, Booking.com certainly has significant distribution power, and there is no doubt that it represents an increasingly significant portion of the income of numerous hotels throughout the world.
>
> Adapted

4

Facilities

banks, are using hospitality not only to attract customers, but also to retain them. In retail, service provision has always contained a degree of hospitality and this continues to evolve. For example, elements borrowed from the traditional hospitality industry are high levels of customer engagement, free coffee and tea, bottles of water and treats for the children, and improved customer facilities. Retailers spend billions annually to make the retail environment more hospitable and thereby influence customer decision-making. From the customer's perspective, these investments could be crucial for success. If faced with very similar products at the same price and readily available would you choose to buy them in a store with friendly staff and nice facilities (tea/coffee/air-conditioning/trolleys/games for children), or a store that does not offer these elements?

Clearly, if an organisation incorporates hospitality elements in its business model better than its competitors, this creates competitive advantage. Sometimes, introducing these elements can even influence the price levels that customers are willing to accept.

Price

On the other hand, some companies also choose to compete on price. Some companies, such as Rabobank Ireland in the banking industry and Ryan Air in the air travel industry, have successfully opted for low-cost business models. The trade-off incorporated in these business models means that lower prices must be accompanied by lower costs and usually this means a lower quality hospitality element in the end product they provide. They focus on a core product no-frills experience. Rabobank Ireland offers only an online service, with no branch network, while Ryanair only offers flights to destinations outside capitals or major cities. It remains to be seen if these are truly sustainable business models. We cannot say that these are non-hospitality service offerings, but we can say they are less hospitality-focused and more product-focused. Interestingly, such organisations outside the hospitality industry have indirectly contributed to a reassessment of the link between hospitality and choice by players in the hospitality industry. Some are questioning whether hospitality must always be a luxury offer and, as a result, we have seen the rise of alternative business models in the hospitality industry, such as budget hotels and self-service concepts.

Special experiences

Indeed, many more changes are taking place both in and outside the hospitality industry. Again, the concepts of information and choice are a driving force behind many of these changes. Increasingly, guests are looking for new and special experiences that go beyond the standard hotel stay or – in contrast – are simply viewing a hotel room as a place to sleep and nothing more, while they visit other sites or conduct their business. Many guests find standard hotels too expensive, staid or unimaginative, and are looking for something different. Some new business models emerging in the hospitality industry as a reaction to these developments are illustrated by the following examples:

- Capsule hotels provide budget accommodation, where guests sleep in closely stacked rectangular containers, with little room for much else besides sleeping. These are common in Japan.

Capsule hotel

- Novelty hotels, such as the ice hotels in Jukkasjärvi in Sweden and the Hotel du Glace in Canada, which melt in spring and are rebuilt every winter.
- Garden hotels, established to show off famous gardens, such as Cliveden and Gravety Manor, in England. Here, the reason for the accommodation is the garden, and the hospitality establishment exists as a secondary entity.
- Underwater hotels are becoming increasingly popular accommodation. A few examples are Utter Inn in Lake Mälaren in Sweden, Jules' Lodge in Key Largo, Florida, where guests have to get to their rooms using scuba equipment, and some of the rooms of the Atlantis Hotel in Dubai.
- Tree house hotels, constructed in trees or in forests, are aimed at providing people with a chance to experience nature among the tree tops, combined with ecological values and uniquely designed houses.

These examples represent just a few types of the new business models emerging in and outside the hospitality industry that are related to hospitality experiences, as we defined them in Chapter 1. A crucial element of that definition is the word 'interaction'.

New business models

4

The view from the underwater hotel suite of the Atlantis Hotel, Dubai

A tree house hotel

The following MGM Grand Hotel example illustrates how this interaction should not be limited to the provision of food, drink and accommodation in today's business models, both in and outside the hospitality industry.

That's grand…

Entertainment and hospitality are interchangeable elements. Alternatively they can also be seen as strategic enablers for the delivery of either of these interchangeable elements in a business model. If you extrapolate this, hospitality can also be viewed from the standpoint that it is about the enjoyment of human experiences.

In the hospitality industry a prime example of this is the MGM Grand in Las Vegas. Billed as the city of entertainment, Las Vegas offers gambling, swimming pools, carnivals, Broadway and Hollywood productions, and provides accommodation (including state-of-the-art in-room entertainment) combined with food and beverage services.

To define the MGM Grand in terms of its hospitality product/service can be a complex issue. There is an alternative view to its hospitality offering. Through its more traditional elements, such as providing accommodation and service bundles of food and beverages (F&B), hospitality is essentially used as a strategic enabler of a more dynamic business model.

At MGM Grand, hospitality is about the provision of time and space. The role of the hospitality element is to provide the customer with the time (no cooking, cleaning or travel) to enjoy the virtual and physical interactions of the space around them. Entertainment is on the doorstep of all the customers. The hospitality element provides the time and space (intangible exchange) for social interactions, which in this case are the wide array of entertainment provided.

All this facilitates increased profits by selling ancillary services in the form of entertainment thus providing multiple revenue streams and a more viable, sustainable and profitable business. Consider for example the revenues of the MGM Resorts (parent company of the MGM Grand). In 2011, it made $4.7 billion in gaming, retail and entertainment revenue, whereas it generated revenues of $1.5 billion and $1.4 billion in accommodation and F&B respectively.

The article on the 'knights of old' at a motorbike rally is another example and shows how these interactions can have many different forms.

● news.carjunky.com

Be like the knights of old!

A motorcycle rally is a gathering of motorcycle riders, usually sponsored by specific motorcycle clubs or organizations. These rallies may be attended by anyone but there are some that are only open to adults. Accommodation is provided, though often of a rudimentary nature, and there are usually vendors present at these rallies who offer all kinds of motorcycle accessories and services. Attending a rally, you will find a variety of events and entertainment. During the day you will also have the opportunity to view many different new, custom and vintage bikes, and you may be able to test-drive the latest bikes offered by the top manufacturers. In the evening you can relax in your hammock or sleeping bag in your tent or bungalow, swap stories over a campfire and enjoy a home-cooked meal. So, what else might you find at a rally? Music is a big thing, which is why there are some rallies that combine music festivals together with other great, live entertainment. You will find that these rallies are scheduled events and not just random gatherings. In fact, most of them take place each year and grow bigger and better every year.

This motorbike rally case illustrates a less structured hospitality offering than we are used to in the traditional hospitality industry. Here, the provision of food, drink and accommodation enables people to share a common interest. The hospitality enables 'petrol heads' or Harley lovers to express a passion or fulfil their desire to hit the open road, then rest and share their stories. While this event may be less structured than the MGM Grand, the underlying principles of creation of time and space for human interaction or exchange (in this case a common interest rather than a Hollywood show) remain the same.

Role of hospitality

This view allows us to identify a main role of hospitality in industries outside the traditional hospitality industry. In some respects we can see that using hospitality has brought about an improved service offering in many industries. In these situations, hospitality is often described as the ability of an organisation to be a good host and thereby improve the experiences of customers and employees, either to attract new ones or retain current ones. All this is directly related to the resources available to provide the services needed to host customers and employees.

Consider the two cases of ING and Caring Homes as further illustrations of non-industry hospitality experiences.

● linchikwok.blogspot.com

ING

Yesterday, I visited the ING Direct Café located at the corner of Post St and Kearny St in San Francisco. ING Direct Café is an innovative banking concept, currently available in major cities like New York City, Chicago, Toronto, Las Angeles, and San Francisco. So, what makes this bank so special?

There is big open space in this two-story 'bank', with free Wi-Fi and many electronic outlets.
Instead of counters or desks for tellers or bankers, ING puts a nice café that sells coffee, tea, and snacks to customers.
The only ATM in the bank is 'hiding' somewhere behind the stairs.

There are professional bankers in the store, providing banking services if needed – promoting the services offered by the bank and helping customers navigate the bank's online banking systems.
There are multi-purposed functional rooms in the basement. Customers can use the space with reservations.

I like this concept. With more customers are using online and mobile services, companies need to come up with innovative business models for day-to-day operations. By adding hospitality services to a traditional bank, ING Direct Café creates a welcoming and cosy atmosphere for customers, promoting B2C (business-to-consumer) and C2C (consumer-to-consumer) relationship. Hopefully (and I believe that), business opportunities will come along while customers are enjoying the hospitality services provided.

I can see that hospitality management, as an emerging discipline, will play a more important role in business in general. What do you think?

January 2012

● www.caringhomes.org

Caring Homes

As a Hospitality Assured organization, Caring Homes is committed to ensuring that each of our residents receives first class hospitality above and beyond the traditional expectation of a 'care home'. Our homes employ qualified chefs, who work with the care teams and residents to deliver menus that not only meet nutritional requirements, but also provide outstanding choice and quality. Savoury mince and mashed vegetables are definitely not the order of the day at Caring Homes.

At the beginning of the day residents may relax with breakfast in bed, or enjoy the companionship of friends in the dining room. A choice of continental style or traditional English breakfast provides a pleasant dilemma.

4

Lunch is the main meal of the day, ensuring that residents enjoy a fine meal and the opportunity to savour it over time, aiding the digestive process. Residents always have a menu choice at lunch and, where dietary requirements allow, may enjoy a glass of sherry or wine with their meal.

Evening meals are normally served at around 6pm and tend to be lighter than lunch, again to facilitate digestion. Whilst we encourage residents to enjoy meals in the social milieu of the dining room, as this is an important component of daily interaction, residents may of course choose to have meals in their room.

Very special consideration is given to the dietary requirements of residents living with a form of dementia. Meals are carefully prepared to ensure they support hydration and those residents who may not be able to eat a main meal are supported to eat little and often throughout the day.

We are proud to meet the Hospitality Assured Standard, which is traditionally associated with service and business excellence in the hotel industry. An organization is only awarded this standard following a rigorous inspection process undertaken by the Institute of Hospitality.

These two cases represent two very different environments, which use hospitality as a means of improving the delivery of the core product or service. This is achieved by using traditional elements of hospitality to improve the human exchange element. In these circumstances, hospitality can be interpreted as the management of the time and space to permit and facilitate meaningful human exchange experiences.

Again, all this shows that hospitality provision today extends beyond tangible goods and services and has evolved to include intangible resources such as space and time. It has become more transferable between industries and cultures. Together with the characteristics of today's customers and employees, operating in today's society full of information and choices, this explains why staging appropriate hospitality experiences is playing more of a crucial role in deciding who will be successful and who will be not, even beyond hospitality industry borders.

4.4 Hospitality and networks

Network view

A final aspect that deserves attention in this chapter is the role of networks in today's society. More and more, the literature and business model experts apply the network view of organisations, focusing on the environmental interfaces that play a crucial role in these networks. This perspective highlights some important links and parallels between the internet and the physical environment (virtual and physical), the tangible and the intangible. It is important for us to understand these connections, as hospitality principles can be crucial to successful management and development. How these principles support the management of an organisation and its environment depends on the exact role and position of the organisation in a network.

Networks are not static constructs. By their very nature they are multi-dimensional, usually governed more by and consisting more of social constructs than physical ones. Ultimately, networks consist of individuals and their perceptions of the relationships with all other individuals that together constitute a network. The human element in the network is the basis of connections. Put simply, human beings and the nature of their relationship structure is the unit of analysis for a network perspective. Obviously, many elements that describe and explain what a network is are very similar to the elements and constructs that define hospitality experiences (see Chapter 1). Therefore, it should come as no surprise that hospitality plays an important role in organising and managing networks, regardless of whether they are located in or outside the hospitality industry.

Networks

4

Roles in a network

A key element is the role of the individual in an organisation (no matter the industry). First, it is important to realise that networks look different depending on from where you look at them. A supplier and customer may have two very different views of the relationships that make up a successful network, and these views may change over time and not always be strictly defined nor separated.

Let us use a hospitality example to illustrate this blurring of roles. On the one hand, someone staying in a hotel or enjoying a hospitality experience is a customer. On the other hand, the customer is in fact (partly) responsible for managing their own hospitality experience in that they have made the reservation for accommodation or food and beverages, and have particular expectations. Increasingly, today's customers want and can customise their hospitality experiences and make changes or manage a booking at will, whether in or outside the hotel. So hotels and other businesses are looking for new ways to accommodate this new type of customer and enhance the guest experience. The story on iRiS Software illustrates some recent developments in new business models and applications in this context.

Blurring of roles

● www.irisvalet.com

iRiS Software Wins Travolution 2012 Technological Innovation Award

Prominent hospitality applications provider, iRiS Software Systems, is thrilled to have scooped the 'Best Technological Innovation' accolade in this year's Travolution Awards held in London on 23 October.

The Travolution Awards recognise businesses that lead and innovate in digital development and strategy in the travel and hospitality industries and the iRiS win was for its market-leading iRiS Valet application. iRiS Valet is presented as a room-paired app called Guest Valet that enables hotels to present their services to guests via an in-room iPad or other tablet. It offers a nifty and invaluable interactive in-room service that allows guests to view hotel facilities, reserve a restaurant table, book a spa treatment or order room service, all at the touch of a button, and it even translates into their own language to avoid miscommunication.

The design, look and feel are tailored to each property. iRiS Guest Valet is fully integrated into the hotel's systems and can be instantly updated. As well as enhancing the guest experience, iRiS Guest Valet has been proved to reduce costs and significantly increase revenue. iRiS CEO, Jason Jefferys says, 'The Travolution Award is a great recognition for us. Consumers are increasingly adopting apps to find information and we are seeing a rapid rise in demand for this type of technology in travel and hospitality. This is an exciting time for the whole industry and at iRiS we are pushing the boundaries of mobile capability and interaction.'

The latest development is the iRiS Mobile Valet that allows guests to download their guest services app to their own device or smart phone. Available for both IOS and Android, this removes the requirement for hotels and cruise lines to provide the hardware in rooms or cabins, and guests download and browse the app prior to arrival.

October 26, 2012

With applications such as iRIS Valet, people have increased control over their hospitality experience and are becoming more like managers of their own hospitality experience. Obviously, this change not only has implications for the role of the customer, in this case the guest, but also for the role of the professional hospitality manager. A shift from standardised service design to doing 'whatever it takes to make the guest's stay memorable and happy'. In the future, this role could very well be more like a network or systems administrator and facilitator than a traditional hospitality provider.

All this illustrates that the roles of people in networks, such as customers and managers, are fluid and the way this network is managed needs to adapt to this. If we take into account that most businesses, and not just hospitality businesses, represent similar networks with similar degrees of fluidity of roles, for customers, employees and managers alike, this simple example shows that organisational boundaries, the determinants of organisational effectiveness, and the processes of managing a business all need to be re-evaluated as well.

Connectivity

Mass information age

All this also means that organisations have had to re-organise the way they allocate resources for service provision. Increasingly, the fast and open provision of information has become a must – information on demand, much like movies or TV on demand. Connectivity has translated into the customer expecting that all the elements of the service offering are readily available, and they expect to have real-time information on and during the delivery and consumption. The mass information age has given way to the individual information age, for example internet banking. And, once again, it is clear that hospitality principles can play a crucial role in successfully managing these networks, as a means of managing the multitude of relationships

Networks are key

that affect the individuals that make up the business environment. Hospitality principles can facilitate the human exchange in these networks and allow for the necessary time and space. More and more organisations have recognised this role of hospitality in the modern business environment. They see the benefits to network and relationship management they can achieve by creating far more 'hospitable' business environments.

If we refer back to the opening case of this chapter and the ING case, the roles of Pierre, 'the good salesperson', or 'the professional banker' at ING are now clearer. The salesperson role is as much about understanding the needs of the customer as it is about selling. By listening and providing distractions for a customer who did not want to return home, Pierre could sell more goods. First he managed the relationship and the person. In the case of the bank official the role is to facilitate, book meeting rooms, and serve F&B products. Contrast this to the bank official of 50 years ago. Security doors and guards controlled the door into the bank and there were iron bars between the teller and customer. The environment hardly encouraged friendly human interaction and information exchange.

Obviously, these developments are influenced by the transformation effect of new technology. One example of this was the iRIS case. Another example is Kodak's 'listening managers'.

Transformation effect

Kodak's listening managers

I'm so intrigued by your title. I have some preconceived notions about what your responsibilities might be, but I'd like to hear it straight from you. So, Beth, what exactly is a Chief Listening Officer?
Beth LaPierre: Simply put, a CLO is something of an Air Traffic Controller. Just as an Air Traffic Controller facilitates the safe and efficient flow of air traffic, I am responsible for the safe and efficient flow of social media data. I manage the strategy, processes and technologies to handle more than 300,000 new mentions of 'Kodak' each month for both our consumer and B2B businesses.

What specifically are you listening for and how does Kodak use that information?
BL: For the most part, my role supports three main listening functions:
Social intelligence – This data is used to drive product innovation, monitor sentiment and inform marketing and PR strategy.
Brand communications – When we launched our SoKodak campaign in September, we could tell right away that it resonated with consumers by looking at social media data. It's hard to get that from a cable box. We are able to tell very quickly whether or not an ad campaign or PR initiative will be successful.
Customer experience – Kodak's owned media channels on YouTube, Facebook and Twitter are also becoming a medium for customers and fans to contact us for help or to ask questions. Kodak's customers are at the heart of every listening function.

What are some triggers that you hear that alert you to engage in conversation and respond?
BL: More often than not, Kodak employees are the trigger. Each product category has an incredible dedicated team ; they live, eat and breath this stuff. Product teams keep an eye on relevant online spaces and will even engage themselves. For example, Kodak Video Camera Marketing Manager David Snook, vlogs as Vlogger Dude to understand how consumers actually use our video cameras.

Social Intel also helps with Risk Mitigation and reputation management. When a Florida news site falsely reported we had pulled our advertising from a popular NickTeen show, we immediately went to work. Fortunately, our internal PR teams are incredibly social-savvy and understand the immediacy of social engagement. With a few rules of engagement in place, I identified and reached out to influential fan blogs, Twitter users and even the show's Executive Producer. I sent them personal messages to let them know it was just a planned break in the media schedule and that we'd be running spots the following week. They then let their fans know what was going on. This is much more productive than personally responding to hundreds of users. Plus, it's coming from a source that they trust.

Roles of hospitality

The Kodak example shows how important it is to understand the various roles in a network and the role of hospitality in managing those networks. Is your role as a manager to provide administrative and technical support to customers (the new bank managers in an ING Café), or to listen to, understand and connect with people? Managers can use hospitality elements to create the optimal mix of services, time and space for their customers, their employees and themselves to improve human interactions in different micro and macro environments.

Connect with people

In Section 4.1, we established that hospitality involves people, facilities and locations. Based on all the above, we can now conclude that it still does. However, the contexts for applying hospitality have changed dramatically. Therefore, how hospitality is interpreted and how and where it is applied in today's society have changed as well. Hospitality is used in all kinds of industries globally to improve and differentiate service and product offerings. It is becoming an individual management competency and, in turn, is weaving itself into organisational cultures. As competition and information flows increase, organisations and individuals need to be able to attract and retain customers and employees. When customer power increases through increased information and choice, the ability of product innovations can no longer be the only source of competitive advantage. Then hospitality has an increasingly important role to play in organisations of all types. Similarly, employees no longer respond the way they did in the past and, instead of picking job security and an attractive pay cheque, opt for a boss who makes them feel welcome, appreciated and facilitated.

Improve and differentiate

Clearly, hospitality can and should also exist outside the traditional confines of the hospitality industry. Hospitality experiences are found everywhere and, you could say it has always been like that. Obviously, hospitality continues to be found in bars, restaurants and hotels, but it may equally be found in banks, IT stores, at motorcycle rallies and in hospitals. As a result, the concept of hospitality has become far more dynamic and needs to be viewed in a manner that is open to changes in society, technology and the ever-changing needs and demands of customers, employees and managers. While the hotel industry may well be the yardstick, the principles and theories of hospitality are not only integral to many other industries, businesses and institutions, but also inherent and implicit. By its very nature, the borders of hospitality will always remain permeable and fluid.

Everywhere

4

Summary

► Today's society is changing rapidly.

► As a result, hospitality plays an increasingly important role in companies and organisations outside the hospitality industry.

► Some key developments that are linked to these changes are:
  • a growing concern for sustainable development
  • dramatic shifts in the economy and financial markets
  • the internet

► We can distinguish two types of change when it comes to products and
services:
  • evolutionary
  • revolutionary

► Hospitality principles can be applied in various contexts:
  • at the core of a business model, such as in the hospitality industry
  • as a supporting element, such as in the leisure industry
  • as a related supporting element, such as in the travel industry
  • as a means to create competitive advantage, possible in many differ-
    ent industries
  • as a crucial element to address in revolutionary developments, e.g.
    the internet

► Networks play a crucial role in business environments and models in today's society.

► Multi-dimensional networks are based on social constructs and blur traditional roles.
  As a result of all the above, hospitality is becoming a:
  • generic management competency
  • principle that is interwoven with our societies and almost all of our
    businesses

Food for thought

This chapter discussed the concept of hospitality in its non-industry guises, while highlighting some major changes and developments in our society and business models, and linking these to the role hospitality principles can play in dealing with them. Based on the content of this chapter, the following questions, challenges and topics could serve as interesting starting points for further discussion:

1   Can you describe the networks you belong to and what role(s) you play in them? Elaborate on that by discussing the importance of hospitality principles in fulfilling those roles, How can others support and facilitate you?

2   Sustainable development and hospitality are intertwined concepts. Can you explain why? Refer to what we called the 'Triple Bottom Line' (People, Planet, Profit/Prosperity) in your explanation.

3   Even though the internet is a virtual environment, without physical food, drink or accommodation, it is closely linked to the definition of hospitality experiences, as we introduced it in Chapter 1. Can you elaborate on that?

4   Chapter 4 presented several examples of companies and events outside the hospitality industry that incorporate hospitality principles. What would be the most extreme example you could come up with?

5   Many hospitality companies are not yet sure of how to deal with social media. Based on this chapter, what would be your advice?

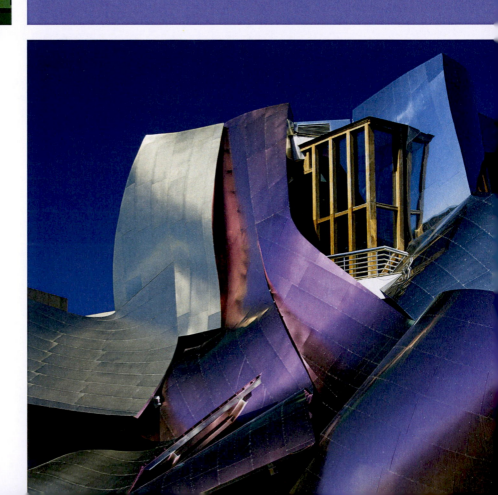

5

The future of hospitality

Annemieke de Korte, Jeroen Bosman, and Robert Blomme

Exploring the future means dealing with uncertainty and identifying new business opportunities. This chapter takes you into the future of hospitality and argues how important it is that hospitality leaders have a clear vision of future developments. Under the influence of societal developments, leaders must develop the competencies that enable them to foresee developments, to be successful today and in the future.

5

Futuristic technology and customisable rooms

Guest room access that reads your fingerprint instead of a key card... wall colour that changes at the click of a button... design elements chosen by the guest before arrival... microwaves that heat up anything you want... a robot butler serving your every whim. These are just a few features in children's vision of the hotel of the future.

A roundtable, organised especially to find out what children want from hotels, conveyed the need for hotels to focus on personalisation and customisation for their youngest guests. Highlights include:
- Customised experiences with a tech twist. Aside from whimsical desires for endless free ice cream, water slides and entire floors dedicated to 'FUN,' kids want to be in control of their travel experiences, from pre-ordering in-room snacks to deciding hotel room amenities. Hoteliers should not underestimate the importance of the bed itself. Ideas ranged from mattresses/pillows that can adjust firmness based on personal preference,

to mechanisms specifically designed for light sleepers (sound proofing) or heavy sleepers (an alarm-enhanced pillow).
- Emotional motivation of family time on the road. When asked to cite the best part of travelling with their families, the kids mentioned the emotional experiences and importance of sharing memories. Connecting with family, seeing relatives who live abroad and spending quality time with loved ones ranked most meaningful.
- Getting there is half the fun... or at least it will be in the future. Forget long family road trips packed into a station wagon. Flying cars, teleports, Google driverless cars, hovercrafts and jet packs are the predictions that the roundtable kids made for future transportation methods. In fact, half the attendees believe that they will one day have the option to holiday on the moon.

Source: adapted from http://www.hospitalitynet.org/news/4061808.html

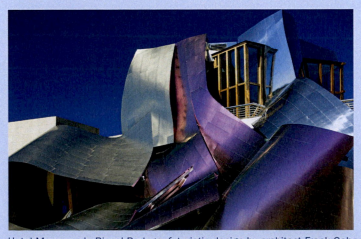

Hotel Marques de Riscal Bodega, futuristic design by architect Frank Gehry

5.1 Predicting the future?

This first section is based on an interview with Dr Ian Yeoman, the world's first professional crystal ball gazer or futurologist specialising in travel and tourism. After successfully establishing future thinking at Visit Scotland, Yeoman currently conducts research on future scenarios in tourism and hospitality from a dual base in New Zealand and in the Netherlands. The interview with Dr Yeoman was conducted by Dr Jeroen Oskam, who is affiliated with the European Tourism Futures Institute at the University of Stenden, Leeuwarden.

Futurologist

How do you, as a scientist, conduct research on the future?
Studying the future is both a science and an art. Formerly, our idea of the future was based on things continuing as they were in the present. We would make extrapolations of trends to predict where a certain development would lead to in the future. This process does not take into account sudden changes and paradigm shifts, such as the ones in geopolitics and technology that we saw at the turn of the century. So, future studies do not predict the future, they analyse what may happen if conditions change. Futurologists combine a variety of techniques, including economic modelling, trends analysis and scenario construction. The field also requires creative thinking, since you have to be able to think beyond existing paradigms.

FIGURE 5.1 Bergman's typology

	Making truth claims	Not making truth claims
Making explanatory claims	*Prediction* Example: Kahn & Wiener: The Year 2000	*Science fiction* Example: Rand: Atlas Shrugged
Not making explanatory claims	*Prognosis* Example: Toffler: The Third Wave	*Utopia/dystopia* Example: Vonnegut: Player Piano

Source: Bergman, Karlsson & Axelsson (2010)

We see this if we look at Bergman's typology of future paradigms (Figure 5.1). Bergman distinguishes forecasts with and without a truth claim – where the author states that what is predicted will actually happen or not. He also distinguishes forecasts with or without an explanatory claim – where the author does, or does not, describe causal mechanisms behind the predicted events. This leads to four types of future studies:

1 *Predictions*, truthful and certain. Here, you can think of predicting the weather for the next seven days or using econometrics tools for an economic forecast.

Predictions

2 *Prognoses*, dealing with uncertainty but looking for relationships. This all boils down to systems thinking.

Prognoses

Utopias

3 *Utopias*, untruthful and uncertain. These concern a perfect land or place. They are about painting pictures and about creativity.

Science fiction

4 *Science fiction*, fuzzy futures of truth and explanation. This is about understanding technology, with grains of truth, and about thinking the impossible.

What are the most important drivers of change for the long-term future?
In general, our scenarios are based on three drivers. First, we have the ex-

Technology

ponential development of technology. Just think where we were 20 years ago with the internet and mobile phones, and try to imagine where we may

Distribution of wealth

be in 2040. Second, there is the distribution of wealth around the world. We see important shifts here, both inside countries and globally. Think of today's shifts from West to East, for example. It is obvious that changes in purchasing power will also affect travel behaviour. And, finally, we have to

Availability of resources

consider the availability of resources such as energy, water and food. How will we be able to feed, for instance, the population of megacities such as Seoul, predicted to have as many as 100 million inhabitants by 2050?

How do these drivers affect the hospitality industry?
If we look at these same megacities, revolutionary sustainable designs become essential. The Songjiang Hotel near Shanghai is a perfect example. As far as the hotel's rooms are concerned, by 2050 they will be so technologically advanced that they will seem to be almost alive. Cutting-edge technology will monitor tourists' energy levels, physical well-being, emotions and mood to help ensure a good night's sleep. Dream management education systems will help us learn new languages. A bed will have built-in memory to remember a guest's preferred settings and adapt to changes in body posture. Taking this concept one stage further, claytronics will allow the bed to re-configure itself based upon programmable information. Fundamentally, hotel bedrooms constitute a place between science fiction and reality, where anything is possible. The application of nanotechnology – like self-cleaning surfaces – will have an enormous impact on housekeeping.

Global food consumption will double between now and 2050. This has to do with changes in the diets of millions of people in a developing world. In turn, this will lead to food inflation and the world looking for answers to supply problems. At the same time, gastronomy will become more and more important as cooking and baking are the last crafts we can master. It speaks to our urge for creative expression. *Food is bling*, and men especially become gastro-seducers.

5.2 Managers and envisioning the future

Future developments

When we consider potential future developments and their consequences for a hospitality company, an important first step is to examine possible environmental developments in the near future. We can specify the full spectrum of these developments in the form of elaborate scenarios. We often

Scenario thinking

use scenario thinking if the future is highly uncertain. It is a well-known stepwise method to develop more than one plausible future world for a hospitality company. These scenarios then become the basis upon which an enterprise can build strategies to adapt to these possible environmental developments. Scenario development is an 'outside-in' approach.

Applying a future-oriented approach is not so much about predicting the future, but rather about developing sensitivity and openness to the 'early warning signals' of environmental shifts. In terms of strategy, it is important to identify the environmental changes that might have an impact on hospitality organisations in the future. For example, new technology that enables remote meetings such as videoconferencing will affect hospitality, because in future business guests will be able to 'visit' another place from the office, or even from home. More than likely this new technology will influence consumer behaviour and needs, and thus how hospitality should be organised.

Dealing with and deciding on future uncertainty is the essence of manage-   **Uncertainty**
ment. Exploring the future is about dealing with uncertainty and anticipating change by taking the 'right' decisions, based on:
- Adequate information (predominantly rational)   **Information**
- Human judgement and sensitivity (predominantly creative)   **Human judgement**

The latter urges managers to stretch their minds about what is possible or likely to happen, to 'think the unthinkable' in an optimistic as well as a pessimistic sense. It is worthwhile to envision future dreams and ambitions, but also to be aware of possible nightmare scenarios to avoid negative outcomes or even the bankruptcy of a business. Additionally, we need a sound comprehension of potential gradual or disruptive changes in the mind-sets and needs of people because of societal changes. This is an important prerequisite for the definition of possible scenarios. For example, the global awareness of the impact of our (Western) lifestyles on our planet has resulted in many fundamental changes with regard to awareness of sustainability, in particular in many people trying to be more careful with natural resources. Managers should be able to develop insight into future developments affecting the environment of their organisations and to find ways to anticipate the future, for instance by using scenario thinking. This allows them to develop future-proof visions and strategies for their enterprises to become and stay successful.

Contemporary visionary: Ray Kurzweil

One entrepreneurial visionary is futurist Raymond Kurzweil, a graduate of the famous and widely acclaimed Massachusetts Institute of Technology, MIT. Kurzweil is a strong believer in the 'trans-humanist movement', which is about integrating technologies into the human body. One of his recent bestsellers is entitled *How to Create a Mind: The Secret of Human Thought Revealed*. It deals with the topic of building the human brain architecture in machines, which could then lead to artificial super intelligence. Over time, Kurzweil's visionary ideas have been criticised because of ethical dilemmas.

Google recently appointed this controversial thinker Director of Engineering. Technologies similar to Kurzweil's disruptive technologies are also expected to influence the hospitality industry, for example, virtual agents will assist travellers, or artificial humans will facilitate the delivery of hospitality services. Similar developments will likely be witnessed if 'organisms that mimic and support consumers' different mood and energy requirements are implemented', or organisms which embed 'emotional technology that senses and responds to consumers' physical and mental needs in invisible ways'.

5.3 Environmental analysis

Environmental analysis

It is now clear that we need an environmental or external scan of future trends to identify key drivers of change as the fundament upon which to develop future visions and strategies. The following sections elaborate on major changes in the environment that will shape the future of hospitality. Conducting an environmental analysis will enable managers to envision the impact of global and industry changes on their current hospitality businesses. This is primarily related to anticipating changes by developing future-proof strategies for hospitality organisations, as 'resistance to change has become one of the primary causes of business failure' (Cline, 2005). An important aspect of environmental analysis involves looking for trends. Trends are long-term changes in the environment that are in progress for a considerable amount of time. Trends are different from hypes, fads or temporary fashions, all of which rise and fade away quickly. Once identified, we can evaluate a trend as either an opportunity or a threat to the organisation.

Trends

Hypes

Fads

Fashions

5

Agility

Some companies aim to study the future with a time horizon of a mere year or two (or less). Others may look further ahead, with time horizons spanning decades. A company's future horizon is connected not only to the dynamics of its markets and its environment but also with the organisation's agility, a term used in business for 'the capability of rapidly and efficiently adapting to changes'. Most strategic management models emphasise the need for periodic evaluations of current strategy and for embracing a global change orientation.

A sound comprehension of developments occurring in the hospitality environment is an important condition for defining, maintaining, and altering a strategic course since the environment is complex and multi-layered. Moreover, each layer in the environment has its own pace and will affect an organisation in its own way, directly or indirectly. Hence, in examining the differences and effects of environmental changes, we need to distinguish between a context that influences at its own pace societal development in general, and a context that directly affects a hospitality organisation. Before we can examine how the environment directly and indirectly influences an organisation, it is helpful to go back to the essence of a hospitality organisation. We will use the work of the great organisational thinker Russell Ackoff to build our understanding of organisations, the influence of environmental developments and the need to catch trends.

First, Ackoff (Ackoff & Emery, 1972) defines an organisation as:

> 'a complex adaptive social system which finds itself in an on-going struggle to deal with its stakeholders, including employees, labour market, customers, shareholders and competitors, to reach its own strategic goals'.

Optimal transactions

From this perspective, the most important purpose of strategic management is to establish optimal transactions with the stakeholders. Transactions include attracting and retaining the best employees from the labour market as well as offering and selling the best possible services to consumers in relation to competitors. In turn, this is reflected in establishing high sales and profits, in attracting capital investors for investments in future business and in outperforming competitors and gaining competitive advantage. Ackoff defines the environment that directly affects the organisation as the *transactional environment*. Movements in the transactional environment are often the result of movements in society. These movements, which can lead to trends, have their own pace of change and are often emergent. Changes happen spontaneously without an apparent direct cause and are hard to catch and predict.

Transactional environment

Ackoff defines the *contextual environment* as one in which emergent processes of change and trends occur in societies and in which these changes and trends affect each other. Trends emerge in the contextual environment and might affect the changes and trends in the transactional environment. This means that to gain an understanding of future trends in the overall environment of your organisation, we need to catch the contextual environment and to estimate the consequences for the transactional environment of your organisation.

Contextual environment

The last step is to examine the effects on your organisation and define the measures you need for your strategy. Again, once identified, you evaluate trends as an opportunity or a threat, or even as an opportunity *and* a threat at the same time. This distinction, often known as the OT (or SWOT analysis) seems simple, but its application is often complex. As many other sources cover this topic, we will not dwell on it here.

SWOT analysis

In summary, we can distinguish two categories of environment:
- Contextual environment, where overall developments, changes, and trends occur, often grounded in societies
- Transactional environment, where your organisation interacts with other parties to establish continuity and profit, which is influenced by the contextual environment

In the next sections, we will examine some of the most important future trends for hospitality organisations, first in the contextual environment and second in the transactional environment.

5.4 The contextual environment

We use four perspectives to analyse changes in the contextual environment:
- Political and economic
- Sustainability
- Demographic and cultural
- Technological

We can distinguish interesting major changes when we apply these four perspectives to the contextual environment of hospitality organisations. Here, in light of the topic of this book, we mostly focus on examples that illustrate how, over time, customer experiences are affected by these changes.

Meeting of leaders of the BRICS countries

Political and economic perspective

Economics

In terms of economics, the hospitality business has had to deal with a major global shift of economic progress and power, influencing its growth opportunities. Financial crises, resulting in periods of economic recession in the first decade of the 21st century, have put more emphasis on costs and revenue management practices. Due to fading borders and the fact that financial systems are strongly intertwined, the global economy has been unstable and unpredictable over the last decade. Moreover, emerging new economies have caused a shift of power from the West to the East. These

BRICS
MIST

countries are generally referred to as BRICS (Brazil, Russia, India, China, South Africa) and MIST (Mexico, Indonesia, South Korea, Turkey) countries. Inhabitants of these countries are projected to travel more, on their own continent or by visiting other places overseas.

This longer-lasting economic turmoil as seen on a global scale is an important driver of change. In the long term – due to issues such as scarcity, distribution of wealth and the urgency of creating a sustainable world – this will most likely result in a transformation, and it will likely force us to reconsider the paradigm of endless growth.

On a macro level, the globalisation trend will have a major impact on future jobs. Since the hospitality industry is highly internationally oriented, almost by definition, the latest globalisation waves will definitely affect employees in this industry, for instance with regard to their attractiveness on the global labour market. The economic outlook will also directly affect consumers and their demand for travelling, holidays, and entertainment. This has formed a push for creativity in finding smart but affordable solutions and for an increased emphasis on value-for-money. Many consumers have shifted to a lower level of luxury in accommodation or food. They may also spend their limited budgets on 'affordable luxuries' or ad hoc/last minute purchases. This latest shift seems irreversible, even when the economies will recover.

From a political perspective, the hospitality industry may be affected by changing regulations influencing businesses in this industry, for example by laws affecting labour markets or expansion. The political situation and (potential) conflicts in certain parts of the world have an impact on their attractiveness and therefore on the possibilities to conduct business. To illustrate, political instability in government, environmental structure and changing rules and regulations in Northern African countries have had to be assessed critically these last few years, not only from a safety and security point of view, but also with respect to growth strategies for large hotel chains. Not only the economic powers are about to shift from the West to BRICS and MIST countries but henceforth, political power as well.

Political perspective

Now we see that the political force field in the world is about to change fundamentally. Although the European Union is in the process of further integration for developing more political and economic power on the world stage, the member states struggle with internal dissension and endure problems in unified decision-making. The United States is expected to remain the strongest political power, but despite this we see a shift of political power from the West to upcoming countries including the Russian Republic and China. The rise of these two countries has consequences on legislation and exploiting business activities. Examples of this are the Russian Republic's increased political influence on the former countries of the Soviet Union and the economic activities China deploys in African countries. The latter means that they are increasing in political influence and gaining access to valuable resources, including coal, oil, and scarce metals, necessary for their economy.

Sustainability perspective
The economic rise of the BRICS and MIST countries and the efforts of Western economies to maintain economic growth increase the demand for fossil fuels and other resources. The current stocks of oil (30 years), natural gas (50 years) and coal (200 years) can supply the current demands of the world's economies. However, demand is expected to grow in the following years, especially in emerging countries. Moreover, the stocks of fossil fuels are distributed erratically. A few partly politically instable countries and regions control a considerable part of the world's total production of fossil fuels, leading to constant political manoeuvring of countries in securing access to these resources. This political manoeuvring, deploying activities globally, will influence the strategy of hospitality organisations. As we said in the previous section, the battle for resources can lead to instability in regions and countries, leading to threats to in-depth investments.

The thirst for fossil fuels in securing economic prosperity has led to growing emissions of carbon dioxide and thus climate change. Climate change will have an important effect on how consumers will experience hospitality. First, destinations will become less or more attractive for travellers. For example, flooding will appear more frequently in northern Europe, while droughts will appear more frequently in southern Europe and the American Mid-West. Hence, destinations will change.

Carbon dioxide

Climate change

Another issue related to the economic rise of countries is world population growth and the need for fresh water and food. With on-going climate change leading to problems in food production and the unequal distribution of fertile farmland, producing and distributing enough food for a growing world population is becoming problematic. Hence, increasing food prices will co-erce people in developed countries to become far more aware of what and how much they eat. People will be more aware of menu choices in securing a smaller ecological 'footprint'. This awareness will have its effects on consumer behaviour. Becoming more 'green' will thus be more important for hospitality organisations to attract and retain guests.

● www.ameinfo.com

Ramada Ajman reaps crops from urban farm

A month after launching its first urban farming project, Ramada Hotel and Suites Ajman harvested vegetables and crops for the hotel's kitchen for hotel consumption. As part of the property's continuous commitment to the

Wyndham Green Programme, urban farming aims to promote sustainable measures in the field of hospitality.

Iftikhar Hamdani, general manager, Ramada Hotel and Suites Ajman, said, 'We are delighted to harvest the fruits of our labour. Our first yields are rocket leaves, and we plan to work further on this project by growing more crops and possibly increasing farm size. Our team is strongly committed to sustainable projects and we hope that other organisations, especially in the hospitality sector, will also take part in our cause by initiating various green initiatives.'

The 430-square metre urban farm was converted from the property's vast parking space in April, to coincide with the observance of Earth Day. Abraham Cherian from the Engineering Department, was appointed Urban Farm Committee Head and leads the team looking after the farm in assigned periods to ensure good care of the crops.

Adapted

5

The theme of sustainability in relation to the environment is becoming more important to consumers and is likely to increasingly affect their choice of hospitality provider and type of experience. Businesses are expected to be more transparent and contribute to the community beyond current levels of corporate social responsibility (CSR). Still, current initiatives by hospitality businesses are often considered mainly as window dressing, instead of 'shared value', which involves creating economic value in a way that also creates value for society by addressing its needs and challenges. Filling in sustainability means carefully considering a balance between people, planet, and profit. Hence, the sustainability megatrend in increased awareness and environmental consciousness has proven to be an important driver for 'back-to-basics' trends and hotel businesses will likely be forced to address this trend more seriously. Simultaneously, sustainability is also related to finding new ways of making use of goods without owning them, leading to the 'ownerless' trend.

Corporate social responsibility

● www.greenhotelier.org

Eco chic: The Green House Hotel

Winner of this year's Considerate Hotelier of the Year Award and runner up in the Green Hotelier 2013 competition, The Green House Hotel is now one of the most sustainable hotels in the UK.

The Green House is an independent luxury four-star eco hotel, with 32 guest rooms, restaurant, bar and private event facilities. The hotel opened in July 2010 following an 18-month refurbishment of an existing Grade II listed building. Since then the hotel has achieved a gold rating under the Green Tourism Business Scheme and won the AA Eco Hotel of the Year. Throughout the refurbishment, and since the hotel opening, the environmental impact of every decision has been taken into account – and I mean every. Never before have I been to a hotel where so little eco potential remains to be fulfilled. From the paints on the walls to the beer barrel cleaning system, pretty much everything has been thought of.

The Green House Hotel is clearly a great example of how the sustainable agenda is creeping into the minds of guests. Business at the hotel has increased by 37% over the past year, and from their guest questionnaires the hotel know that for 35% of their guests, environmental performance was a key factor in their decision to stay at The Green House.

Adapted

Demographic and cultural perspective

In developed countries including Western Europe and the US, we see two trends:

- *Continuing increase in longevity.* Considerable progress in health care and quality of life is more the rule than exception, and life expectancy is still rising, with the gap between male and female life expectancy closing. It will not be uncommon to see four surviving generations of the same family. But individual members will move more and not always live as near to each other as they did in the past. The growth in the number of workers over 60 will continue, and will stop only around 2030, when the baby boomer generation becomes 'elderly'.
- *Continuing low birth rates.* The baby boomer generation had fewer children than previous generations because of many factors including difficulties in finding a job, the lack and cost of housing, the older age of parents at the birth of their first child, different study, working life, and family life choices. Almost everywhere, fertility is below the population replacement level.

The structure of society is changing radically. Family structures are changing. There are more older workers (55–64), elderly people (65–79) and very elderly people (80+), fewer children, young people and adults of working age. The bridges between the various stages of life have become more complex, particularly for young people, who are experiencing certain life events later (e.g. graduation, first job, first child). If we look at younger generations, we observe a rise in single households, a change in family compositions, the involvement in various social and professional networks and the willingness to travel in maintaining these networks.

To compensate for the predicted fall in the working age population, governments advocate greater employment participation, particularly by women and older people. Governments encourage investment in human resources and higher productivity through economic reforms, research and innovation. Due to the challenge for governments to maintain reliable pension funds, the age of retirement will go up and disposable income on retirement will drop significantly. Generations who are about to enter the workforce will, contrary to previous generations, pursue non-linear careers, alternating between employment, study, unemployment and retraining or updating skills. These structural changes in society will impact the hospitality industry. Elderly people are becoming increasingly important market segments with their own needs for hospitality services.

Non-linear careers

In countries demonstrating rising economic prosperity, including China and India, we see similar trends. Although the population will increase in the near future, leading to the growth of the world's population. In the long run, with the further development of prosperity, the population will decline, following the Western trend. In this economic and numerical growth, the middle class will become more important. An emerging middle class is more readily inclined to travel and to spend money on hospitality services. With the increase of their prosperity, these countries will have to deal with the same challenges Western Europe and the US are facing such as dropping birth rates and fewer younger people available to meet the challenges of an ageing society.

5

Collaborative consumption: sharing and renting

Less ownership is better for the environment. It is space efficient and cheaper, but more importantly there is the social aspect. By sharing or lending goods, customers build trust in the community to which you and they belong. Popular examples of this trend are sharing a car (e.g. electric car sharing scheme Car2go, electric SMARTs for share as launched in bigger cities), sharing your house as a place to stay (e.g. coachsurfing. com or Airbnb), neighbourhood rental programmes (e.g. sharesomesugar.com and spullendelen.nl), sharing gardens with neighbours or friends (crop swaps), wardrobe sharing (e.g. H&M Recycled initiative) or sharing expensive, luxury designer goods such as a handbag (bagborroworsteal.com), sharing money (LETS-Local Exchange Trading System), private jet share (Flyvictor.com), and sharing rides (erideshare.com).

Besides these structural changes in Western society, we also recognise an upcoming trend in a larger degree of collectivism. After decades of individualisation, communities and sharing facilitated by social media now seems to have become the new norm. Over time, we have seen a declining belief in institutions, but a larger degree of trust in peers. This has contributed to the popularity of review sites as an influential information source. These

Collectivism

Individualisation

observations will have an impact on the design of hospitality experience concepts and how and where these are offered (see Chapters 2, 6 and 8).

Connected society

The way the digital world is transforming our modern society into a networked and permanently connected society has a major impact on the way we live, leading to new ways of working or learning and requiring other organisational structures and leadership. We know that in today's globalised world there are fewer places that a person cannot reach in a day's travel, and there are fewer people who a person cannot reach by telephone or the internet. Because of our modern modes of travel and communication, citizens have become more conscious of the world at large and may be influenced by other cultures in a variety of ways. This will influence their expectations. In fact, it will be quite a challenge for hospitality businesses to exceed these expectations if everything seems to be available practically everywhere. This further emphasises the need for uniqueness and authenticity and what we may term a 'globalised' approach, combining the global perspective with local specific possibilities.

5

Technological perspective

Technological developments

Technological developments have had a considerable impact on economic growth the last two decades. The most important technological change concerns the computer's role in economic transactions, on labour, and on the transfer of information. Distance has become a less important obstacle for doing business, which is an important condition for globalisation. In addition, repetitive and routine labour in industrial organisations has shifted from human operators to robots.

Communication and information technology will enable new ways of collaboration, new service designs and improvements to the operational efficiency of service staff and information flows to management. They will lead to greater transparency as well as empowered, well-informed customers and self-supportive local communities.

Information and communication technology

Data mining

These new technologies will enable hospitality businesses to design and deliver state-of-the-art services and add to the customer experience. Employing information and communication technology (ICT) is vital to virtually every aspect of operations. ICT enables hospitality services in two critical areas, sales and marketing, and service delivery. Upcoming technologies such as mobile internet and a new version of the internet, virtual and augmented reality, data mining tools and intelligent profiling will enable smart hospitality operations to fulfil customer demands quickly and accurately. In an industry with high fixed costs and high labour intensity, improving labour productivity must be a goal for forward-looking organisations.
ICT will further speed up the pace in our real-time society and economy. Organisations will have to react even faster as customer´s expectations of quick responses are still rising. That is why ICT must operate on a decentralised basis, delivering the right information to the right people at the right time, for example on-the-go check-in data when guests arrive at a hotel.

The use of mobile internet will expand quickly and provide new solutions as an additional distribution channel that supports order and delivery on the spot (see Chapter 3, online travel agencies). Data mining tools and intelligent profiling will likely enable highly personalised services and enhance guest experience. Combined with location-based and context-aware tools and systems (knowing where I am and what I am doing), personalised, multi-sensory enriched services will be available for people to stay in constant touch with social networks. Ever more sophisticated applications will enable seamless simultaneous translation that will take communication between people from different cultural and linguistic backgrounds to another level.

Virtual environments will create many new possibilities for adding information in a user-friendly way and for enriching experience. Intelligent objects will add functionalities in the environment. The engineering of nature will enable new possibilities in the design of hospitality environments. The fact that you can construct several environments, such as meeting rooms or a travel experience, at a distance may also be a threat for the travel and tourism business.

The innovation of 3D printing will highly affect not only the design of hospitality environments but also food and nutrition. Similar to what is happening elsewhere, we may expect nanotechnology – using extremely small structures – to be the next big thing in the hospitality industry. We can think of all kinds of smart materials and futuristic products to create a comfortable experience, for example sheets that adjust to a guest's body temperature and accommodate the environment to personal wishes. Alternatively, you can think of developments that will contribute to improved sustainability and cost savings in the cleaning of spaces or that will improve the freshness of food, thus reducing waste.

Main drivers of change

In summary, generic key drivers of change in the contextual environment will influence the hospitality industry and individual businesses, particularly when they concern:
- Demographic changes and the need to cater for new customer segments such as the ageing population
- Demographic changes resulting in greater diversity of the labour population and an expected war for talent
- Economic turmoil and a global shift in power, which creates an uncertain, turbulent business environment and a need to reduce risks
- Upcoming economies with an emerging middle class (such as BRICS or MIST countries) and new markets for travel, both inbound and outbound
- Changing moods in society with greater emphasis on sharing and sustainable development
- New enabling technologies that support new ways of working and communications or a higher quality of life

⬤ 5.5 The transactional environment: consumers

In this section, we consider the consumer lifestyle trends relevant to the future of customer experience, which in turn are unavoidably related to innovation and service design. Trend analysis can give us a deeper understanding of patterns of change in consumer behaviour and future needs. From the perspective of concept development or in service design practices (as we discuss in more detail in Chapter 6), scanning the environment for

Consumer lifestyle trends

5

consumer lifestyle trends provides the 'design space', the context for design. It aims to find insights into design drivers (Osterwalder & Pigneur,
2010) as a starting point for concept development. Innovation is based on
this insight into consumer behaviour, to meet their needs and exceed their
expectations (Zaltman, 2003).

A new collaborative consumption way of life

Ownerless trend

Visionaries

An important development in consumer experience is the 'ownerless' trend,
where access is more important than ownership. Visionaries like Kevin Kelly, founding executive editor of the influential Wired magazine foresaw this
trend, 'the end of an ownership culture', as early as the end of the previous
century. It brought about a change to new business models such as pay-
per-view, or pay-per-use. Over time, new generations of consumers have
made use of digital content, but also of cars, equipment, or software without having to own any of it. This ownerless or non-ownership trend has several drivers. It is likely to grow, probably turning into the 'New Normal', the
state a trend reaches once it no longer implies change, but 'becomes common, ubiquitous, and finally so pervasive as to be invisible, something that
the really profound changes happen to be' (Shirky, 2008).

5

● www.slideshare.net

Mainstream sustainable consumption:
moving beyond dreams

We can work out possible future worlds that focus on consumers' attitudes
and purchasing behaviours by exploring how key environmental, economic,
and social trends might play out over the next few years. There is a clear
opportunity, today, for smart brands and businesses to make money by ac-
celerating the transition to a sustainable future. It means making it easy for
consumers to go green by offering products and services that are not just
better for the environment, but healthier, cheaper and longer-lasting.

- Smart growth is characterised by 'decoupling' commercial success from
  environmental impact, often by delivering more economic value per unit
  resource used
- Smart use is characterised by closed loops, where someone's waste is another's raw material: take-back schemes, where used goods return to the
  manufacturer; product to service shifts, and different ownership models;
  consumers do not need to possess something just to derive a benefit
- A better selection of choice, where the unsustainable product or service
  is no longer available, and consumers are choosing from a set of sustainable options. By deciding what to stock, and what to make, retailers
  and manufacturers have already made choices on behalf of their consumers
- Positive social impact, smart consumption involves transactions for
  goods and services that have a positive social benefit, where novelty and
  implied personal status are far less important than they are today

Adapted

New enabling technologies facilitate interlinks between the physical (things) and virtual (information) worlds, making use of proximity (where you are) or matchmaking between supply (I have on offer) and demand (I am looking for). Combined with the fast adoption of social media, ownerlessness has evolved into mesh networks, built upon the premise that 'the future of business is about sharing' (Gansky, 2010). In addition, networks speed up many things and enable a real-time economy, raising consumers' expectations and impatience. Consumers want what is new and cool, on the spot, and immediate answers to questions without having to buy any of it. This same phenomenon is related to trends such as localism, energy sharing with solar panels (e.g. sun-sharing via solarcity.com) and the longing for authenticity or the real thing, as illustrated by connections between travellers seeking authentic experiences with home stays and hosts all around the globe offering unique spaces.

Authenticity

Although the new collaborative consumption approach to life partly stems from ecological awareness, not all new consumption is 'green'. Younger generations of consumers are raised in an era without strong attachments to objects. Instead, they learn to use objects and simply replace them with new ones soon after they have lost their function. Future consumers *do* want to be involved. They want to take initiative, co-create with brands or manufacturers, and engage in do-it-yourself (DIY) activities. Hospitality organisations will have to focus on their customers and less on their hotel assets as measures of success. 'To accomplish this, however, customers need to participate in the product or service development process' (Cline, 2005), as we discuss in Chapter 8.

The vital role of social networks
Over time, flexibility and mobility have been highly rewarded, and freedom is another common reason for detaching from property. You might think of the ability to work from anywhere in the world or the need to switch to a new job in another city, country, or even continent in a world where lifelong jobs are an exception and employees are required to be very flexible.

A growing number of professionals in our all connected, networked societies are less bound to a specific location. We call them nomadic workers, or global nomads (Matthewman, 2011). Social networks have begun playing a vital role in this movement. It underlies the success of intermediary platforms such as Tripadvisor, for example. Along with the strong need for transparency and openness, hospitality organisations need to develop strong social media 'listening skills' to understand customer needs and perceptions of brands and service quality.

Networked societies

Global nomads

Citizen brands will arise wherever a group of followers are attracted and involved in creating brand value. New possibilities such as data jockeying, powerful connectivity, rating companies, social awareness, and social involvement are valued more highly than before, and this will increase even more over the next few years. We must recognise this fact in the hospitality sector, too, and not underestimate it.

Citizen brands

Hospitality companies will have to learn to cater specifically to different generations (see Table 5.1 for some of the main characteristics of various generations) and thus also to the younger generations who are accustomed

Millennials
Generation Y
Generation C

to 'having it their way', in any form imaginable, including wanting direct influence on what companies develop and produce for them. This generation belongs to the Millennials or Generation Y, and is called 'Generation C' (where C stands for content). Members are creative and increasingly often have access to professional content-creating tools. Thus, the major challenge for companies is 'to get them to create, to produce, and to participate' (Godin, 2003; also see Trendwatching.com).

TABLE 5.1 Generations

	Baby Boomers (1946–1965)	Gen Xers (1966–1978)	Millennials (1979–2001)
Characteristics	*The 'me' generation* • Narcissistic • Intellectual renaissance • Judgemental	*Disillusioned cynics* • Cautious and sceptical • Searching for self • Alienated and confrontational • Alternative	*Optimistic and confident achievers* • Disciplined and accepting of authority • Well educated and competitive • Upbeat and open-minded • Entitled
	Baby Boomers came of age post WWII, at the height of an intellectual reawakening in America. Boomers rebelled against the establishment and the over-idealised, team-oriented generations before them.	Gen Xers are a product of a strongly individualistic society. Thought of as slackers with little drive and no direction, Gen Xers are anti rules and anti groups. They rely on the self over others.	Reared in a youth-centric culture, Millennials are self-assured and civic-minded. With sophisticated social awareness, Millennials believe community extends beyond their own backyard, and feel empowered and compelled to make the world a better place.
Defining experiences	• Summer of love • Civil rights • Vietnam war • Sexual revolution	• Aids • Recession • Soaring divorce rates	• Digital age • Terrorism and natural disasters • A global economy
	Social change and political push-back marks the Baby Boomer era. Boomers fought against race and gender inequality, participated in anti war protests, and supported sexual freedom, all in the refuge of an affluent America. This highly politicised generation was intent on challenging the status quo.	Gen Xers were faced with a social climate in the midst of advancements in medicine and technology, the War on Drugs, a new and deadly disease, times of recession, and the splintering American family. Collectively, Gen Xers were not considered capable of rallying together to improve the state of the world.	Millennials have grown up in a world where technology is a platform for customisation and immediate gratification in all aspects of life. News and information travel freely across continents, with acts of terrorism and natural disasters touching more than the people directly involved. Millennials have been instilled with a far-reaching, global social conscience.

Source: adapted from www.centerforgiving.org

Younger generations

An effective generations approach is focused on trying to understand the characteristics of different age groups. Often, people belonging to a certain generation are influenced by the period that shaped their main values, beliefs, moods, and mentality. The Baby Boomers and Gen X are referred to

Gen X

and agreed upon the most. The most frequently cited sources are the historians Strauss and Howe and their book *Generations: The History of America's Future, 1584-2069.*

The term Baby Boomers covers a large group, with members sometimes divided into two subgroups: Younger versus Older (Howe & Strauss, 1991; Howe & Strauss, 2007). The generation following Generation X is labelled the Millennials or Gen Y (Y follows X), but other also called other names such as Generation MTV, Generation Einstein, Net Generation or Digital Natives. Before the Baby Boomers came the Silent Generation, also named Traditionalists or Veterans.

Baby Boomers

Note that the age limits of the generations should not be interpreted as absolutes. There is a transitional period of approximately five years and age ranges vary between sources. In addition, exact time frames may differ between countries or regions as their historical developments and events may vary. Generation watching, combined with customer-centric approaches and new methods in service design such as empathy mapping will provide insights into consumers' changing life styles over time. The question is how to cater to newer generations that are starting to have economic power and the still influential Baby Boomers entering another life stage. What will the new hotels for Gen Y look like? Gen X is still around but will probably be overwhelmed by Gen Y in terms of influence. The Baby Boomers are ageing, but they remain an influential economic entity to be reckoned with.

5

● business.time.com

Marriott and IKEA launch a hotel brand for Millennials: What does that mean?

Most hotels are marketed to a specific group, travellers. Not Baby Boomer travellers or Gen X travellers or Millennial travellers – but *all travellers*. But a new hotel brand called Moxy has been specifically 'designed to capture the rapidly emerging Millennial traveller.'
This week, hotel giant Marriott announced that it was partnering with the Swedish furniture maker IKEA to create a new brand called Moxy Hotels. The first location will open near Milan's Malpensa airport in early 2014, and the plan is for roughly 150 Moxy properties to be launched all over Europe during the next 10 years.

Designed to capture the rapidly emerging Millennial traveller, the new brand combines contemporary stylish design, approachable service and, most importantly, an affordable price. Moxy was created for 'the next generation traveller, not only Gen X and Y but people with a younger sensibility.' So what do Millennial travellers want in a hotel, according to Moxy's designers?

'Economy Tier'
Moxy rooms will be offered at price points and amenity levels somewhere in between a hostel and a four-star hotel.

'Wildly Self-Sufficient'
'We learned that these confident explorers are wildly self-sufficient, but still want a chance to connect with each other in inviting social spaces in person or digitally.' In this case, being 'wildly self-sufficient' translates as being OK with self-service. Staffing will be minimal, which helps Moxy keep prices down. Self check-in will be available via mobile devices, in an overall atmosphere designed for 'savvy travellers who thrive on self-service and embrace new technology.'

'Tech-Savvy'
'Guestrooms will be functional and well-designed,' the Moxy announcement states. Read, small and uncluttered. Again, both of those characteristics help control costs.

March 8, 2013
Adapted

Generational effects

Generational effects in the labour market may also influence hotel styles in the next decades. For a certain period, Gen Y will profit from the small size of Gen X and the retirement of Boomers. They will have power during this period and will command higher salaries for more interesting jobs. Hotels will be forced to incorporate technology into new processes to find ways to improve salaries and enrich jobs while maintaining margins (Zaltman, 2003). Multi-divergence of tastes and needs takes place, across generations and in Gen Y. The industry will continue to be challenged in terms of balancing industrial economies of scale against boutique customisation. Successful companies need to be ahead in providing options appropriate to today's influential generations if they wish to be perceived as market leaders.

Mentality concepts

New moods or mentality concepts in society will drive the creation or foundation of innovative hospitality concepts. This requires a group of followers that feels attracted to the concept and who will be involved in the development. In this case, the terminology of the current customer group will no longer apply, as it is impossible to determine previously defined socio-demographic customer buying behaviour.

Groups and tribes

Tribe

Although the concept of the tribe is relatively new in service design, it is of course a century-old tradition in many countries across the globe. In hospitality, a tribe stands for people who share a preference and collectively feel

Tribal movements

Tribal movements (Raymond, 2010) are also the focus of Claus Sendlinger (founder of Design Hotels) for the benefit of the transient passenger, always depending on the very specific settings of a hotel. Considerations include the property, the district, and the design. The last is always the catalyst, and the architecture needs to embody the soul of the hotel. The involved parties are currently planning, in cooperation with Crane TV, a series of worldwide 'conversations' with invited experts and celebs in design, art, architecture and fashion as well as entrepreneurs and selected media focusing on Millennials. This is definitively considered not only an event, but something that needs to happen organically. People should want to meet at a certain venue because they like the atmosphere, the people, and the place.

Heretics are the new leaders (Raymond, 2010). They challenge the status quo, they get out in front of the tribes and create movements. But leadership is not the same as management. Management is about channelling resources to get a known job done. These new leaders know exactly what they need to deliver and are given resources to do it at low cost. They manage known processes and react to the outside world, making processes lean, fast, and cheap. Managers have employees and make widgets. They often use policies, procedures, bureaucracy, and hierarchy to manage. New leadership is about creating change that you believe in. Leaders have followers and make change happen. Leaders are inspiring, passionate and connect with others around to believe in an idea.

5

attracted to a new concept. In the future, followers will be easier to target than existing target-defined markets. Followers will go through existing socio-demographic markets, starting with a small core of followers. In other words, 'You don't create a new product, but a new group of followers. Human beings need to belong' (Raymond, 2010; Godin, 2008).

As Godin says, 'It's a survival mechanism to be part of a tribe, to contribute to (and take from) a group of like-minded people. We are drawn to leaders and their ideas and can't resist the rush of belonging and the thrill of the new. Preferably, people belong not only to one, but to many tribes. A group of followers can be defined as a growth potential group, as the first fans will spread the words and thoughts of the group by word of mouth. And, in turn, this will result in the increased volume of this particular group. Groups are therefore not measured in terms of potential volume of revenue as has been done in traditional marketing. Only afterwards can it be determined how large the group actually is and which type of people were attracted' (Godin, 2003).

Traditional marketing

Geography used to be very important to tribes. Coordination and leadership were difficult, but the internet has eliminated the problems. Internet has caused a true explosion of new tools: Facebook, Twitter, Craigslist, Meet up, Blogs, Online Video, and LinkedIn, to name but a few. Nowadays, tribes are far bigger, quicker, broader, instantly communicating and with more impact than ever before. New technologies are designed to connect tribes and broadcast their work. Still, the internet is just a tool, an easy way to play out certain tactics. The real power of tribes has nothing to do with the internet but everything to do with people. Each of these tribes is a movement waiting to happen, a group of people waiting to be united.

Geography

Thrilling tribal movements are the work of many people, all connected, all seeking something better. Tribal movements want to make things happen and get things done. Tribes are about faith, about belief in an idea and in a community. Tribes are grounded in respect, belief, and admiration for a leader, an idea, and their members.

5

● Nino Caceres, Rijnders, Lub, 2012

Lifestyle Hub: a possible future for the hotel

The concept of a 'lifestyle hub' depicts the future of the hotel as an integrated space in constant evolution that serves the highly dynamic lifestyles of tomorrow. Its key attributes involve a clear assembly of single services upon physical and mental evolving and sophisticated requirements. It provides clearly separated functions to work independently and with others, to relax, sleep, nap, recharge and eat. The space transforms and caters to the needs of consumers along their active and demanding journeys in one place.

In the lifestyle hub, consumers can find appropriate spaces to be highly pro-active in isolation with the environment, cancelling what they might consider obstructive 'noises' and allowing only predetermined sounds for increased concentration. Other spaces spark equal physical and mental agility and engagement with peers through walls and tables as interfaces that support easy projections, idea clustering, and mind mapping activities, instead of working in individual screen-based options. For recharging purposes, there are special devices such as floating tanks that allow people to fulfil reenergising purposes in easy and more effective ways. For relaxation, there are special spaces, tools, and food depending on the type of relaxation expected.

The lifestyle hub's spaces are organised according to consumers' moods or the expected activity performance. The hub is a platform to achieve overall mental and physical well-being and high personal and professional prolificness along the course of the day. The hotel of the future is not a place for sleep, but rather a highly engaging and active concept that moves with peoples' changing demands in the day.

Adapted

Higher standards

Hospitality experience is about exceeding customer expectations. The future of hospitality is about being pro-active and interacting quickly, instead of waiting to see what will happen. Interacting with customers to meet their various needs is what lies at the heart of most hospitality firms as they, by definition, are well-tuned to changing customer needs, expectations and values, especially with respect to lifestyle (Zaltman, 2003). Here, we explore how this will impact the core concept of this book, the hospitality experience.

Lifestyle

Experiences follow every form of consumption and behaviour. They are not the privilege of a select group. They are something that will be remembered and differentiate the company from its competitors, simply by putting the individual centre stage and building an experience (i.e. product) around him or her.

Consumption and behaviour

This customer focus implies a significant shift in what drives a hospitality business. A consistent predictable level of service is the expected standard, not the exception. In addition, companies aware of having to woo their customers are not satisfied with a consumer review below '8', and strive to turn this into at least a '9' or even a '10' out of 10. Still, with regard to operations, it is a challenge for the hotel industry to meet the standard of zero defects in service, as services are based primarily on people including customer interaction, and not on computers or other equipment. Yesterday's surprising product or service is today's status quo (Cline, 2005). For many hospitality organisations, this requires a shift from the traditional hierarchy to a flatter organisation with transparent connections between leadership and employees. The flatter organisation is closer to the customer, speeding communications up and down the organisation.

Flatter organisation

5

The 21st century customer
In the above section, we examined changes and trends in consumer experiences. Due to various trends and changes in the contextual environment, shifting consumer behaviour will require a pro-active response on the part of hospitality organisations. We discussed the following trends:
- A new collaborative consumption way of life
- The vital role of social networks
- The increasing importance of the new Gen Y
- Tribes make groups more fluid
- Guests require higher standards

5.6 The transactional environment: the industry

In the previous section, we identified several key drivers of consumer behaviour. Here, we examine the developments and trends in the hospitality industry that are influenced by changes in the consumer market. Under the influence of changing consumer needs and requirements, the hospitality industry in general is slowly shifting from an asset focus to a customer focus. Here follow nine of the most important trends.

Asset
Customer focus

1 Consumers from different generations are seeking new experiences
Hospitality businesses are discovering the need for a shift from market share thinking to customer perspective thinking, as consumers in the Western world are seeking highly personalised brands and products that can enhance their own identity. The Experience Economy (or 'Exponomy' – the Economy of Experiences, also known as the Surprise Economy or the Economics of Emotion (Boswijk, Peelen, & Olthof, 2012)) will evolve even further, building upon previous stages that developed in parallel with increasing welfare, which has enabled consumers to spend more on entertainment or memorable experiences and the like. The most recent insights incorporate new ways of value engineering, for instance via social innovation or experience co-creation, with a strong focus on user-centred design of sustain-

Exponomy

Value engineering

able innovative concepts (Boswijk et al., 2012). Existing products owned by all are no longer interesting, and customers are no longer accepting forced lifestyles. They are far more willing and motivated to create their own world and express themselves by combining different styles, brands, and social media such as Pinterest or Facebook. They seek exposure, 'This is me'. Looking at the role and the impact of the internet, and more particularly the effect of social media on today's society, we see that memorable experiences have recently evolved combined with an increased interest in the search for exposure and the sharing of those memorable, unique experiences in the Experience Economy 2.0.

2 Repositioning

Lifespan

Each product has its own lifecycle and a decreasing lifespan that will end if nothing happens. Hence, hospitality organisations have to make sure that they develop new business concepts in a timely manner. Innovation seems to be necessary as early as a product's growth stages. Innovation should also take place in the maturity stage of the existing product instead of its decline stages. This makes it possible for organisations to introduce new concepts when old concepts are declining, all the while maintaining sales, and profit.

The Kodak example demonstrates the importance of keeping an eye on innovations and not delaying their introduction.

● www.independent.co.uk

The moment it all went wrong for Kodak

The trouble began 20 years ago, with the decline of film photography. In the 1990s, Kodak poured billions into developing technology for taking pictures using mobile phones and other digital devices. But it held back from developing digital cameras for the mass market for fear of killing its all-important film business. Others, such as the Japanese firm Canon, rushed in.

So who invented the digital camera? Ironically, Kodak did – or, rather, a company engineer called Steve Sasson, who put together a toaster-sized contraption that could save images using electronic circuits. The images were transferred onto a tape cassette and were viewable by attaching the camera to a TV screen, a process that took 23 seconds.

It was an astonishing achievement. And it happened in 1975, long before the digital age. Mr Sasson and his colleagues were met with blank faces when they unveiled their device to Kodak's bosses.

For Kodak's leaders, going digital meant killing film, smashing the company's golden egg to make way for the new. Mr Sasson saw in hindsight that he had not exactly won them over when he unveiled his toy. 'In what has got to be one of the most insensitive choices of demonstration titles ever, we called it 'Film-less Photography'. Talk about warming up your audience!'

5

In 1976, Kodak sold 90% of the photographic film in the US and 85% of the cameras; 10 years later it still employed 145,000 people worldwide compared with a global payroll today of 18,000. Historians may one day conclude that most of the company's slow unravelling can be traced to the failure of its leaders to recognise the huge potential of Mr Sasson's invention.

Don Strickland, a former vice-president, who left the company in 1993 because even then he couldn't persuade it to manufacture and market a digital camera, put it this way, 'We developed the world's first consumer digital camera but we could not get approval to launch or sell it because of fear of the effects on the film market.'

Adapted

3 Increased pressure on shorter time-to-market
The innovation process or design and development cycles (time-to-market) are shorter than before because of increased pressures from the contextual environment and fast-changing consumer behaviour. Commercial ideas based on upcoming trends today require rapid prototyping, and innovations are more often launched at the stage of 'minimal viable products and services'.

4 The emergence of open service innovation
Hospitality organisations are trying to create innovative partnerships with other industries such as retail or design, fashion and art, for example a fashion hotel (The Exchange in Amsterdam) or a luxury brand exploiting hotels (Armani hotels). Firms are looking for innovation as a new source of profit.

5 New business models
Hospitality organisations are forced to look for possibilities to facilitate strategic collaboration with key partners, new cost and pricing models, new unbundled roles (such as owner, management, branding) and asset management strategies. Examples include emerging unbranded hotel groups offering 'white label solutions', sophisticated marketing, very high standards of service and advanced technology support while allowing owners to develop their own brands.

Strategic collaboration

White label solutions

6 Streamlined distribution
Technological developments, including the growing importance of mobile devices and the internet, force hospitality organisations to compete and collaborate with online travel agents. In addition, new challenges arise with regard to the seamless use of mobile applications, cost management and hence transparency, which leads to the need to consider the use of technology for optimising operational processes and acquiring competitive advantage.

7 Brand management and customer engagement
The concept of tribes and their fluid needs force hospitality organisations to reconsider the concept of branding. While branding initially concerned activities using traditional media, hospitality organisations should realise that

Branding

social media and themes such as simplicity, sustainability, and scarcity are becoming more important today. Additionally, in relation to new generations, organisations should explore the possibilities of edutainment (fun and knowledge) and experience marketing (content culture and content brands) in attracting and retaining consumers.

Edutainment
Experience marketing

8 Special attention for human resources

Management capabilities

Catering for impassioned people providing the heart, soul, and spirit of the customer experience has been affected by an ageing and more diverse population. Organisations of the future must build management capabilities to deal with critical challenges, such as diversity. In addition, the introduction of newer generations in the workforce urges managers to think about new ways of leadership, including supportive leadership and empowerment.

The hospitality industry can learn a great deal from developments and trends in other industries, also when it comes to HR. The Semco example challenges the traditional way of human resources management. Would it work in an exclusive hotel? Would it enhance the hospitality experience?

● www.freibergs.com

Semco, insanity that works

Semco is a Brazilian company led by Ricardo Semler. The company was founded in 1952 by Semler's father, Antonio, and specialises in manufacturing marine pumps. Ricardo took over in 1980 at the age of 21, his head brimming with radical ideas about how businesses should operate. Within a few days, he had dismissed 75% of the senior executives and began putting his ideas into practice.

Semco has no job titles, no organisational charts, and no headquarters. If you need an office, you go online and reserve space at one of the few satellite offices scattered around Sao Paulo. Semler explains, 'If you don't even know where your people are, you can't possibly keep an eye on them. All that's left to judge is performance.'

Many workers, including factory workers, set their own schedules and their own salaries. They can also choose their own form of compensation based on 11 different options. What prevents associates from taking advantage of this freedom? First, all of the company's financial information is public, so everyone knows what everyone else makes. People who pay themselves too much have to work with resentful colleagues. Not long ago union members argued that their pay increase was too high and would hurt profitability. Second, associates must reapply for their jobs every six months. Pay yourself unfairly, and you could soon be looking for a new job. Finally, employee compensation is tied directly to the company's profits – there is enormous peer pressure to keep budgets in line.

Semler, who, of course, has no title, has built a reputation for encouraging people to fearlessly ask 'why.' Why do we have job titles? Why do we need a headquarters? (According to Semler, 'It's a source of control, discrimination, and power-mongering.') Why shouldn't employees have access to detailed financial information? Semler believes that challenging assumptions, rather than conforming to them, is the key to building an adaptive, creative organisation. The company has a policy of no policies. Instead, Semco offers employees a 21-page 'Survival Manual' filled with cartoons and brief declarations designed to help assimilate people into its culture.

Adapted

Ricardo Semler

9 The need for new collaborative leadership

A collaborative corporate culture is often regarded as a culture of trust, where the company's vision, mission and values provide direction to handle new requirements dealing with diversity, ageing and longevity. Hence, the challenge for hospitality organisations and their management is to co-create trust and collaboration.

Culture of trust

These trends will urge hospitality organisations to comprehend contextual trends and ever-changing consumer behaviour. Dealing with trends from the contextual and transactional environments has become a necessary competence to tune into the needs of tomorrow's guests and to stay successful.

The changes we discussed in this section raise fundamental questions for hospitality organisations. They must introduce new concepts and services, while giving increasing customer expectations full attention, as generational effects are likely to affect successful concepts over the next decades. In the next section, we elaborate on the future of hospitality. It demands pro-active behaviour and a quick response to changing needs.

5.7 The future of hospitality

Market volatility

This chapter began by emphasising the importance of further developing the ability to think ahead and, we concluded, market volatility has become the norm, also in hospitality.

Consumer groups have become more fluid so companies have to come up with new ways of interacting with their customers and be able to understand how they can link with their tribes or even initiate them. This requires considerable creativity, maybe the most vital future skill to develop. Studying the future of hospitality, we attempted to give you a deeper insight into the many perspectives you should use in forecasting future trends for your organisation. In many cases, we ourselves have experienced that if a business is aware of the most relevant drivers of change and perspectives for key strategic issues, it is in a better position to anticipate changes at a strategic level. We presented visions of the future that can facilitate hospitality businesses to improve their decision-making and their ability to deal with uncertainty. In the elaboration on new technologies, we pointed at new technologies that will reshape the future hospitality context.

In terms of exceeding customer experiences, there are challenges ahead. Your future guests' needs have become increasingly fragmented and diverse. Future leaders have to develop the sensitivity to see what others do not see yet and foresee what the majority or particular market segments might be interested in. A major challenge for future hospitality practices will be fulfilling the needs of ever more educated and demanding customers with individualistic expectations. Contemporary thoughts and views on studying the 'signs of the times' have pointed to a shift in terms of consumer insights and lifestyles. Insights into changing customer behaviour will help you find new opportunities and define what kinds of innovations are needed. We presented many examples linked to different contexts in hospitality, together with consumer insights based on trends. We hope these examples inspire you to design new concepts and innovations to cater for rapidly changing customer habits and tastes. In the end, you may want to become (or hire, or connect with) a 'lifestyle detective' (Raymond, 2010) trying to trace and understand the needs of future tribes and creating or finding your own followers to lead one. Intuition, communication, innovation, and emotion should lead you to adapt to changing societal challenges, instead of a purely analytical and rational focus.

Visionary leadership

To achieve all these things in day-to-day business life, you may wish to set up diverse teams with a mix of talents and to nurture your networks, as they will be a vital source of inspiration and help. And do take care of your employees and/or colleagues, as 'service experience is heavily affected by interactions with front-line staff, attitude towards customers, empathy and attentiveness' (Stickdorn, 2011). In the end, visionary leadership is essential to lead successful businesses. It must be linked to business operations that emphasise empowered employees, flexibility, learning, and cooperation. In this way, you can embrace changes that enable employees to manage their own roles and actively use serendipity principles and teamwork skills.

In the next chapter, we explain how you can recognise the trends discussed in this chapter and design hospitality experiences that meet the changing needs and requirements of today's and future consumers.

Summary

▶ You should use an outside-in approach in studying the future.

▶ We distinguish two dimension of the environment:
  • Contextual environment, where overall developments, changes, and trends occur, often grounded in societies
  • Transactional environment includes the parties that hospitality organisations interact with in establishing continuity and profit, which are influenced by the contextual environment

▶ In the contextual environment, we distinguish the following six trends:
  • Demographic changes and the need to cater for new customer segments such as the ageing population
  • Demographic changes resulting in greater diversity of the labour population and an expected battle for talent
  • Economic turmoil and a global shift in power, which creates an uncertain, turbulent business environment and a need to reduce risks
  • Upcoming economies with an emerging middle class (such as BRIC or MIST countries) and new markets for travel, both inbound and outbound
  • Changing moods in society with greater emphasis on collectiveness, communities, sharing and sustainable development
  • New enabling technologies that support new ways of working and communications or a higher level of the quality of life

▶ In the transactional environment, we can distinguish the following five consumer trends:
  • A new collaborative consumption way of life
  • The vital role of social networks
  • The increasing importance of the new Gen Y
  • Tribes make groups more fluid
  • Guests require higher standards

▶ In the transactional environment, consumer trends have the following eight consequences on the hospitality industry:
  • Consumers from different generations are seeking new experiences
  • Old product/concept has reached its end, requires repositioning
  • Increased pressure on shorter time-to-market
  • The emergence of open service innovation
  • The need for new business models
  • Streamlined distribution
  • Special attention for human resources
  • The need for new collaborative leadership

▶ Hospitality leaders must study the future of hospitality.

Food for thought

This chapter introduced you to the future of the hospitality industry, high-lighted the on-going debate on what it means for the hospitality industry and staging hospitality experiences. Based on the content of this chapter, the following questions, challenges and topics could serve as interesting starting points for further discussion:

1   Which developments discussed in this chapter can you see in society nowa-days? What impact do they have on how the hospitality industry works?

2   Which other developments are possible in the future? How would they af-fect the future of hospitality?

3   In this chapter we mainly addressed developments in the hospitality indus-try. In Chapter 4 we discussed the integration of hospitality in other indus-tries. What crucial developments can you identify in other industries and what do they mean to the role of hospitality in these industries?

6

Designing hospitality experiences

Bert Smit, Monique van Prooijen-Lander, and Frans Melissen

This chapter focuses on designing hospitality experiences. First, we revisit the implications of today's 'experience economy' and discuss the importance of accounting for the interaction part of hospitality experiences and the need for hosts and guests to really understand each other. We then discuss specific tools and methods to ensure a full understanding of your customers, part of the first step in the process of designing successful hospitality experiences. Subsequently, we explain the remaining steps in the process and illustrate them with supporting theories, models, and practical examples.

citizenM

citizenM is a new breed of hotel now in Amsterdam, Glasgow and London, and coming soon to New York, Paris and a city near you. citizenM welcomes the mobile citizens of the world – the suits, weekenders, explorers, affair-havers and fashion-grabbers. So if you travel with an open mind, a love of free movies on demand and free Wi-Fi, come in and take a room tour. The inspiration hungry: meet citizenMag, our lifestyle magazine. The gung ho: jump straight to reservations.

Source: http://www.citizenm.com/trendy-boutique-hotels

citizenM is a hotel driven by one desire, to create affordable luxury for the people. By 'the people', we mean a smart new breed of international traveller, the type who crosses continents the way others cross streets. This includes the weekenders, the suits, fashion-baggers and affair-havers. The explorers, adventurers and dreamers. Those who travel the world with big hearts and wide eyes. Those who are independent, yet united by a love of the five continents. Those in search of business, shopping or art. In short, everyone who is a mobile citizen of the world. Most likely, that also means you.

Source: http://www.citizenm.com/hotel-technology-concepts

6.1 Reference points for the design process

Getting the design right so that you can stage the right hospitality experience in the right situation is extremely important for the financial viability of companies. In this section we address hospitality experience design in the commercial context. We focus on the characteristics of the design that make a hospitality experience appropriate for a specific context. The principles we discuss here also apply in non-commercial contexts outside the hospitality industry.

Characteristics of the design

'For the first time in the hotel industry, we're defining customers by a mind-set rather than a price point.'

— Steve Porter, president for the Americas, InterContinental Hotels Group at the opening of the first Indigo hotel.

To ensure financial viability or adapt successfully to a changing world, it is crucial that we stage the right hospitality experience for a particular context. Hospitality experiences come in so many different forms that the key question is often not whether we should stage one, but which one would be best for the circumstances. As we saw in Chapter 1, a hospitality experience relates directly to the interaction between a host and guest, who both engage voluntarily in the interaction. It involves the host providing accommodation or food and drink to the guest and the context in which this interaction takes place determines the applicability of specific rules and norms.

Financial viability

6

This definition tells us three important points that you need to consider in designing a specific hospitality experience:

1 *In the interaction between host and guest in the commercial setting, the host creates economic value by delivering accommodation and/or food and/or drink to the guest.*

When you, the host, stage hospitality experiences for guests in exchange for money (or other economic value) with the goal of making a profit, then the hospitality experience must be worth more than the monetary value of the goods and services. A guest will pay extra for the added value of the experience connected to the goods and services. How much extra depends on the choices made by the host and their interaction with the guest. Most guests do not find it strange that dinner in a Michelin restaurant is more expensive than in a fast food restaurant. The promise a Michelin restaurant makes to its guests is very different from the one a fast food restaurant makes, in terms of what they offer and what the role of the guest will be in the experience. This promise is called the value proposition.

Economic value

Value proposition

In general, to create and maintain loyalty, hotels especially aim to meet guest expectations that result from this promise to at least a satisfactory level. Hotels determine their part of the interaction based on the expected lifetime value of a guest (not just the value of one stay but of all stays and expenses together). Similar mechanisms seem to apply in restaurants, theme parks, theatres and many other types of accommodations. Within the hospitality industry, there seems to be a connection between *expectations*, the *value proposition*, *satisfaction*, and *loyalty*. Chapter 1 dealt with another important reference point: companies need to account for the principles of *the experience economy* in order to be successful. This chapter further explores the link between expectations, value propositions, satisfaction and loyalty on the one hand and the experience economy on the other.

Expectations
Loyalty
Satisfaction

2 *We design voluntary interactions between the host and the guest.*

Choice

It is important to realise that 'voluntary' implies a choice for both host and guest to engage in the interaction. As we saw in Chapter 3, the commercial domain of hospitality comes in many different forms (hotels, restaurants etc.). Guests can choose any form based on what they want and expect to get or do. Simultaneously, hosts have a number of choices available to them, regarding the type of interactions, accommodation, food, and drink that they want to provide and the price at which they want to provide them. Given the many different successful forms of hospitality businesses, this implies that not all guests want and expect the same. In this chapter, we look at the choice element from the guest's side and at how companies try to influence that choice by creating *concepts or brands, touchpoints, roles* and *scripts*.

Concepts or brands, touchpoints, roles and scripts

3 *The context determines the rules and norms of the interaction.*

The host's offer and the guest's expectations are largely determined by the context of the interaction. Guests of a five-star hotel have different expectations of their room than guests of a hostel. A restaurant in Macau has a different set of rules and norms than a restaurant in Madrid. Guests and hosts interact differently in the Starbucks on 52nd street in New York than in the bar of St. Regis in Aspen. This chapter will show how the context of the hospitality experience influences the rules and norms that apply to both host and guest. It will also show to what extent the context can be purposely designed, by creating *concepts and brands* that come to life in the design of *guest journeys and touchpoints*. This chapter explores *morphological charting*, and *service blue printing* as tools to create consistency in a hospitality experience.

Guest journeys
Morphological charting
Service blue printing

6.2 Setting the stage for experiences

Customising

Pine and Gilmore (1999), the authors who pointed out that today we live and work in an 'experience economy', claim that economic value of a certain product is enlarged by customising it to the needs of customers. The more something is customised to meet the wishes of an individual customer, the more it is worth. Figure 6.1 visualises this idea.

FIGURE 6.1 Progression of economic value

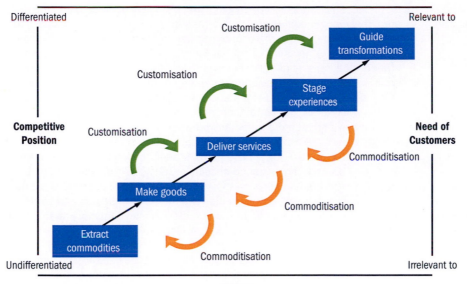

Source: Pine & Gilmore (1999)

Pine and Gilmore use three axes to explain the concept of economic value:

The first axis they use is 'pricing' (market-driven versus premium-driven pricing), meaning the extent to which the market determines the price versus the extent to which the premium determines the price. For example, the price of a barrel of crude oil is determined by supply and demand in the world market, whereas the price of a litre of processed diesel at a full-service petrol station is determined by the cost of all the refinery and production services added to the original crude oil before it ends up in your car.

Market-driven

Premium-driven

The second axis, 'competitive position' shows the level of differentiation a specific value proposition has relative to those of competitors. For example, you could say that a source material, cocoa beans from Ivory Coast, does not differ from one producer to the next (undifferentiated). However, the products they create, for instance a Mars bar sold at a petrol station or a Sacher Torte cake served in Hotel Sacher are recognisably different (differentiated).

Differentiation

The third axis covers the extent to which the 'needs of customers' are taken into account. Is every element of the final product completely customised to your wishes or are you buying a highly standardised product or service. Do you buy any one of a million standard bikes on the planet or are you a bike freak who wants to determine every little detail of your bike up to the last screw and bolt. Both are possible, but option one will probably be cheaper than the second (pricing), and only a limited number of suppliers can offer the second to you (differentiation).

Needs of customers

6

Different types of economic offering and their links are positioned in this framework. At the basic level (bottom left) it says 'extract commodities'. This is, for instance, the price you pay to extract a barrel of crude oil. In the next step, these commodities are transformed into 'goods' (such as plastics, diesel, or kerosene). When the economic offering using these goods is further customised they become part of the 'delivery of a service' (diesel at a petrol station, clothing sold and handed over to you in a branded bag at ZARA). When a service is customised to the needs of the customer, it becomes part of a 'staged experience'. For instance, a staged experience is when petrol station workers fill your petrol tank, and check your oil level and tyres, clean your window and stop the traffic for you when you re-enter traffic. If you are willing to pay more for this experience, apparently you like having it, and so choose not to go to a self-service petrol station. Economic value is created by staging an experience around specific products and services. The combination of products and services tailored to the needs of customers creates an experience that is worth more than the individual products and services. If performed well, the experience can create a positive memory related to a specific petrol station or brand, which can lead to a form of loyalty.

It is like theme parks and zoos stating that what they actually sell are fond memories of a day with family or friends. They claim to stage meaningful experiences for their guests. Theme parks invest a lot of money to make sure this memory is linked to their park and brand by creating experiences that are unique for the park, but also by emphasising the connection between the group members (i.e. other parks linked to the same brand). Compare that to a couple looking for a restaurant to have a romantic dinner. If the services the host provides are tailored to their needs, and in the style they like, the couple will have that romantic feeling they are looking for, creating that memory of spending quality time together. They opt for a specific combination of products and services; the menu, the type of waiter, the linen used in the restaurant, candlelight, music and other characteristics that create the opportunity to have the restaurant experience they want. To be able to customise the products and services on offer, the host needs to know what feeling his guests are expecting to have. That is the reason behind the following common question in the hospitality industry, 'May I know the purpose of your stay?' Obviously, the more a guest is willing to share, the better the host can adapt his offer.

As we said before, in the hospitality industry, staging experiences takes on and will continue to take on many different forms, based on the presumed expectations of particular target groups and the host's view of what his value proposition should be. And many different experiences have become successful. From Starbucks and McDonald's to Six Senses Resorts and the Burj al Arab, all of these companies have a value proposition that attracts enough guests to keep them in business. All have been able to create a 'set of benefits and values that they promise to deliver to customers to satisfy their needs' (Kotler, 2004) to enable them to have a large base of loyal customers. For some reason, their guests return regularly. Some guests say they would never consider going to a different company. These guests must feel that the offer made to them (or how they have experienced that offer in the past), is better than any other offer they expect to get somewhere else. In other words, loyal guests have a certain expectation of what they will get from a provider, which apparently matches their needs and serves the purpose to at least at a more than satisfactory level.

Commodities

Experience

6

Guests

Provider

Interactive experiences

As we said in Chapter 1, at the core of a hospitality experience lies the interaction between a host and a guest. In fact, understanding the nature of interactions in the context of experiences has been an important topic for researchers in many fields. They have widely analysed such concepts as optimal work experience, peak experiences in leisure, tourism and sports, and experiences in education.

Nature of interactions

The interactive experience model of Falk and Dierking (1992), depicted in Figure 6.2, is one of the most commonly acknowledged frameworks for the influences of interactive experiences, such as hospitality experiences. This model was originally used to understand the experiences of museum visitors. Nowadays, it is widely used to help companies understand how interactive experiences work. Falk and Dierking discovered that the way a guest participates in and interprets a museum experience is first influenced by his personal context: his motivation to be there, his personality, expectations of the specific museum, skills, knowledge, and previous experiences.

Personal context

Secondly, the social context in which the person operates in the museum influences the experience. The social context consists of the people with the visitor (he behaves differently when he is with his kids, just his wife or by himself), and the way other visitors and staff behave in the museum. The experience is different when it is extremely busy or when an interpreter is present to explain certain objects or artefacts. The social context, to a certain extent, also dictates what behaviour is expected. For instance, the fact that most people are very quiet in a library also influences the volume at which you will talk to your friend sitting beside you.

Social context

Thirdly, the physical context influences the experience: the layout of the building, signage and routing of the museum, ambient conditions such as light, smell and air, and of course the design of the exhibit itself. The three contexts together create the interactive experience.

Physical context

FIGURE 6.2   The interactive experience model

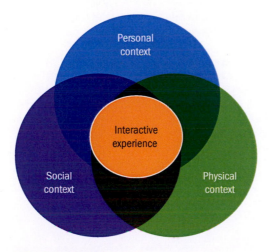

Source: Falk & Dierking (1992)

Staging experiences

Given that hospitality experiences imply an interaction between hosts and guests, when we design such experiences, we clearly want to influence or steer this interaction. The literature on experience and service design often uses an analogy with the concept of theatre to illustrate this (see e.g. Schechner, 1988 ; Pine & Gilmore, 1999 ; Stuart & Tax, 2004). Let us consider the following example to illustrate how this theatre analogy, also depicted in Figure 6.3, could be applied to a hospitality context.

Theatre analogy

When you dine in a restaurant with two Michelin stars, as a guest you know that you are not supposed to walk up to the bar to order a beer. Normally you would wait at your table for a waiter to ask whether you would like something to drink. Somehow, even though this rule is not communicated to you explicitly when you enter the restaurant, both you and the waiter know how you need to behave and the type of interaction that you will have. This shows how guests and staff perform specific roles following a predefined script that all involved consider appropriate for that situation, much like actors do in a play. The same logic applies to the physical context. In the same restaurant you would not expect to find a pinball machine, plastic cutlery, and loud music. This decor and these props would not fit the context. Like in a play, specific roles, decor, and props support scenes that together create the scenario appropriate for the hospitality experience. Therefore, when you design an experience, you not only need to establish the desired interaction between your staff and guests, but also the physical context supporting this interaction. The literature usually refers to this as the 'servicescape'.

Servicescape

Thinking about the appropriate interactions and servicescapes that, put together, create a hospitality experience, you need to realise that both constantly influence each other. This means that the designer of a hospitality experience needs to base his choices of interactions and servicescapes on the full guest journey (or play) that a guest will engage in. It is crucial to realise that the journey that you are offering is not the only one available to a potential guest. Your competitors will offer different journeys. Ultimately the guest decides which journey best meets his needs and expectations. Simultaneously, as a hospitality provider you also have a choice in the guest journeys that you are willing to create and offer. Once again, these choices illustrate the voluntary character of a hospitality experience.

Needs and expectations

The logical starting point for any design is thinking about how your specific choices can meet the needs and expectations of specific (groups of) guests with respect to the guest journey you are willing and able to offer. The latter is usually referred to as the value proposition. The remainder of this chapter focuses on the various choices you can make for all the elements in Figure 6.3. The order in which this is done is outside-in, which means that the starting point is to understand what the guest wants and needs, and the result is a detailed script for the interactions that together shape the guest journey.

FIGURE 6.3   Theatre analogy of interactive hospitality experience

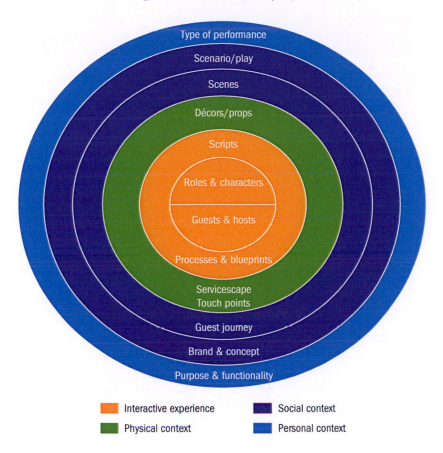

6.3   Personal context

Different people like and dislike different experiences. To design an experience a guest is hoping for and a host (a hospitality company) is willing to stage, it is important for both parties to understand each other. For the host, it is crucial to attract the right kind of guest. For the guest, it is crucial to pick the right host. The Ritz-Carlton does not want to attract backpackers. For a five-course dinner you do not go to Starbucks.

All consumer-purchasing decisions are made in the same basic way and follow the same five steps (Mowen & Minor, 1998), as highlighted in Figure 6.4.

Step one of the decision-making process starts with an awareness of some kind of need (e.g. for food or a place to sleep). Marketers distinguish two types, utilitarian needs and expressive needs. Utilitarian needs involve the consumer's desire to solve basic problems and are mostly related to innate needs such as the need for food or safety. Expressive needs involve the consumer's desire to fulfil social and/or aesthetic requirements, which are mostly learnt. Ultimately, the hospitality industry provides services aimed at utilitarian needs, but adds value by considering and providing for expressive needs.

Utilitarian needs

Expressive needs

FIGURE 6.4 The consumer decision making process

Source: Mowen & Minor (1998)

The situation can provoke the consumer's awareness of needs (you feel hungry and realise you want food), but this awareness can also be triggered by marketing messages. Surfing online, many of us have experienced how personalised advertisements on internet pages contain selected content that is based on our surfing behaviour and the websites that we have visited in the past. Seeing these ads can trigger our desire for a specific product or service but our awareness of this desire seemingly pops up out of the blue. Up to that point, you had not thought of buying that product or service, but now you realise that it might be a good idea. In fact, we often do not remember the specific advertisement that triggered our desire, but now that it has, we are fully aware of our need.

When a consumer is aware of a specific need, he looks for information on possible alternatives that can satisfy the need. As a consumer you are now creating a long list of possibilities. This gathering of information and listing of possibilities is the second step in the consumer decision-making process. The third step is the evaluation of all the alternatives. As a consumer, you now start to create a shortlist of interesting, attractive alternatives to satisfy your need. In the fourth step you make the actual decision to buy one of the alternatives. The fifth and final step is the purchase evaluation, in other words establishing your level of satisfaction with the purchase.

The designer of hospitality experiences has to understand and consider all five steps in the process, especially the mechanisms in steps three and four, because the success of the designed experience depends on your offering getting onto the shortlist of the right consumers and being chosen as the best alternative by the right type of guest.

Getting onto the shortlist

As we mentioned above, a guest creates a shortlist of alternatives and compares the options to come to a purchasing decision. The selection of alternatives is based partly on situational elements and partly on the personal characteristics of the guest. The designer of hospitality experiences needs to take all of them into account to make sure he meets the guest's expectations.

Selection of alternatives

The situational elements that influence decision-making are the actual purpose of the purchase and the amount of effort needed to acquire each alternative, which influences the level of involvement in the purchase and its importance. In other words, your choice of hotel depends on why you are travelling (leisure, meeting, or conference), ease of booking, where your hotel is located relative to where you need to go, and, of course, price. These days, another influential aspect is often how other guests have experienced a specific hotel and their comments about that experience on review sites such as Tripadvisor or social media.

Review sites

The personal characteristics of the guest that influence the selection are the combination of psychological and social factors (linked to expressive needs) that make up the symbolism of his consumption pattern. You could say that by consuming (specific products or services), the guest is actually communicating what is important to him (see e.g. Veblen and Almy, 1899 ; and Beck, 1992). The psychological and social factors mentioned above include such aspects as personality and personal values, type of upbringing, financial resources, and previous experiences in hospitality settings. In other words, a guest chooses his hotel based on how open he is to other cultures, how important fun and enjoyment of life is to him, and the kind of relationship he would like to have with the hotel. The choice also depends on how much he can afford to spend and his expectations of certain hotels based on his own or others' previous experiences.

6

Designing for a specific group of guests

All this means that different hospitality experiences appeal to different guests or consumers. The same hospitality experience might be perfectly acceptable and appealing to one group of consumers, but not even remotely appealing to another. That is why designers use market segmenting to tailor the design of specific experiences to the right type of guests. Segmentation divides the heterogeneous (widely varied) market into smaller, more homogeneous (similar) segments based on specific variables. Potential guests in one segment are more homogenous in their behaviour, motives, and expectations. As a result, you can tailor the design of an experience to their profile. Segmentation for new experiences is done by combining several segmentation types. Usually a combination of psychographic, behavioural, and sometimes demographic segmentation creates a clear view of who the potential guests are and what they are looking for.

Segmentation

Psychographic segmentation divides the market based on personality traits, personal values, lifestyle, and social class. This type of segmentation is important if you aim to satisfy expressive needs of guests. A shy guest who

Psychographic segmentation

likes modern design and being alone is very different from a sociable guest who likes vintage design and thinks sustainability is important.

Behavioural segmentation

Behavioural segmentation divides the market based on guest knowledge, attitude, or response towards a product or service. What is the *occasion* for visiting, what is the *benefit* the guest is looking for and is he a *loyal* guest? A guest checking in into the Four Seasons in New York every month to have a business meeting in the morning in an office one block away is very different from the guest who is there for the first time to explore the city and came here for the view over Central Park.

Demographic segmentation

Demographic segmentation helps to narrow the market further if needed by adding variables such as income (or spending power), age, occupation, race and gender. Obviously, 88-year-old male guests have different needs and expectations than eight-year-old female guests.

You could say that demographic segmentation is usually the starting point for marketers, but for experience designers in the hospitality industry, psychographics and behavioural segmentation probably provide more useful information.

6

Personas

Many companies in the services and hospitality industries use personas to help design appropriate experiences. Personas are descriptions and visualisations of fictional characters that represent different (groups of) guest types, or segments. A persona is the prototype of a guest from a specific segment that a company is aiming for. The persona description in terms of individual and situational characteristics helps with internal communication when a company is designing a new experience. A persona usually has a name, age, marital status and is linked to specific concepts and brands he likes or buys. A persona also has a specific set of skills and a certain education (level).

Given the fact that most companies provide products and services to more than one type of customer, they usually also use more than one persona to create their value proposition. However, when designing one experience in the wider set of experiences on offer, they tend to customise that experience for a particular persona.

Personas in practice

To illustrate the use of personas, consider the Royal Dutch Touring Club ANWB. ANWB offers a wide range of services related to roadside assistance and medical and repatriation assistance abroad. Besides their websites, ANWB has many shops throughout the Netherlands for their tour operating business, where they sell travel information, insurance and many other products and services in the areas of recreation, tourism, and mobility.

ANWB used these personas to create customer awareness and customer focus in their product development, marketing, and communication teams. The personas improved internal communication and helped to create a common understanding of why customers choose ANWB and what they expect of ANWB. The ANWB personas Bert, Arthur and Margo are of course fictitious. Each persona has its own personality and values and its own vision of why they like ANWB and what ANWB should provide for them.

Bert

Bert is a safety seeker with traditional norms and values. He likes his daily routine and believes he must work before he can enjoy himself. He is involved with his local community. Family is important to him. He values his cosy home and what his community brings him. Bert's main descriptors are security, discipline, traditional values, cosiness, citizenship, tradition, respect, and retention. His slogan is 'ANWB, stay who you are!'

Arthur

Arthur is an ambitious, lively hedonist. He focuses on his career, which is also the main driver of his social status. Arthur is individualistic but has a large social network. He strongly values his individual freedom and he seeks a wide variety of activities every day.

Arthur's main descriptors are freedom, ambition, impulsive, work, busy, personal development, enjoyment, consumption, career, materialistic, social climber, money, success, gadgets. His slogan is 'ANWB, what can you do for me and where can you get me?'

Margo

Margo is self-conscious and socially critical. It is important to her to find the right balance between her work and private life. She loves nature, is keen on culture, and is in-

volved in her community, the environment, and politics. Margo's main descriptors are social, self-conscious, environment, work, moral, tranquillity, life, improvements, being authentic and social norms and beliefs. Her slogan is 'ANWB, involve me in what you do.'

The ANWB used these personas to reach a common understanding of typical customers and why they chose ANWB. Armed with this understanding, interdisciplinary teams found it easier to discuss new product developments because they could talk about 'real' people rather than target groups. Everyone understood immediately if you said, 'Margo wouldn't like that' or 'Bert is definitely looking for this'.

Source: Composed in consultation with the ANWB and used with their consent.

---

6 Targeting

6.4 Social context

Looking back to the definition of the hospitality experience, two key elements are (1) 'the interaction between host and guest is voluntary' and (2) 'the interaction context determines the rules and norms'. As we mentioned in the introduction to this chapter, the word voluntary means that both host and guest have a choice. And, as we have shown in the previous sections, a guest actively chooses a host. Similarly, a host chooses the type of guest for whom he wants to provide accommodation and/or food and/or drink. By segmenting the market and targeting a specific type of guests, based on for instance the behavioural and psychographic characteristics mentioned above, the host also chooses which type of guest he does not want to serve.

Scenario

The key element in this part of the design process is the scenario of the interaction. Ultimately the scenario determines which concept or brand you will offer to the potential guest. Later on, the choice of concept or brand helps you determine the rules and norms that apply to each interaction with the guest and thus also the appropriate form of accommodation and/or food and/or drink that you will provide.

When asked about successful hospitality experiences, many of us will mention the likes of Sheraton, British Airways, Subway, and other worldwide brands. Others would mention that one little B&B they once visited that really felt like home. All of these companies, even the little B&B, have a crucial characteristic in common; they are all very clear on who and what they are and the scenario you enter when you visit them. They have a clear value proposition with a clear and consistent concept or brand promise.

Creating a brand and a brand promise
There are many ways to define 'brand'. Without going too deeply into the history, you could say that over time brands have evolved from a sender perspective to a receiver perspective, and now, roughly since the turn of the century, to an interaction between sender and receiver.

Kotler (2004), representing the sender perspective, defines a brand as 'a name, term, sign, symbol, or a combination of these that identifies the maker or seller of the product'. The brand in this sense is merely used as a way to recognise the producer, but does not say anything about the intended audience.

Aaker (1991), representing the receiver perspective, defines a brand as 'a set of assets (or liabilities) linked to a brand's name and symbol that adds to (or subtracts from) the value provided by a product or service.' The best examples (or maybe worst, if you were to apply a public health perspective instead of simply assessing effectiveness) of this type of branding are the cigarette brands from the nineties, such as Marlboro and Pall Mall, that communicated a certain lifestyle preference through their value proposition. These brands made themselves attractive by identifying with certain lifestyle segments.

In contrast, Kapferer (1997) was one of the first authors to recognise that a brand is actually created in the interaction between sender and receiver and that the interaction itself creates value. Kapferer says that 'a brand is not a product. It is the product's source, its meaning, and its direction, and defines its identity in time and space'. What Kapferer means is that a brand's behaviour is predictable to some extent. The source and identity tell the consumer what to expect from the brand, what kind of performance it will deliver and how it wants to interact with the consumer, and how it would like the consumer to feel and act. Kapferer (1997) uses the brand prism to explain that. The brand prism should be seen as a lens to look at different elements of a brand, as Figure 6.5 illustrates.

FIGURE 6.5 The brand prism

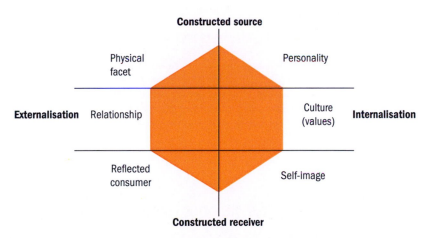

Source: Kapferer (1997)

This brand prism or lens can be used to see how a brand is internalised and externalised. Using one helps you to look closer at the company behind the brand and the consumers who favour that brand.

Brand prism

Using a brand lens to see how the brand is internalised gives insight into the personality and culture of the brand, but also shows what the brand does for its consumers' self-image. Brand *personality* refers to identity, a set of traits associated with the brand, because of what they say about it

Brand personality

Brand culture

and its products. Language and symbols used to represent the brand give the brand character and attitude. The brand *culture* is a result of specific values that explain what it stands for and what it will and will not do. This culture is directly related to the way that brand looks at and interprets the world. Nike's marketing messages, for instance, express a desire to make sure that individuals reach their maximum potential. This desire reflects a specific perspective and represents the culture that Nike stands for. That is backed up by a specific personality that, in turn, is shaped by specific language and symbols used to communicate that desire, that culture.

Self-image

Simultaneously, a brand also has an effect on the *self-image* of consumers. Consumers who favour specific brands usually use them to emphasise certain aspects of who they are or would like to be. This is how they internalise the brand characteristics. For instance, going to Starbucks makes a consumer feel young and hip, whereas going to the Ritz-Carlton makes a consumer feel well respected and successful.

Externalisation

Physical facets

Relationship

Reflected consumer

Looking through the brand lens to the outside world shows the externalisation of the brand. This externalisation relates to the way the brand looks (physical facets), interacts (relationships) and the way the brand sees its consumers (reflected consumer). *Physical facets* of a brand are tangible elements that make the brand visible and recognisable. A physical facet can be all kinds of things: a building (e.g. the Burj al Arab), a person (e.g. Steve Jobs for Apple), a logo (e.g. J.W. Marriot), or, for instance, a flagship product (e.g. the Waldorf Astoria in New York). The *relationship* element refers to the typical mode of conduct that identifies the brand and is at the heart of all consumer interactions. The core relationship element of Apple is user-friendliness, Ritz-Carlton conveys sophistication, and Starbucks wants to be personal and intimate. Finally, the *reflected consumer* is the prototypical consumer, from the brand perspective. The reflected consumer is very similar to the personas we discussed earlier in relation to market segmentation. The opening case of this chapter gave another example of this form of prototyping. We saw that the reflected consumer for CitizenM is 'a new breed of traveller [...] the mobile citizens of the world'. By formulating it this way, CitizenM creates a picture of who they see as their ideal customer.

● www.craplogo.me

New Gap logo, despised symbol of corporate banality, dead at one week

The new Gap logo, which was unveiled last week to a chorus of caustic criticism, died yesterday at the age of one week. The logo passed after a brief and ignominious battle with stage IV banality.

Brought into the world on Gap.com on October 4, 2010, the logo was supposed to signify Gap's transition from 'classic, American design to modern, sexy, cool,' according to company spokesperson Louise Callagy. The gods of graphic design though, had other plans. 'It looks like the emblem of some failed low-fare spinoff of a major airline,' wrote Slate's Tom Scocca. Refinery29 compared the logo to 'that awkward cap-sleeved tee with the rhine-stone letters you find while thrift shopping that's neither vintage nor new, but definitely not cool.'

The advent of a create-your-own-Gap-logo website called 'Crap Logo Your-self' dragged the design ever closer to the brink of death. After suffering emotional injuries sustained upon reading the satirical Gap Logo Twitter feed, the infantile imprint was rushed to Facebook, where it underwent an emergency resuscitation attempt. 'We know this logo created a lot of buzz and we're thrilled to see passionate debates unfolding!' Gap's Facebook status reported on October 6. 'So much so we're asking you to share your designs. We love our version, but we'd like to see other ideas. Stay tuned for details in the next few days on this crowd sourcing project.'

Details would come less than one week later; crowdsourcing would come nev-er. 'We've learned just how much energy there is around our brand, and after much thought, we've decided to go back to our iconic blue box logo,' Callagy, the spokesperson, told Bloomberg.com of the logo's passing. The new Gap logo is survived by its antagonistic Twitter feed and a dozen 'failed branding strategies' slide shows, in which it will be archived in the annals of history.

October 12, 2010
By Juli Weiner, adapted

This Gap logo example illustrates the importance of getting it right but when constructed and applied correctly the six elements of the brand prism can create a coherent brand. It has a constructed source, comprising physical facets and personality, and a constructed receiver consisting of the reflected consumer and self-image elements. The way the source and receiver interact is determined by the culture and relationship elements of the brand prism.

Obviously, the key in designing hospitality experiences is to make sure that this interaction with culture and relationship creates a natural fit between receiver (the guest) and source (the host company). The brand personality and culture create the rules and norms a hospitality company will live by. You could say it is the *why* of their existence. In combination with the physical facets of the brand it is the promise they make to the guest. The promise of *what* the brand will provide but also *how* the brand will provide it to the guest. As such it should set the guest's expectations for the experience the brand wants to stage. It also indicates the type of character, the role, the designer would like the guest to play in the interaction. These principles stay applicable even when a stand-alone concept represents the brand, for instance a B&B or an independent hotel or restaurant. The key to a successful design for any hospitality experience is a clear value proposition that is backed up by creating a fit between what the host can and wants to offer and the characteristics and preferences of potential guests.

6.5 Guest journey and touchpoints

Scenes

Now that we know the type of scenario and characters playing a role in it, the next logical step is to identify all the scenes the guest will be in when interacting with the host. In the theatre world, ultimately, the sequence of scenes creates the play. Designing hospitality experiences is not so different. The sequence of events involving the guest ultimately creates the hospitality experience. This sequence of events is usually referred to as the guest journey. The journey starts when the consumer chooses a provider and for instance contacts the host to make a reservation. This is the first moment of interaction between the guest and the host. After that moment the sequence of separate scenes, or events, starts and these are usually called touchpoints. A touchpoint can be defined as the moment that the guest and the host (concept or brand) 'touch' or interact. Some authors also refer to 'the moment of truth' or 'attribute' when they talk about touchpoints. They can be interactions between a staff member, representing the host, and a guest, but also between the guest and the website, the hotel room, advertisements or even a toilet. As we saw in Kapferer's brand prism, how the concept or brand communicates and its physical facets are both elements representing the concept or brand.

Guest journey

Touchpoints

Customer journey canvas

Stickdorn and Schneider (2010) use a customer journey 'canvas', depicted in Figure 6.6, to put all the touchpoints in a timeframe. They divide the various touchpoints in three time-related categories:
1 pre-service period: when the concept or brand promise is made and expectations are created
2 service period: all the touchpoints from the moment of booking, till the moment the guest leaves
3 post-service period: after the guest leaves, all possible forms of evaluation including comparing expectations to actual experience that indicate whether the guest was satisfied. The host's follow-up influences this evaluation further in terms of aftersales or customer-relationship management.

FIGURE 6.6 Customer journey canvas

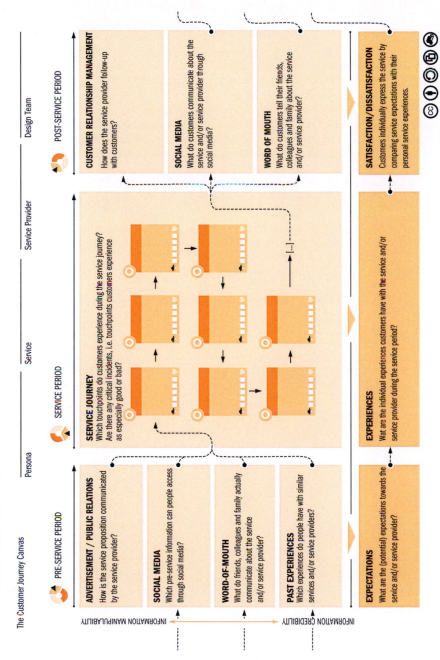

The Customer Journey Canvas

Source: Stickdom & Schneider (2010)

Aligning every touchpoint with the concept or brand promise can be a big challenge when designing experiences. Every interaction between guest and host needs to 'support the overall design' to create the right storyline for experiencing the concept or brand. It can be hard understanding guest expectations with regard to certain elements of the experience and translating them into specifications for the various combinations of personal interactions and physical settings for specific touchpoints.

Satisfaction and loyalty

Satisfaction

Loyal customers

Meeting or exceeding expectations is crucial to satisfying guests. Having satisfied guests is just as crucial if you aim for returning customers and positive word of mouth. The higher the satisfaction, the more likely a guest will turn into a loyal guest. Some authors (e.g. Heskett, 2008) say that satisfaction has to be at least eight on a ten-point scale to create truly loyal customers. Any grade below that means the guest is not truly loyal.

Authors like Pine and Gilmore (1999) and Wilson et al. (2008) state that customers define their level of satisfaction by looking at what their expectations were and comparing that to their perception of what they received. If the perception of the experience is in the 'zone of tolerance', between desired and adequate performance, as illustrated in Figure 6.7, the guest will be at least satisfied.

6

FIGURE 6.7 The zone of tolerance

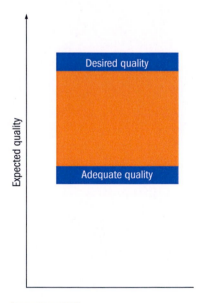

Source: Wilson (2008)

Servqual model

The servqual model (Parasaruman et al., 1985) was developed to link the design of services to customer expectations and perceptions of *service quality*. In a way, servqual was the first attempt to analyse customer experience by looking at the design of the host performance, and comparing that to guest expectations and perceptions. Servqual does not look into the actual interaction between customer and service provider, but takes the customer's perception of the interaction as its focal point.

Wilson, Parasaruman, Zeithaml, and Berry (2008) identify five basic service quality dimensions in their more recent version of servqual:

1. tangibles: appearance of physical facilities, equipment, personnel, and written materials **Tangibles**
2. reliability: ability to perform the promised service dependably and accurately **Reliability**
3. responsiveness: willingness to help guests and provide prompt service **Responsiveness**
4. assurance: employees' knowledge and courtesy and their ability to inspire trust and confidence **Assurance**
5. empathy: caring, individualised attention given to customers **Empathy**

These dimensions are used in surveys that aim to identify differences between guest expectations and perceptions of service quality.

Similar to what we saw earlier in this chapter, in servqual, guests' expectations of a service are influenced by their needs, word of mouth, and past experiences, as well as external communications from the host (concept or brand promise).

Bringing these together is far from easy, but that is not the only complication, as Figure 6.8 shows. First, when a designer starts a new design, he tries to understand the guest's expectations, but his perception of expectations might not reflect the actual expectations, creating Gap 1 displayed in Figure 6.8. Then, the designer translates his perception of expectations into service quality specifications, which do not always reflect the more complex and holistic expectations, creating Gap 2. These specifications are the basis of the service delivery that happens on the work floor, but specifications always leave room for interpretation by staff, creating Gap 3. At the same time, the interpretation of service quality specifications might also create a discrepancy between the actual service delivery and the promise made in external communication, creating Gap 4. The guest's satisfaction in the end depends on the difference between the expected and perceived service, creating Gap 5. Of course, every service designer aims to be as close as possible to the desired quality level, and will certainly want to be above the adequate quality level (see Figure 6.7 The zone of tolerance). The customer journey canvas does the same thing. It compares expected service with perceived service, but only considers the consumer viewpoint. The added value of servqual is that it helps us to understand how the service was designed and performed in relation to how it was perceived.

Expectations and perceptions

Now that we have seen how expectations and perceptions lead to a certain level of satisfaction, the next step is to take a closer look at how the appropriate characteristics of a specific touchpoint need to be established.

In servqual, the host's external communication about the offer contribute to the guests' expectations (Gap 4). That communication should reflect the customer-driven design of the hospitality experience and the standards (rules and norms) associated with it.

FIGURE 6.8 The SERVQUAL or gaps model

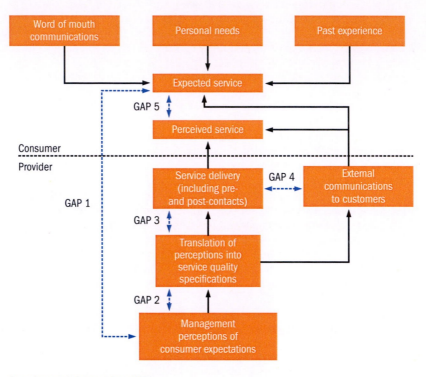

Source: Parasuraman, Zeithaml & Berry (1995)

Perception

The guest's perception of how service was delivered, the actual execution of the design and the standards, compared to the expectations ultimately determine the level of satisfaction. Of course, that perception is not a one-way thing. That perception is always influenced by the interaction between host and guest. It is indeed what this book is all about, the interaction of host and guest in the context of a hospitality experience.

Holistic intangible experience

For the designer it is important to realise that a hospitality experience is always a holistic intangible experience, meaning that a guest will perceive the offer as a total package, as a whole, and not necessarily look at or assess all the individual elements it consists of. The guest will base his level of satisfaction on the full picture, the experience as a whole. However, Brady and Cronin Jr. (2001) point out that when customers look for evidence of the quality of a specific service as a whole, they look at three categories:
1 interaction quality
2 physical environment quality
3 outcome quality

Their research has shown that guests combine these three qualities to come to a judgement of the service quality provided. What is more, the three qualities are each based on three sub-dimensions, leading to nine sub-dimensions in total, as Figure 6.9 illustrates.

FIGURE 6.9 The service quality model

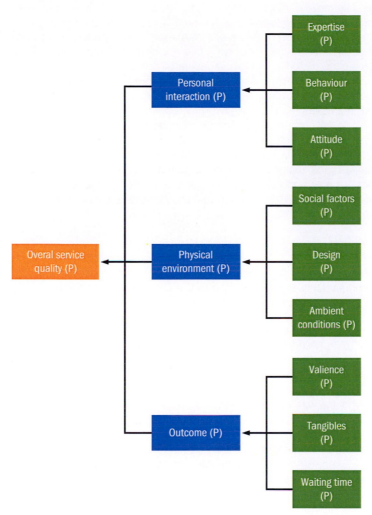

Source: Brady & Cronin Jr. (2001)

Personal interaction
The judgement of interaction quality in Brady and Cronin's model consists
of three factors, attitude, behaviour, and expertise. This means that a
guest's judgement of the interaction quality in a restaurant, for instance, is
based on a snotty waiter (attitude), the way he handles a complaint about
the food (behaviour) and the knowledge he presents (expertise) when serving your wine. As we saw in Kapferer's brand prism, personal interaction in
the form of attitude, behaviour, and expertise should be in line with concept
or brand personality and culture, and at same time it should create the type
of relationship the concept or brand aims for.

**Attitude,
behaviour, and
expertise**

Physical environment
Judgement of physical environment is based on ambient conditions, the
design, and social factors. This means that guests, when assessing the

physical quality of a hotel lobby, for instance, look for the use of plants, art, music and lighting (ambient conditions), the privacy available to them when checking in (design and layout) and the other guests already present in the lobby area (social factor). As we saw in Kapferer's brand prism, the physical elements, together with what Kapferer calls personality, form an important part of the constructed source of a concept or brand. Ambient conditions, design, and social factors should represent the identity, communicate the culture, and demonstrate the relationship the host company would like to have with the customer. The designed physical environment, (see e.g. Bitner, 1992) usually referred to as the servicescape in the literature, forms the landscape in which the service takes place. The servicescapes of Starbucks, CitizenM and, for instance, Aloft Hotels are known for the way they convey their brand identity. These servicescapes are designed in such a way that both host and guest feel the brand culture and simultaneously they facilitate the kind of interaction that creates the relationship the brand is aiming for.

Outcome quality

Outcome quality

Judgement of the final dimension, outcome quality, is based on the assessment of waiting time, the tangibles, and valence. In a restaurant, for example, outcome quality would be judged by the time it takes for a waiter to bring you the menu (waiting time), the food quality and cleanliness of toilets (tangibles), and a guest liking or disliking other elements of the restaurant visit, such as feeling welcome and cared for, or the behaviour of other people at the table (valence). Outcome quality does not link directly to one of the brand prism elements, although the self-image element has similarities. Self-image is the way the concept or brand makes the consumer feel about himself. The sub-dimension valence relates to it in that outcome quality should be in line with what the guest expected that this specific hospitality experience would do or contribute to his self-image.

Nine sub-dimensions

All these nine sub-dimensions of the three main quality indicators (interaction, physical environment, and outcome) are influenced by the factors responsiveness, empathy, and reliability, which we saw in the servqual model. Servqual dimensions 'tangibles' and 'assurance' have become part of physical quality and personal interaction, respectively.

When we look at how expectations influence the guest's overall perception of quality, we must conclude that although guests have a holistic perception of a certain experience, this holistic view is formed by their perception and expectations of three key elements, interaction quality, physical environment and outcome quality.

Research by Bitner et al. (1994), among others, has shown that interpersonal interaction has the biggest impact on the overall perceived quality of services. So we can assume that interaction quality is more important than the other two key elements for designing hospitality experiences. You have probably been in a restaurant where at the end of the evening you said something like, 'Great food, but that waiter couldn't tell a steak from a pork belly.' Outcome quality apparently matched or exceeded expectations (food), but you were less happy with the interaction quality. If there was no direct remark about, for instance, the comfort of your chair or the music volume, the physical environment was probably equal or above what you thought was adequate and equal or below desired level.

All this means that overall expectation, beyond what we have already seen in servqual, is influenced by our expectation of the three quality dimensions discussed above. The expected level of quality can be different for each of the three. That also means that there is not just one zone of tolerance when it comes to expectations, but a different one for each of the three dimensions, as Figure 6.10 depicts.

Three quality dimensions

FIGURE 6.10　Three zones of tolerance

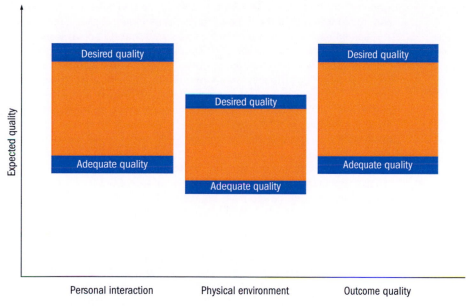

Source: Wilson et al. (2008)

6.6　Guest journey design: choosing touchpoints

In the previous sections, we saw all the elements that create a hospitality experience. We saw how the characteristics of guest segments determine what kind of experience fits them. We saw how companies use brands and concepts to create a promise of the experience they offer. We saw that a hospitality experience could be mapped in a guest journey that puts touchpoints, in the form of personal interactions and/or physical environments, in a chronological order from the guest perspective. And we saw how guests evaluate experiences in relation to expectations they formed before entering a specific experience. When we want to design hospitality experiences we need to combine all these insights to create the appropriate holistic experience.

Holistic experience

Steps of the design process

Again, the logical starting point for any design is the user. For hospitality experiences, that means starting with a very clearly defined target segment or

segments based on psychographic, behavioural, and demographic characteristics of the guests or personas belonging to these segments.

The first step in the actual design process is formulating a (concept or
brand) promise that represents why (the purpose you want to serve) and how
(the value proposition) you want to stage a specific hospitality experience.

The second step is creating the guest journey by mapping all the touchpoints needed to create the value proposition, thereby creating a clear overview of what you want to offer.

Sub-solutions

In the third step, you generate possible ways to shape individual touchpoints. Obviously, touchpoints need to be aligned with the brand or concept.
Therefore, the outcome of this step is a list of possibilities, called sub-solutions, to create each of the needed touchpoints in line with the brand promise. Each sub-solution needs to be described so that it is clear what type of
personal interaction and (physical environment creating the appropriate)
servicescape is linked to this touchpoint. This third step is directly related
to what we often call the mysterious or creative part of the design process.
The terms mysterious and creative indicate that there are no predetermined
rules or formulas available to help a designer generate all the relevant, interesting sub-solutions. Ultimately, the designer needs to create a list of
possibilities based on all the information gathered in the previous steps.
He learns from examples of possible sub-solutions known to him, and applies those theories and models that could assist in interpreting and understanding the situation at hand, especially with respect to the target group.
Last but not least, he has to have the creativity, talent and/or courage to
combine all of that into interesting, feasible sub-solutions for specific
touchpoints.

Morphological chart

In the fourth step, we include the sub-solutions for each touchpoint of the
guest journey in a morphological chart (see Figure 6.11). Displaying the
sub-solutions in a morphological chart allows the designer to create an
overview of the full range of alternatives for the hospitality experience overall, or for chosen segments or personas, in step five of the design process.

In the relatively simple morphological chart in Figure 6.11, you can see that
for each touchpoint, one, two, or three sub-solutions fit the brand or concept. In practice, we could possibly identify even more sub-solutions for a
specific touchpoint.

Design alternatives

The next and fifth step in the design process is to combine specific sub-solutions into overall design alternatives, as Figure 6.12 illustrates. In practice,
this means that you would now try to pick one sub-solution per touchpoint to
generate a design alternative that incorporates all touchpoints that together
shape the guest journey. The number of possible alternatives depends on
the number of touchpoints and the number of sub-solutions per touchpoint
that was generated in the previous steps. In theory, this could lead to a huge
number of alternatives to consider in the evaluation stage. However, in reality, not all sub-solutions can be combined with each other in an overall design
that makes sense. Therefore, the resulting number of feasible design alternatives usually is a lot smaller. In this context, feasible relates to design alternatives that can actually be staged in such a way that they answer to the

FIGURE 6.11 Morphological chart: example of a hotel stay

	Scenes/touchpoints		Possible sub-solutions for the various touchpoints	
Pre-service period	Booking	1.1	1.2	1.3
	Travel	2.1	2.2	
Service period	Arrival	3.1	3.2	3.3
	Check-in	4.1	4.2	
	Entering room	5.1	5.2	5.3
	Facilities	6.1	6.2	6.3
	Room service	7.1		
	Breakfast	8.1	8.2	8.3
	Checkout	9.1	9.2	
Post service period	After sales	10.1	10.2	
	Loyalty program	11.1	11.2	11.3

6

FIGURE 6.12 Combining sub-solutions into design alternatives

Guest segment/ persona ....

Brand / concept promise ....

	Scenes/touchpoints		Possible sub-solutions for the various touchpoints	
Pre-service period	Booking	1.1	1.2	1.3
	Travel	2.1	2.2	
Service period	Arrival	3.1	3.2	3.3
	Check-in	4.1	4.2	
	Entering room	5.1	5.2	5.3
	Facilities	6.1	6.2	6.3
	Room service	7.1		
	Breakfast	8.1	8.2	8.3
	Checkout	9.1	9.2	
Post service period	After sales	10.1	10.2	
	Loyalty program	11.1	11.2	11.3

△ = design alternative 1    ⬭ = design alternative 2    ▭ = design alternative 3

overall concept or brand promise and value proposition. It means the designer must take on board all the complications and requirements, such as outcome quality and personal interaction, that affect the logic of combining sub-solutions into a whole. The generated alternatives also need to be feasible from a practical perspective. Alternatives that take years to become reality would not make sense for a company that wants to stage profitable hospitality experiences in the short term. If staging a specific alternative would require investments that a company cannot afford, this would be a perfectly legitimate reason to discard that alternative in this stage of the design process. In other words, the alternatives that you actually generate should represent guest journeys that the company could and would want to stage.

In the sixth step of the design process, a specific design alternative is chosen. Based on all the information gathered in the previous steps, what alternative would best meet the target group expectations? Furthermore, besides meeting guests' expectations, it is crucial to consider the host's goals when deciding on an alternative and, thereby, finalising the guest journey. Once again, aspects such as costs, needed investments, profit margins, and number and characteristics of needed staff (also compared with what is available), come into play when you select one option from the generated list of overall design alternatives.

Detailed design: creating the script

Now that you have chosen a design alternative, the final step is to work out all the guest journey details by creating a service blueprint of the interactions in the hospitality experience to be staged, like the example depicted in Figure 6.13. This helps you to understand all the processes involved, to estimate the amount of time needed, and to guarantee the appropriate interaction between host and guest.

Service blueprint

FIGURE 6.13 The service blueprint for overnight hotel stay service

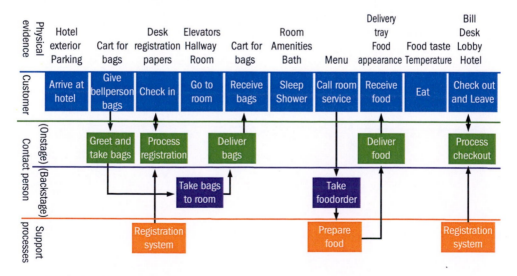

Source: Customer Service Institute of Australia (2011)

A service blueprint takes the guest journey as its basis, and links all the interactions to what needs to happen both onstage and backstage to create the intended experience. Linking interactions between the guest and onstage staff to backstage and support processes creates a timeline (script). What is more, the blueprint includes details of the physical surroundings, providing evidence of services performed and supporting, or more precisely, confirming that the overall hospitality experience design links to the individual touchpoints in the guest journey.

The designer's main objective in this stage is to establish all the details that will encourage both guests and host(s) to interact in accordance with their roles, as designed in the overall scenario. The details should deliver cues that explain not just what the guest can and should expect of the host (company), but also what the host expects of the guest. Ultimately, these details outline how the host (company) can provide accommodation and/or food and/or drink in line with the scenario, or with the brand or concept that constitutes the reference point for the chosen overall design.

As authors like Grove and Fisk (1983) and Stuart and Tax (2004) indicate, when designing a hospitality experience, keep in mind that not just the physical stage, decor, and props have to be designed. Like in a play, it is as important to include all the details of the actors' characters and to have an unambiguous script.

Script

Obviously, you need to manage all these aspects properly to stage a coherent, successful hospitality experience in everyday practice. It should be clear to the guest that he does not prepare his meal himself, or that he should go to the buffet to get his food. The social and physical context of the practical situation should contain clear clues as to the expected behaviour of guests and staff.

As we have seen earlier in this chapter, the concept or brand indicates which characters are expected to play what role in the hospitality experience. The concept or brand sets the expectations for the type of interaction that takes place and serves as input for the actors. Managing what employees do and what they look like on stage is crucial, as they embody the brand's personality and values. In fact, employee behaviour, as discussed in the section on service quality, plays a crucial role in the overall satisfaction of guests. Employee behaviour, together with the physical facets of the brand, should create the right circumstances for the actual hospitality experience to materialise and live up to expectations. That is why we discuss employee behaviour in more detail in Chapter 7.

Employee behaviour

In conclusion, the hospitality experience can only be successful if backstage actions, systems and processes properly facilitate and support on stage interactions. That is why these backstage processes and quality management are the topic of Chapter 8.

Summary

► For hospitality experiences to be successful, from a financial perspective as well, it is crucial to stage the appropriate experience for a specific context and type of customer.

► A specific combination of products and services, supported by specific intangible elements can create more value than the sum of the values of the individual products and services.

► Hospitality experiences are interactive experiences that are influenced by:
  • the personal context
  • the social context
  • the physical context

► Understanding your customers, and their needs and wants, is crucial to designing appropriate hospitality experiences for those customers.

► Market segmenting is used to tailor the design of specific experiences to specific types of customers/guests.

► Establishing a clear concept or brand serves as an important reference point for designing hospitality experiences.

► Guest journeys and touchpoints shape the scenario that your concept or brand offers to customers/guests.

► Touchpoints are shaped by:
  • personal interactions
  • physical environments

► Guest satisfaction is determined by the combination of:
  • personal interaction quality
  • physical environment quality
  • outcome quality

► The actual design process for hospitality experiences consists of the following steps:
  1 formulating a (concept or brand) promise based on target group and value proposition
  2 mapping the touchpoints that together shape the guest journey
  3 generating possible ways, sub-solutions, to shape each touchpoint
  4 drawing a morphological chart that represents all possible guest journeys
  5 generating feasible design alternatives and all feasible guest journeys

6   choosing the best alternative, selecting the most appropriate guest journey
7   detailed design of the appropriate guest journey to create the overall experience

▶ Some relevant/useful theories and models to support a designer in executing these steps are:
- the experience economy
- interactive experience model
- personas
- brand prism
- customer journey canvas
- servqual model
- gaps model
- service quality model
- service blueprint

6

Food for thought

This chapter discussed and illustrated the design process for hospitality experiences. Based on the content of this chapter, the following questions, challenges and topics could serve as interesting starting points for further discussion:

1   What would be the maximum number of target groups that a hospitality company could focus on?

2   The best way to really understand all that is involved in designing a hospitality experience is to do it yourself. This chapter provided a range of tools, theories, design steps, and pointers to do so. Why don't you try to design an appropriate hospitality experience for a target group of your choice, in the context of your choice.

3   Alternatively, you could analyse why specific existing hospitality experiences are successful, or not. Pick a well-known hospitality company. Then try to establish which hospitality experiences it offers to which target groups. Subsequently, use the various theories, models, steps, and pointers provided in this chapter to analyse those experiences. Can you establish some specific improvement points to make them (even) more successful?

7

Delivering hospitality

Rolf van der Veer, Rob Nierse, and Robert Blomme

This chapter discusses the effective behaviour and skills required to stage hospitality experiences so that employees satisfy the needs and wants of the guests. We elaborate on how hosts and managers influence people and explain what behaviour is and how it originates. We focus on the concept of supportive scripts for effective behaviour in interactions with others. In addition, we deal with how professionals manage effective behaviour in commercial hospitality. This chapter should give you solid insights into human behaviour in hospitality and hospitality management, as well as an understanding of what you need to fit human processes into the design of a hospitality experience.

'Why I got kicked out of a restaurant on Saturday night'

[…] But that's as far as I got into the meal. About ten minutes after my party of four sat down, we heard yelling – loud, sustained, top-of-lungs yelling – coming from the kitchen. Mr. Forgione was dressing down a staff member in full view of many customers. The dining room quietened as patrons exchanged uncomfortable glances. No one said a thing. Soon the target of the chef's harsh words delivered our amuse-bouche, and the poor guy was so rattled he could barely speak above a mumble. A few minutes later, the chef was at it again. I waited 15 seconds. Another 15. And without much forethought, I pushed back my chair and walked through the open doorway of the kitchen.

I don't remember exactly what I said, though I did not raise my voice to the point beyond where people in the kitchen could hear it. I told the chef that his behaviour was making me and others uncomfortable. I let him know that I thought it was mean. And I asked him to cut it out. I don't remember exactly what he said in response, but whatever it was, I found it irritating enough that I reminded him that I was paying to eat there and told him again to stop berating his staff at that volume.

Maybe 20 seconds after I had returned to my seat, he approached the table. He apologised, barely, and then let me know that he thought it was incredibly rude of me to come into his kitchen and tell him how to do his job. I repeated the fact that he had been ruining my dinner. But his yelling was all in the interest of maintaining quality, he said.

'I think it's time for you to go,' he said.
'Are you kicking me out?' I asked.
'Yes,' he replied. […]

Source: by Ron Lieber, adapted from http://dinersjournal. blogs.nytimes.com, May 11, 2010

7.1 Hospitality and behaviour

As we learnt in Chapter 6, expectations play an important role in hospitality experiences. They also influence what we consider to be appropriate behaviour linked to those experiences. To illustrate this, consider the following situation.

Not what you might expect...

Two professors, who teach hospitality management, have reason to celebrate because they have just learned that a paper they have written has been accepted for publication in a renowned journal. One says, 'Let's have dinner!'

If you were them, where would you go? Who would you take? What food would you have? Take a minute to think this over. What does 'going out for dinner' mean to the professors, or to you?

Let's imagine the professors invite you to join them for dinner. Obviously, you would dress up to go to a three-star restaurant. This is the kind of establishment you expect your professors to pick for a celebration.

However, the professors actually take you to a restaurant of a fast food chain. There is a big chance that you are at least surprised. You would probably have a hard time hiding your feelings and feel somewhat overdressed.

You decide to tell the professors and they apologise for the misunderstanding. Nevertheless, they are a bit offended. Their tight schedule leaves little room for having an extensive diner. They just wanted to grab a quick bite. To satisfy your needs, however, they take you to a three-star restaurant.

They walk in silence from the fast food outlet to the chosen restaurant. You feel you have overplayed your hand and think it is better to keep quiet for a while.

The above case shows that the expectations we have of a hospitality experience are influenced by what we experienced in the past or by what we feel is normal. It also shows how different expectations have an effect on the behaviour we show or the interactions we have. These expectations also have an effect on what type of hospitality experience we choose to engage in and probably also on how we will perceive and appreciate the choice for a specific hospitality experience.

Specific hospitality experience

From the perspective of the host, all this is related to targeting the right guest for his hospitality experience design. The previous chapter explained that the designer of a hospitality experience has to design and deliver the total package. We illustrated this with the service quality model (Brady & Cronin Jr., 2001). This model states that there are three groups of dimensions of influence on the overall experienced service quality. The group of outcome dimensions (waiting time, tangibles, and valence) are strongly influenced by the previous experiences and knowledge of the guests. The personal interaction dimensions refer to the behaviour, knowledge, skills, and attitude of the employees working in, for instance, the restaurant. And the third dimension is the physical environment where the guest is welcomed and served.

This chapter focuses on the effect these dimensions have on the interaction between guests and employees. It also investigates how an understanding of these perspectives can help management lead and ensure that their staff's behaviour is aligned with the designed experience and meets the needs and expectations of the guests. In other words, a manager needs to care for his customers through caring for his staff. This is not always a given in the hospitality industry, as the following quote reveals.

> '... employees and how they are managed are key determinants of service quality, customer satisfaction and loyalty, competitive advantage, organisational performance and business success. The tourism and hospitality industry has a reputation for poor human resource practices and managing people in a traditional and exploitative way. Accordingly, tourism and hospitality firms are described as Bleak Houses or ugly and bad establishments in employment terms.' (Kusluvan, Kusluvan, Ilhan, & Buyruk, 2010)

Motivation
Expectancy Theory

In fact, one of the most important aspects in any line of business is the behaviour of the people working there. The performance of employees in hospitality partially depends on the motivation they have to show certain behaviour. As Vroom (1964) argued in his Expectancy Theory, the choices employees make between various behavioural alternatives is a function of three distinct perceptions. These are expectancy, instrumentality, and valence. Expectancy is the belief that employees have that if they work very hard, their job performance will improve. Instrumentality is the reward employees think they will receive from doing a job well and valence is the reward or outcome that motivates them to work (Chiang, 2008). These perceptions define the amount of effort employees put in showing the desired (hospitality) behaviour. As Chiang (2008) shows, intrinsic valence motivates employees to take more responsibility and make full use of their capabilities; also explained as skills and knowledge. These skills and knowledge will thus be used more effectively if employees feel motivated to show certain behaviour.

Skills and knowledge

7

This clearly shows how important it is to understand what influences behaviour. Such understanding enables hospitality employees and managers to stage genuine hospitality experiences. They adapt their own professional behaviour to change that of others. For example, if a manager has in-depth knowledge on how to tap into an employee's motivation, then the manager can influence employee behaviour and achieve the desired outcome, that is, the right behaviour that matches the needs of the guests and the type of experience offered.

Performance

Although it may be tempting to view behaviour as isolated from its surroundings, human behaviour is often strongly influenced by external factors. This chapter refers to external factors as situations. The situations encountered by staff in a business have an effect on the behaviour they show and thus on their performance. Performance is measured by what we do and show, so a change in behaviour has an effect on performance perceived or measured by others (e.g. guests).

Skills and knowledge are key, but not enough

7

Defining and understanding behaviour

A key question is how to define and explain behaviour. The Oxford Diction- **Behaviour**
ary (2010) defines it as:

> The way in which one acts or conducts oneself, especially towards
> others.

This definition suggests that humans are aware of their own behaviour.
However, most of the behaviour we show is subconscious. For example, **Subconscious**
when we wake up and switch on the light, we are hardly aware of moving to
and turning on the light switch. We usually do it without deliberate thinking.
Moreover, we show different types of behaviour in different situations. Behaviour can also vary over time and shift within seconds. Mostly people behave without being aware of the effect their behaviour has on others, until
the effect of their behaviour suddenly becomes painfully apparent. Imagine
a waiter who has worked in the restaurant for so long that he has grown
tired of it without noticing. He does his job on autopilot. One evening a
guest is angry at the waiter for his sloppy behaviour. Hopefully the startled
waiter becomes more alert right away.

So, all this goes to show that behaviour is tricky to define and possibly
even more difficult to explain and predict. That is why so many researchers
and professionals, over the years, have tried to depict behaviour schemati-
cally or explain behaviour through basic models and theories.

Iceberg

A well-known example of a schematic depiction of behaviour is called the iceberg. Figure 7.1 depicts the iceberg showing the origins of behaviour. It tells us that what we see is not all that is there. It explains what forces drive humans to act the way they act. Above the waterline is the actual behaviour. This is what others can perceive and corresponds with the definition of behaviour given earlier. Behaviour is what we can see, hear or feel by touch and, therefore, it comes across the same to everyone. Under the water surface, we see the causes of our behaviour. This is where we find the important drivers of behaviour, such as the cultural background, intentions, skills and knowledge of the person showing the behaviour. These drivers cannot be seen, heard or felt, but are key to our understanding and trying to influence behaviour.

Causes of our behaviour

FIGURE 7.1 The iceberg

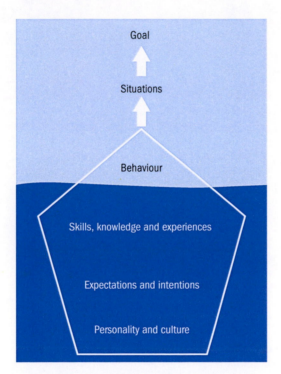

Source: adapted from Spencer and Spencer (1993)

Goal

As Brunner-Sperdin and Peters (2008) and Mohsin et al. (2005) argue, employees' skills and expertise have a strong impact on the expectations and emotional state of guests. From a hospitality management perspective, it is important to understand what makes employees willing to learn skills and develop expertise. Your reasons for learning and developing are often linked to whether you expect or have experienced a reward that is connected to a behaviour. The expectation of achieving a goal creates the willingness to master a specific skill. Expectations of the outcome of a behavioural pattern, combined with knowledge and experience, make someone put effort into using or learning a skill or expertise. The iceberg scheme shows that intentions also affect whether you show a certain type of behaviour.

Intentions

The intention is determined not only by how you value the expected outcome, but also by your belief in making the behaviour successful. Intention creates the amount of perseverance and effort you put into the behaviour and thus serves as a key predictor of behaviour, together with expectations.

The bottom layer of the iceberg is personality and culture, which influence the types of behaviour that you feel strong about. We refer to these as core values and they form the basis of behavioural norms.

Personality and culture

Behavioural norms

> Norms are behavioural patterns that you perceive as normal or the right thing to do.

Culture has a deep and lasting impact on norms and values, which means they cannot be changed overnight, but perhaps the hardest thing to change or understand is personality. Indeed, a full exploration of this topic would take at least a full chapter, probably more, to discuss all the complications and unexplained questions linked to it. Therefore, for now, let us simply conclude that all the above, including the position of personality in the iceberg, tells us that influencing the behaviour of people is, at best, difficult. It is probably more realistic to conclude that we can only influence people to a certain degree, and employees are no exception to that rule.

Culture

Therefore, to ensure that you can stage a hospitality experience as designed, selection of the 'right' staff to deliver hospitality is as crucial, maybe even more so, as trying to influence their behaviour.

Selection

Behaviour and a concept/brand

How can we use these insights to create the *right* kind of behaviour? To do so, let us first take a step back and define what constitutes the right kind of behaviour. In the previous chapter we discussed how to use concepts and brands in market segmentation and how they help hosts choose what type of guest they want to provide for. As an example, we used the prism brand by Kapferer (1998) to create a fictitious brand personality for a three-star restaurant (Figure 7.2).

Right kind of behaviour

7

FIGURE 7.2   Brand personality of the restaurant Chez BéBé

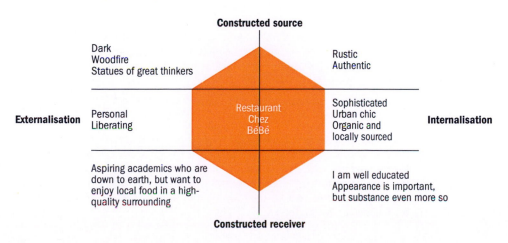

The brand personality attached to this restaurant is sophisticated and rustic authenticity. It seeks to attract highbrow individuals who place great emphasis on style, but equally want an intellectually challenging environment. This needs to be evident in the physical structure. In this case, the wood fire and the statues of great thinkers provide a setting that, in the eye of its owner, fits with the brand personality. However, the personality must also be translated into the behaviour of staff and be visible in their actions. In this example, waiters would be expected to be punctual, courteous, and concise, leaving guests to discuss matters among themselves without too much intervention. While they may have an understated presence, their knowledge of food and drinks has to live up to very high standards to answer the guests' questions, for instance, as to where the food comes from and how it was prepared. Only this behaviour would fit the design of this hospitality experience. Guests visiting this establishment would probably expect this behaviour and would interact with staff based on these expectations.

7.2 Interaction and behaviour

Interaction

The previous section highlighted key aspects of behaviour and how we can explain and influence it. However, a key aspect is still missing, especially from the perspective of staging hospitality experiences; interaction. The following part of our continuing story illustrates how interaction and perceptions steering that interaction influence hospitality experiences.

How to lose a customer, Part 1

We arrive at the restaurant of choice. It is a nice, somewhat posh restaurant and there seems to be a free table. You ask the waiter, 'Do you have a free table?' The waiter answers, 'Yes sir. Would you like a table right away?' You reply in the affirmative. The waiter brings you to the table that you had noticed before.

A guest at another table wants to order. He tries to get the waiter's attention. First, he tries to make eye contact, but the waiter doesn't look his way. After a while, he thinks of something else. He raises his hand slightly, hoping the waiter will notice. Unfortunately, the waiter ignores him. Then the guest gets irritated. He starts waving his hand. This surely must get him attention. Now really irritated, the guest calls out, 'Waiter!' Without bothering to make eye contact or actually walking over to the guest, the waiter replies, 'What do you want now?!' After a while, the guest stands up and leaves the restaurant, shouting, 'I won't ever come back! That'll teach you!'

Therefore, this section focuses on how our perceptions of each other's behaviour lead to an interaction and how changing behaviour can influence the interaction. Indeed, changing or adjusting your behaviour can change the interaction outcome. In a hospitality context, this outcome could refer to the experienced service quality, which in turn will influence your ratings on Tripadvisor, for instance.

When people interact, there is always a goal involved, as discussed in the previous section. The key aspect is not only at the tip of the iceberg (see Figure 7.1) but can also be depicted as in the following simple diagram:

Goal

Goal → Behaviour → Effect

Simply put, when you want to achieve something you behave in a way that you think will help you reach your goal. This also applies in interactions with others. When you act in a specific way while in contact with someone else, you expect, or at least hope, that the interaction will lead to something that comes close to the desired goal. Sometimes, however, you do not get what you expect and do not reach that goal. In those situations, specific behaviour turned out to be ineffective.

This all may seem rather obvious. Still, we have all experienced interactions with other people in which our behaviour was not as effective as we wanted and expected it to be. That is because people do not always react to what we want them to react to. And if they do react, they still might interpret the situation differently and end up reacting differently than we expected. To examine this more thoroughly, we need to understand what people react to, what communication channels we have at our disposal, and how we can use or misuse them.

According to Paul Watzlawick (2011), our communication consists of two layers, content and relationship. We not only send 'plain' information on the content level, but very often we also send numerous other kinds of sometimes encoded information that deals with what we, the sender, think of the receiver of the information. Watzlawick's theory is elaborated by Friedeman Schulz von Thun (1981) into a Four-sided model, depicted in Figure 7.3. This model helps us to analyse the communication between sender and receiver.

Communication
Content
Relationship

Four-sided model

7

Sending and receiving information
All messages we send and receive contain something about the matter at hand, but also about the sender and the receiver.

FIGURE 7.3   Send and Receive

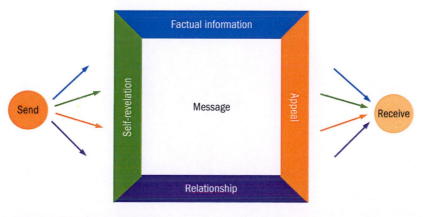

Source: adapted from Schulz van Thun (1981)

Self-revealing

Relationship layer

Appeal

As Figure 7.3 illustrates, in the *Self-revealing* or self-disclosure part of a message the speaker – consciously or unconsciously – tells something about himself, his motives, values, emotions, etc. Similarly, the *Relationship layer* of the message expresses how the sender gets along with the receiver and what he thinks of him. The *Appeal* contains the desire, advice, instruction and effects that the speaker seeks.

However, every layer can be misunderstood individually or in relation to the other layers. Schulz von Thun's (1981) classic example used to illustrate this deals with a back-seat passenger telling the driver, 'Hey, the traffic lights are green.' Depending on the 'ear' he uses, the driver could notice a number of different messages, which would all lead him to react differently.

On a factual level, he will probably notice the simple fact that *'the traffic lights are green.'* On the level of Self-revelation, he could hear something like *'I'm in a hurry'* or *'I'm displeased with your slow reaction.'* On the Relationship level, he could understand the message as *'You need my help to drive well.'* And, as for the Appeal part, he probably hears something like *'Come on, drive!'*

Levels of communication

Communication channels

Schulz von Thun (1981) gives us a model to analyse and explain the origins of many misunderstandings by looking into different levels of communication. Another way to analyse communication failure is to take the distinction between the different communication channels. Basically, in face-to-face communication with others, we have three main channels or tools of communication at our disposal, the words we use, the way we sound and the way we look. In other words, verbal, vocal, and visual communication. The work by Albert Mehrabian (1971), highlighted in Figure 7.4, shows us that in most situations, the actual effect of vocal and visual stimuli by far outweigh the effect of the words we use.

FIGURE 7.4 Components of communication

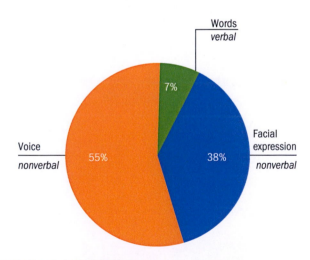

Source: http://www.trendsandstrategies.blogspot.com

Mehrabian argues that tone and intonation (38%) and body language (55%) outperform words (7%) in conveying a message from one person to another person in communication. Especially in *ambiguous situations,* we tend to believe and rely more on the information given by facial expressions and body posture of the sender. Listeners rely on far more than just the message content to make up their minds about the sender and the meaning of his message.

Tone and intonation

Body language

Words

Actions, reactions, tools, and flexibility

Clearly, our actions do not always lead to the reactions we expect and predicting reactions is difficult. In the context of staging specific hospitality experiences, this is an important reference point to be aware of and take into account when implementing our design of those experiences. We need to be flexible in case the effect of our actions is not in line with our goal and change our behaviour if we want to be more effective in our communication. There are so many factors influencing a specific exchange of information that it is not always possible to predefine a set of rules on how to behave. Instead of providing hospitality staff with long checklists of rules or do's and don'ts, we can distinguish the tools people use to communicate and develop the needed skills and expertise to use them as effectively as possible. Most of these tools can be used in various situations to stage hospitality experiences. Although the required approach to the guest may be different in different situations, in different designs or different hospitality experiences, often the tools we use to achieve that approach are basically the same. Different approaches require the same skills and expertise, just used differently. This is why in hospitality practice lots of money is invested in training staff to develop their skills and expertise in using these tools.

Let us focus on the verbal and non-verbal tools at our disposal. Usually, people think about what words to use. We choose our words carefully. We can choose whether we want to use words to send information (sending skills) or to gather information first (receiving skills or listening skills). If sending is the goal, some logical aspects to consider include be concise, structure your information properly, and use attractive language. With respect to gathering information verbally, the focus should probably be on asking questions, paraphrasing and showing understanding.

Verbal and non-verbal tools

Using words as your tool

Different questions have different effects. The first distinction relates to the form, or the difference between open and closed questions. An [] open question starts with an interrogative pronoun like who, what, when, where or how. The question leaves all answers open. You cannot simply answer with yes or no. The question stimulates you to give a detailed answer. The goal of this question type is to get as much information as possible. A closed question is a question that starts with a verb. These questions ask for a yes or no answer. Even though people might answer more elaborately, the goal of this question is usually to check something or get confirmation.

The second distinction relates to content or the difference between 'in questions' and 'ex questions'. An in question is used to obtain more information about the same topic. An ex question delivers information about another topic. We can use paraphrasing as a tool to make our conversations more fluid and show we are actively involved. We use paraphrasing to check if we have understood properly. We repeat the content of the message in our own words, as a question.

The last powerful tool worth mentioning here is showing understanding for how someone feels. When you notice an emotion, you can express that. 'I understand that this might be confusing to you', would show understanding. The effect is that the other person feels understood and becomes inclined to open up to you.

Situational aspects

It would be impossible to list all the non-verbal tools that you could use as the non-verbal details that matter in communication and interaction with guests is endless. However, we can establish six important dimensions (Schnapper, 1975). Again, we cannot give fixed rules for what to do or not to do. This depends on the hospitality experience circumstances, and situational aspects, such as the local/organisational culture, the hotel design and guests involved. However, the following does provide some generic guidelines regarding what to look for when analysing or using non-verbal signals.

Six dimensions of communication

Movements of the body (head, arms, legs, etc.) fall in the category of kinesics. The difficulty of this dimension is that some gestures, like beckoning with a finger, can be normal in one culture and rude in another. Another example is that in Western European cultures big gestures come across as 'loud', whereas southern Europeans consider many big gestures normal.

Proxemics relates to the use of interpersonal space. South Americans and Greeks, for example, usually feel comfortable standing and sitting at a close distance that most north Europeans and Americans would feel uncomfortable with. However, when the latter back away, others might, in turn, perceive them as cold and unfriendly.

The timing of verbal exchanges during conversations is called chronemics. For example, Americans probably expect their partner to respond to statements immediately. In other cultures, people time their exchanges to leave silence between the statement and the response. In yet other cultures, it is more normal to start talking when the other is still talking. This way they want to show they are involved in the conversation.

Oculesics is about eye-to-eye contact or avoidance. In some cultures, making eye contact is a polite way to pay attention. In other cultures, it can be perceived as aggressive and people use elaborate patterns of eye avoidance to show respect. Obviously, this can lead to misunderstandings when guests check-in at a hotel where the employees have a different idea about making eye contact than the guests.

Haptics deals with where, how and how often people can touch each other while conversing. In some cultures, shaking hands is frowned upon, while in others conversation partners hold hands long after the formal greetings are over. Touching or patting on the shoulder or even hugging is often not done in Western Europe, whereas this is considered normal in many Latin American countries.

Dress determines what kind of clothes we should wear in which situations. Most hotels use uniforms to make clear who is a hotel employee. Five-star hotels, usually, prefer a formal dress, while others, like CitizenM, aim to radiate a hip, youthful vibe. Then, the dress code is clearly more low key.

7.3 Behaviour and satisfaction

The previous sections talked about behaviour in relation to its effectiveness and how communication processes work. Engaging with guests is a two-way process in which various levels and flows of information play a role, as well as perspectives based on previous experiences and expectations. The following part of our continuing story only reinforces this point.

Two-way process

How to lose a customer (on purpose), Part 2

Remember that restaurant where we saw an angry guest walk out because the waiter was ignoring him? We decide to give this waiter some feedback. Surprisingly, we get his attention quite easily and discuss with him what we think just happened. We mention the guest's hand waving, his attempts to make eye contact, frowning and rolling his eyes. In our view the guest must have been annoyed because he was kept waiting so long. What just happened makes us wonder whether it was the right decision to have dinner here. We tell the waiter that he made no visible attempt to contact the guest and we feel that he was too preoccupied with other tables. The waiter laughs and explains that before we had come in, he had already asked the guest to leave, as he was a well-known scam artist who had refused to pay twice before. Now we realise that we had judged too quickly. Without hesitation, we order a few beers to flush away the tension.

However, regardless of the hospitality experience circumstances and design, usually we want to make people feel that we are treating them like honoured guests. Based on this reference point, this section discusses effective behaviour towards guests and how it relates to situations in practice.

7

Obviously, the design of a hospitality experience may require extra or even contradicting behaviours, but it is important for hospitality professionals and managers to understand the main facets of behaviour that generally help to establish customer satisfaction. Many studies (see e.g. Winsted, 2003) and anecdotal evidence indicate that the following aspects of behaviour are fundamental to building up a positive guest experience.

Seven aspects

Seven aspects of hospitable behaviour:
- Provide accurate, reliable, and prompt service
- Show civility and respect
- Engage your guests with a smile
- Connect with your guests
- Be sensitive to cultural differences
- Be flexible
- Respond well to service failure

Not a standard recipe

As helpful as this list may seem, it is important to realise that these characteristics are not a standard recipe. How you convey and apply these characteristics to guests depends on the situation. For example, a five-star business hotel will convey the seven facets of hospitable behaviour differently than a fish and chips shop full of people who want to satisfy their appetite immediately. Coming back to the service quality model, as discussed earlier in this chapter and the previous chapter, guests perceive hospitality offerings as a total package. However, when they evaluate the quality of a service as a whole they look particularly at the interaction quality, physical environment quality and outcome quality (Brady & Cronin Jr., 2001). The physical environment provides the setting that may inhibit or enhance certain interactive experiences. In daily business practices, this environment is more or less a given. However, both the interaction quality and the outcome quality depend largely on the quality of staff behaviour. Personal interaction (e.g. attitude, expertise) needs to be in line with the brand personality. Similarly, aspects such as waiting time, the quality and type of service (e.g. intimate or impersonal) or even the cleanliness of the premise all need to align to customer expectations and depend on the qualities of employees.

Standard operating procedures

The seven characteristics listed above are often listed as standard operating procedures (SOPs) in hospitality companies, as a prescription or instruction for employees. However, perhaps this view is too simplistic (Solomon, Suprenant, Czepiel, & Gutman, 1985). The interaction between host and guest is more complex than you can do just following SOPs alone. It takes more effort to tune into the demands of a guest and, simultaneously, take the organisation's interests into account. In practice, front-line employees have to find a balance between what they are supposed to do according to their job description, their role in maintaining the organisation's interests, and their personal role in staging a specific hospitality experience. Executing all these roles at the same time can be stressful because they might require different and occasionally conflicting action.

Scripting

In this context, the concept of *scripting* might be a helpful tool. As we discussed in Chapter 6, a script encompasses the employee's communication and behaviour in the interaction with a guest or with multiple guests in staging the designed hospitality experience. However, scripts are not static.

Scripting is a learning process that can be applied during the implementation stage, in which:

- Employees become aware of the various roles they have in interacting with guests
- They develop communication and behaviour routines that meet the requirements of their roles
- After conducting scripts, they get the chance to reflect on them with the help of colleagues and supervisor
- They get the chance to alter the sets of communication and behaviour routines to improve the effectiveness of their behaviour in the hospitality experience

The benefits of being able to alter a script are illustrated by the story on innovative hotel check-ins.

● www.travelandleisure.com

Innovative hotel check-ins

At the new Andaz Hotel at 75 Wall Street, in lower Manhattan, check-in is also a breeze. There are no glacial queues, no tedious forms to fill out and sign, and no scripted 'How was your flight?' chitchat to endure. In lieu of a conventional check-in desk, a host greets you in the lobby, offers you a seat and a glass of wine, and enters your name into a handheld e-tablet that looks like an iPad. After swiping your credit card and producing a key card, the host escorts you to your room – which, for around $275, features 345 square feet of crisply designed and furnished space, 10-foot ceilings, dark stained-oak floors, and a long, transparent window between the bedroom and the bathtub.

Adapted

Scripts are very different from SOPs. Scripts are not only developed during the design stage, but during the implementation stage and also by involving the front-line employees. Ultimately, this should allow them to develop communication and behaviour sets and routines, which usually integrate the seven aspects of hospitable behaviour. It should help them play their roles in the hospitality experience, handling complex situations with guests while preserving the organisation's interests. Scripts can be very personal and they can be personalised to offer front-line employees the opportunity to use of their own strengths and talents in engaging in effective hospitable behaviour. The opportunity to develop your own scripts could lead to optimal 'tailor-made' responses to guests' demands and needs in a variety of situations, which should lead to higher levels of customer satisfaction.

Strengths and talents

Obviously, all this also has consequences for the role of supervisors. Alongside their own challenge to develop personal scripts related to their own work context, they have to understand how to support their employees in the process of co-developing scripts. As indicated, scripting is a learning process where feedback from colleagues and supervisors is important to further improvement. The following sections focus on the role of managers and supervisors in the development of hospitable behaviour.

7.4 Behaviour and feedback

Feedback

Providing feedback is one of the most important skills in management. It can enable us to effectively improve someone else's behaviour. However, the way you provide feedback is essential to its success, as the final part of our continuing story clearly shows.

How not to give feedback

After our beers arrive we observe an argument between the waiter and his manager. The manager had noticed the incident with the angry guest and in a patronising way shows the waiter how he ought to meet and greet guests. After the demonstration, the waiter tries to explain the actual situation.

But the manager interrupts him right away and tells the waiter that he needs an extra training session. The waiter gets annoyed and tries to explain again, but the manager just won't listen. Now the waiter is really fed up and walks out of the restaurant.

Johari window

Various theories and models are available to help you decide on the appropriate manner to provide and receive feedback. One of these is the Johari window (see Figure 7.5), which may provide insights into how feedback works. As we said before in this chapter, people are often not aware of their behaviour. Sometimes that behaviour may be dysfunctional and, especially in these circumstances, it is crucial to realise that many behaviours are subconscious.

Open area

Behaviour and underlying motives known to both sides involved in the interaction is called the open area. The more the sides know about each other, the larger the open area becomes and the more effective and honest the communication and relationship is. The goal in professional or host-guest relationships is to have the open area as large as possible. The way to get there is by giving feedback and openly discussing what and why both parties feel the way they feel about each other's behaviour (also think of modern social media and review sites). All the behaviour you show that you are not aware of, but others can see, is called the blind area. This is an important area for someone to receive feedback on. In this case, feedback is given specifically on the behaviour that 'hides' in someone's blind spot, that can be observed by the person giving the feedback. If you make sure to discuss this principle, the immediate benefit is that it then becomes part of the open area.

Blind area

The open and blind areas are two 'windows' to providing feedback about the tip of the iceberg, that is, the visible part of behaviour.
In short, feedback has three connected steps:

Observation
1 Observation: what behaviour do I actually see, hear, etc.

Interpretation
2 Interpretation: how do I interpret that behaviour? (grumpy, sad, etc.)

Effect
3 Effect: what does this do to me? What do I do because of this?

FIGURE 7.5 The Johari Window

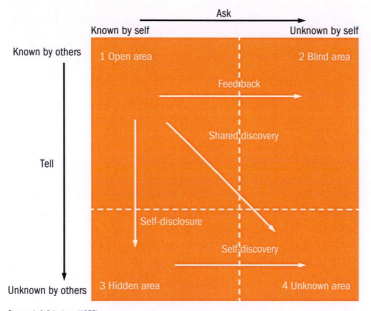

Source: Luft & Ingham (1955)

Feedback generally starts with describing what someone does. This is called the observation. A proper observation states what everyone would and can observe, rather than what we think or feel about it. Second is the interpretation of that behaviour. In this phase, we reflect on the behaviour. What do we believe the behaviour means? Interpretation is important as the same behaviour can have very different meanings. For example, if a person looks away, it may be that they are shy, angry, or uninterested. When providing feedback, it is important to highlight how we interpret behaviour, to improve understanding by the person receiving feedback. The idea is to express the feelings, either positive or negative, that you feel are connected with the behaviour someone shows. The third step of feedback is used to enlighten the person receiving feedback on what reactions may follow from their behaviour. How did their behaviour make you feel and why? For example, a person constantly looking away (step 1) could lead someone else to interpret this as that person is not really interested (step 2) and, therefore, it could result in them not feeling welcome (step 3).

It is important to realise that feedback is a two-way process. To feel safe giving feedback, the other person should also be willing to receive feedback. People often feel vulnerable when they receive feedback on their blind area (fig 7.5). This might trigger a defensive response, leading to them not taking the feedback on board. In these cases, it is essential to provide constructive and meaningful feedback.

Two-way process

Hospitality often involves diverse groups of people, lots of nationalities, and different backgrounds and (sub)cultures. So it is important to consider how these elements influence the way we perceive and interpret actions. Failing to take personal and cultural differences into account can lead to miscommunications when delivering or receiving feedback. It can actually make feedback counterproductive. For example, in a business where people voice their opinions rather bluntly, newcomers may mistake well-meant feedback for rudeness. They may not only fail to adjust their behaviour as a result of this, but also gain a negative opinion on the person providing feedback. Alternatively, in businesses providing subtle feedback, certain employees may not even notice they have received feedback until they 'suddenly' receive a negative evaluation.

7.5 Leadership

The previous section showed that it is not easy to use feedback to improve behaviour. In this section, we continue this discussion by examining ways of providing leadership that will ensure staff deliver the desired hospitality experience. In other words, we investigate how leaders should behave to ensure their employees show the desired behaviour.

Know-how

Show-how

To work at their best, people need both 'know-how' and 'show-how'. Know-how refers to the knowledge, skills, and expertise that are needed to do the job right. To a large degree show-how depends on the self-confidence, intention and motivation of the employee.

Hersey and Blanchard (1975) discuss two types of leadership behaviour that managers can focus on to develop the competence (know-how) and commitment (show-how) of their employees. First, *directive behaviour* is particularly suitable to increase competence (skills). For example, if employees are new to a job and lack the expertise to perform their work successfully, they need direction, in other words, to learn from your directive behaviour.

Directive behaviour

Here the emphasis is on teaching how to do the task, rather than providing support. To increase the competence and achieve a goal, employees need direction from someone who will (Blanchard et al., 2005):

1 Set a clear goal
2 Instruct the task
3 Generate an action plan
4 Show and train how to do the goal or skill
5 Clarify roles
6 Provide timelines
7 Establish priorities
8 Monitor, evaluate, and provide feedback on work

Besides setting an achievable goal, you need to show that you are committed to the behaviour you want your employee to show. In terms of leadership, this requires you to show support to your employees. This leads to the second type of leadership behaviour, *supportive behaviour*. Supportive leadership is appropriate if we want to increase motivation and/or self-confidence. For example, the willingness to learn a skill partially depends upon the self-confidence of an individual. People with low self-confidence find learning a skill harder and are less likely to demonstrate that skill. Here the leader's focus should be on making someone feel able to do the task at hand. Supportive behaviour is also more important when more experienced employees can do the task without much intervention. Then leadership takes on a more facilitating role.

Supportive behaviour

To build commitment to achieve a goal, employees needs support from someone who (Blanchard et al., 2005):

• Listens
• Praises and encourages
• Facilitates problem solving
• Asks for input
• Reminds staff about the why
• Shares information about experiences relevant to goal

Different employees have different needs, so good managers can adjust their leadership style to the needs of the employee. Figure 7.6, distinguishes four main leadership styles according to how much directive or supportive behaviour they show. The lower the competence of the employee, the more important directive behaviour is. The lower the commitment (either motivation or self-confidence), the more important supportive behaviour is. Additionally the more experienced staff is, the more likely their work will be of a certain quality and the less effort it takes to lead them. As a manager, you want all staff to be able to deliver the same quality of work. When staff show a low level of task maturity (i.e. they are inexperienced or lack competence, S1 and S2) SOPs could be useful prescriptions for required staff behaviour, and feedback and scripting, as we discussed in the previous sections, could also help in further developing effective behaviour.

Task maturity

Nowadays there is a trend to provide employees with more of their own individual responsibilities. This leads to the need for employees with a high task maturity (high competence and high commitment). Able and willing employees can make decisions by themselves without consulting supervisors all the time. If and when employees have reached the stage of task maturity (S3 and S4), managers need only support and facilitate employees to develop their own scripts for effective hospitable behaviour.

Individual responsibilities

FIGURE 7.6 Leadership styles

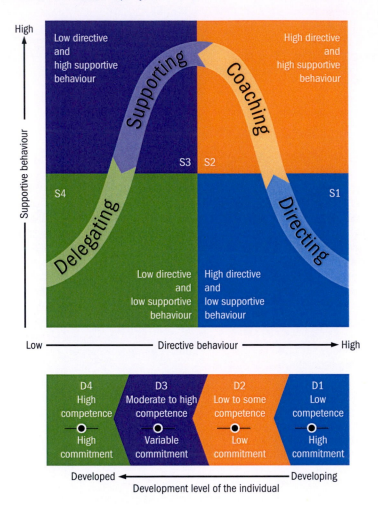

Source: Blanchard, Fowler & Hawkins (2005)

As we said earlier in this chapter, on an organisational level the behaviour of staff must match the design of the hospitality experience you want to create. The goals you set for employees should be aligned with the organisation's goal as a whole. To motivate people to show the desired behaviour, **Goal setting** proper goal setting is crucial. The 'why' of doing things (awareness) enables employees to choose if and how they want to comply. Freedom of choice usually leads to open intention and increases the willingness to learn. If employees understand the underlying hospitality experience design, and the identity and culture of the business they work in, they are more likely to change their behaviour to fit the business goals. Additionally, setting reachable and agreeable goals for staff leads to increased motivation, as we mentioned before in relation to the iceberg metaphor. As Chiang (2008) showed, intrinsic valence motivates employees to take more responsibility and make full use of their capabilities (skills, knowledge).

Ultimately, though, it is important to note how hard it remains to make employees show exactly the kind of behaviour that is conducive to the desired experience, even when you are dealing with task-mature and motivated staff. In fact, this is why organisations maintain on-going debate on how to motivate employees effectively. Solid understanding of the iceberg and different leadership styles helps, but even then, many other factors influence the behaviour of employees. People differ strongly in how and how far they want to be led. It appears that the only real truth we can establish is that different kinds of people require different leadership styles, depending on the context.

7

Summary

▶ Behaviour is a crucial element in the staging/delivery of hospitality experiences.

▶ Behaviour is how we act or conduct ourselves, especially towards others.
Important drivers of behaviour are:
- Cultural background
- Personality
- Intentions
- Skills
- Knowledge

▶ Through interaction, a person's behaviour can affect the behaviour of another person.

▶ Communication layers include:
- Self-revelation
- Factual information
- Relationship
- Appeal

▶ The content of words is usually far less important than tone and body language.

▶ Seven generic aspects of hospitable behaviour are important for a positive guest experience:
- Provide accurate, reliable, and prompt service
- Show civility and respect
- Engage your guests with a smile
- Connect with your guests
- Be sensitive to cultural differences
- Be flexible
- Respond well to service failure

▶ A script encompasses the employee's communication and behaviour in the interaction with a guest or with multiple guests in staging a designed hospitality experience.

▶ Feedback is an important skill, which managers use to improve the behaviour of co-workers. Feedback has three connected steps:
- Observation: what behaviour do I actually see, hear?
- Interpretation: how do I interpret that behaviour?
- Effect: what does this do to me? What do I do because of this?

7

► To develop the competencies of co-workers, managers could:
- Set a clear goal
- Instruct the task
- Generate an action plan
- Show the goal and train skills
- Clarify roles
- Provide timelines
- Set priorities
- Monitor, evaluate, and provide feedback on work.

► To build commitment, managers could:
- Listen
- Praise and encourage
- Facilitate problem solving
- Ask for input
- Remind staff about the why
- Share information on experiences relevant to the goal

Food for thought

This chapter discussed the importance of behaviour in staging hospitality experiences for guests and how you can influence other people's behaviour. Based on the content of this chapter, the following questions, challenges, and topics could serve as interesting starting points for further discussion:

1   Can you influence a person's behaviour? To what extent? And how?

2   Sometimes people resist your interventions. Why would a person resist? How can you deal with resistance?

3   If you are introducing a new brand, what steps are needed to make sure that all the relevant people behave in a way that supports the brand?

7

8

Quality management in hospitality

Alinda Kokkinou and Stan Josephi

Customers hold specific expectations about the quality of the hospitality experience they will engage in. This chapter discusses the definition of quality, and subsequently how it can be measured. This knowledge is used to design and manage processes that must be put in place to consistently deliver a high quality hospitality experience. We discuss the targets you can set, based on these processes, and we discuss and illustrate the associated costs with examples.

8

Bad service at a restaurant: What would you do?

This past weekend, I dined out in a restaurant (not one on the OpenTable network, and, on behalf of my fellow diners, I am glad for that) and experienced really poor service. I've waited tables at many restaurants. Because of that, I am always apt to cut servers a lot of slack. It is a difficult job and, as a waiter, you cannot control every element of the dining experience, even though you are the face of the dining experience. That said, I usually don't complain about service unless it is abominable. And this was.

After the server botched every possible aspect of our meal, I voiced my opinion. The manager, with whom I'm friendly, came over and offered various amends, such as other dishes, or free drinks and dessert. I told him I wasn't interested in any of that as we had to leave, and the point wasn't that I was looking for money off my bill. It occurred to me, though, that I didn't know what I wanted. Probably an apology from the server. Ideally, a do-over on the whole meal, which came at the end of a very stressful day. Looking back, I think I should have asked the manager for a different server as soon as things got off course.

I'm reminded of a silly (and – WARNING! – often off-colour) film starring Ryan Reynolds (aka Mr. ScarJo) called *Waiting*, about servers toiling away at an awful chain restaurant. In one scene, a patron wants to send her food back, and the poor server points out, 'Ma'am, I don't doubt the steak was overcooked, but did you have to eat it all before you complained about it?' Diners can behave badly, too, and negatively impact their own dining experience. However, great service has the transformative power of making a mediocre meal fantastic. Terrible service can overpower any food, no matter how carefully prepared and delicious it may be.

How important is quality service to you when you are dining out? What do you do when the service is less than stellar? What should I have asked for from the manager after my experience? Weigh in here or over on Facebook.

Source: adapted from http://blog.opentable.com, 2010

8.1 Processes and quality

As we discussed in Chapter 6, designing hospitality experiences can be a complex process, and its success depends on the involvement of many actors. For example, employees play an important role in staging the hospitality experience, as you learned in Chapter 7. However, being successful in the hospitality industry requires more than just an appropriate design and people showing the right behaviour. As the example of bad service showed (above), hospitality experiences can fall short of expectations if they are not carefully managed. Hospitality managers need to monitor the processes involved in the delivery of the hospitality experiences to meet pre-specified targets. Among the most common are quality targets, which we set by translating customer needs and wants into measurable objectives. Typically, achieving these objectives means that the customer's wants and needs will more likely be met. Simultaneously, the cost of staging the hospitality experience needs to be managed, to ensure that the hospitality company can be profitable. Even when demand is high, too many very successful businesses are unable to translate this booming demand and revenues into profits. Oftentimes, this is because they do not make efficient use of their resources and fail to convert the potential into revenue and profits. Besides quality targets, it is thus imperative that cost targets are set and carefully managed to ensure that the needs and wants of customers are met in a commercially sustainable way. It means that you, the manager, must have the right processes and resources available to allow you to stage hospitality experiences in a way that serves both the interests of the customers and your company.

Process

Quality targets

Processes and resources

The dining out experience described in the opening case illustrates the need for hospitality organisations to remain in touch with the needs and wants of their clientele. And as you have learned from previous chapters, a hospitality experience consists of both *tangible* as well as *intangible* components. To satisfy your customers' needs and expectations, both components need to be addressed simultaneously. In addition, a hospitality experience is often staged in the presence of a customer who consumes it at the same time as it is produced, or who is even part of the production process. This is in sharp contrast to a physical or manufactured product, which is the result of a *production process* (Grönroos, 2001). Hospitality organisations rely heavily on resources, such as their employees, systems, as well as their customers, 'and a governing system that puts these resources to use when the customer requests a service' (Grönroos, 2001, p. 150). Therefore, once you have designed the various layers of your hospitality experience, it is imperative to deliver consistent quality. To do this, you need to put processes and procedures in place and subsequently manage them.

Consistent quality

8.2 Quality defined

The American Society for Quality defines quality as:

Quality

> the totality of features and characteristics of a product or service that bears on its ability to satisfy stated or implied needs.

A limitation of this definition is that it is subject to interpretation. Not everyone agrees on which features and characteristics have the ability to satisfy guests' needs (Bugg Holloway, & Beatty, 2008). Consequently, the definition has been interpreted in several ways, ranging from very broad (customer satisfaction), to narrower (perceived quality), to much narrower (satisfiers and dissatisfiers).

Customer satisfaction

Customer satisfaction interprets the definition of quality broadly, not by focusing on particular features and characteristics of an experience, but by asking whether it satisfies the customer, making it a very practical performance measure. It is a self-explanatory concept, easy to communicate to employees and customers. In its 2011 annual report, Starwood told stockholders, 'We drove guest satisfaction scores to record levels.' Customer satisfaction is easy to quantify and use when setting and monitoring objectives. For example, Radisson guarantees '100% guest satisfaction'. NH Hotels reports that customer satisfaction increased to 8.41 in its 2010 annual report as a key performance indicator.

With this wide variation in interpreting individual customer satisfaction, organisations staging hospitality experiences usually express overall customer satisfaction as an aggregate number. This method, however, fails to address any quality flaws in the hospitality experience. Ask a guest about his experience with your organisation, and he could reward you with a score of four out of five for his stay, even if the annoying noise from the lift shaft beside his room kept him awake at night. In his experience, though, the concierge who managed to get him a ticket for a very popular sold-out play made up for this abundantly. Management might consider his stay successful without learning about the technical shortcomings, since the hospitality experience is evaluated on an aggregate level. Therefore, the simplicity of customer satisfaction as a performance measure is also its main limitation. Companies can easily set and monitor satisfaction targets for their guest experiences using customer surveys. However, if satisfaction targets are not achieved, the company may not have enough information to explain why not. Conversely, if a company does a superb job at meeting or exceeding their satisfaction targets, they may not have sufficient information to replicate the success. That is why hospitality organisations want to collect more detailed information about the various components that make up the hospitality experience, as this allows them to improve the product and enhance the experience further. However, although customer satisfaction as a measure of quality clearly has some shortcomings, it is still widely used in the hospitality industry as a leading indicator.

As our definition of quality suggests, the quality of a hospitality experience is linked to its ability to satisfy customers' needs. To provide an objective view of the quality of a hospitality experience, organisations need to solicit feedback from their customers. Guest satisfaction surveys are thus a necessary evil in the hospitality industry. The majority of hotel firms use some form of guest satisfaction survey as a proxy to monitor service quality.

Guest satisfaction surveys
Satisfied customers are more likely to become loyal customers, engage in repeat purchase, and spread positive word of mouth or 'mouse'. Therefore, companies track customer satisfaction very conscientiously with customer satisfaction surveys that include questions such as 'how satisfied were you

---

Customer satisfaction

Key performance indicator

Measuring guest satisfaction

Customer satisfaction surveys

8

with your dinner experience', or 'how satisfied were you with your hotel stay?' Respondents are asked to rate these questions on scales typically ranging from 1 (very dissatisfied) to 5 (very satisfied) or from 1 to 10.

You can conduct guest satisfaction surveys in various ways. Some firms prefer to have short, paper-based surveys available at the front desk while other firms prefer to hire a third-party company to conduct these surveys by e-mail. Both approaches have their advantages and disadvantages.

Short surveys have the advantage of a higher response rate. Guests are more likely to fill a short survey than a long survey, as they do not need to invest a lot of time in it. Conversely, a short survey has the disadvantage in that it provides little information beyond whether the customer is satisfied or not. Longer surveys can provide valuable information to the firm, but guests are far less likely to filled them out. Motivated to express their opinion, typically overly satisfied or dissatisfied customers are more likely to fill out long surveys, resulting in a biased view of customer satisfaction.

Readily available paper-based surveys are also more likely to be filled out and returned by guests. However, the results of these surveys can be compromised should an employee selectively remove less favourable surveys.

Guest satisfaction survey

Online surveys prevent such situations, although guests are far less likely to respond to an e-mail received a few days after their stay. Another limitation of guest satisfaction surveys is language. While surveys can be easily provided in a large number of languages, especially online, they are commonly offered only in two to four languages, including the local language and one or two major ones. This restricts responses to speakers of that language. Furthermore, subtleties are lost when survey participants respond in a language other than their native language. Like many other service-related issues, modern technology provides a solution to overcome this problem and allows customers to rate their experience electronically *even when they are still on the premises*. Customers can use their smartphone to scan *quick response codes* (QR codes), a two-dimensional barcode that links the customer directly to a website.

Quick response codes

8

These codes can be printed on restaurant menus, on the displays in the lift, or even on special cards placed in reception. The QR code could send your customers to the website where they have the opportunity to review their experience online, in their own language of course. This way you capture their opinion immediately when their memories are still fresh and that adds valuable data to evaluate your product.

Reliability

The number and types of respondent to a satisfaction survey have huge implications for its reliability. Guests are more likely to fill out a guest satisfaction survey if they are extremely dissatisfied or, less often, extremely satisfied. Guests that are merely satisfied are less likely to fill out such a survey.

This polarisation of responses can make it very difficult to get a true measure of customer satisfaction.

Guest satisfaction measures

Guest satisfaction measures are used at several levels of the organisation. Front-line managers use them to improve on service delivery. In certain organisations, compensation of upper management is tied to customer satisfaction measures. It is not unheard of that general managers can earn a bonus of up to 25% of their yearly salary if they achieve customer satisfaction targets. Finally, for publicly traded companies, guest satisfaction measures are communicated to shareholders, as a hospitality company's ability to satisfy customers is tied to its long-term financial success.

Service delivery

Other avenues for feedback

For better or for worse, customers nowadays have other avenues to express their satisfaction or dissatisfaction with hospitality companies. Specialised websites such as Tripadvisor or Zagat are popular destinations for those who wish to share their impressions of a hotel or restaurant with other customers. Many hospitality businesses encourage their customers to post positive reviews, which is illustrated by the impact of guest reviews on the rates that, for example, hotels may charge. Data show 'that if a hotel increases its review scores by one point on a five-point scale (e.g., from 3.3 to 4.3), the hotel can increase its price by 11.2% and still maintain the same occupancy or market share' (Anderson, 2012, p. 5).

● www.nytimes.com

To hotel guests, sleep is a start

Hotel reviews on sites like Tripadvisor are useful for judging a specific property, to find out whether the elevators are slow or the location is grim. But ranking one brand against another or evaluating the industry as a whole requires a broader view – and new surveys indicate that although guest satisfaction is improving, travellers do have some complaints.

8

For its July issue, *Consumer Reports* asked more than 22,000 readers about their stays at 44 chains. It found scores for service, hotel upkeep and the check-in and checkout process had improved since 2006. Yet a quarter of respondents had at least one complaint, with inadequate beds, noise, outdated décor, cramped bathrooms and poor heating or air conditioning dominating the list.

'The key thing about a hotel is how good a night's sleep you were able to get,' said Todd Marks, a senior projects editor with *Consumer Reports*. 'An uncomfortable bed is one of the things that always seems to stand out in terms of problems.'

July 23, 2012
By Susan Stellin, adapted

User-generated content

For organisations, these review sites have become a very rich source of feedback from customers on the quality of their product and services. The reviews and ratings are also known as user-generated content and have become one of the most influential tools used to support customers in their purchase decisions. At the same time, it has put hospitality companies in the challenging situation that feedback on their product and its possible flaws is now available for all to see. But advancements in technology have enabled them to respond immediately to comments and engage in a personal conversation with guests, even online.

As the Kempinsky example illustrates, technology not only leads to a swifter process, it can also enhance the guest's experience.

8

● www.kempinski.com

Kempinski Hotel Mall of the Emirates drives guest satisfaction and operational efficiency through technology innovations

The result, a digitally enhanced check-in experience, greener operations, and a hotel technology innovation award.

Kempinski Hotel Mall of the Emirates has introduced a number of technological innovations over the past few months, including tablet-based express guest services, iPads in the hotel's restaurants and limousines, and a new in-room energy management system that is already seeing a significant reduction in the hotel's carbon footprint. The hotel was recognised as one of the 2012 EMEA Hotel Technology Innovators during the Hotel Technology Next Generation (HTNG) European Conference held in Austria earlier this month.

Opera2Go, the hotel's property management system, went live last month and has already received very positive feedback from guests. Through tablet devices employees can now wirelessly connect to instantly respond to guest on-the-go queries and manage a guest's check-in and checkout with much greater efficiency, hence significantly improving the whole experience.

Adapted

Customers are also increasingly vocal on their personal blogs, which are easily accessible through search engines. Venting on social media such as Facebook, Twitter, and LinkedIn, customers can also reach a narrower audience of like-minded individuals, who are more receptive to their feedback. Situations that ten years ago went unnoticed can now go viral in a matter of days. As early as 2002, two travellers arrived at their hotel in Houston at 2:00AM only to find that the hotel had given away their guaranteed room. After being dispatched to a 'dump' the two travellers created a humorous complaint on PowerPoint entitled 'Yours is a Very Bad Hotel' and sent it to the hotel managers and a few friends. Very soon, thousands of people had viewed the document and e-mailed their support (Shea, Enghagen, & Khullar, 2004). While much managerial attention is devoted to the consequences of negative reviews, hospitality managers increasingly see the benefits of pro-actively managing positive reviews, as it seems that positive reviews have a much bigger effect (Litvin, Goldsmith, & Pan, 2008).

In addition to its simplicity limitation, customer satisfaction as a performance measure can be influenced by many other factors beyond the control of the hospitality organisation. Customers are savvy enough to distinguish between poor service and poor weather, the question 'how satisfied were you with your beachside dining experience?' cannot differentiate between the two. Similarly, a particular guest's satisfaction can be greatly influenced by his or her emotions during or after the hospitality experience. A guest who asked his girlfriend to marry him and was rejected during the beachside dining experience is very likely to rate the experience poorly. Instead of responding to 'how satisfied were you with your beachside dining experience?' by thinking of the actual experience and its tangible and intangible components, he will focus on his anger and disappointment. Conversely, a beachside dining experience that ends in an engagement is likely to be rated highly by the customer, who will base his judgement of satisfaction on his positive emotions.

Perceived quality
The lack of more detailed information and insight into individual aspects of the hospitality experience can partially be overcome by expressing service quality on a narrower scale, as the perceived quality (Cronin Jr, Brady, & Hult, 2000). Perceived quality expresses the difference in the customer's expectations and the actual staging of the hospitality experience and it shares many common characteristics with customer satisfaction. Both definitions take the view that quality lies in the eyes of the beholder. Both are overall judgements of a product or hospitality experience's ability to satisfy

Perceived quality

8

Firm performance

needs, both explicitly and implicitly. Like customer satisfaction, perceived quality is positively related to firm performance through increased customer loyalty, repurchase intention, and positive word of mouth. Customers' perceived quality is often measured by asking respondents to rate statements such as 'the service I received was of very high quality' and 'the quality of the food was very high' on scales ranging from 1 (I completely disagree) to 5 (I completely agree).

Unlike customer satisfaction, perceived quality is easier for customers to distinguish from other factors affecting their experience as it is more closely linked to a product or experience's actual performance. In other words, customers' perceptions of quality are less biased by other factors than their satisfaction ratings. Therefore, perceived quality is also commonly used by companies to monitor their performance. Specifically, companies can set perceived quality targets and monitor whether they achieve them.

Perceived quality is one step closer to providing an unbiased view of whether the company succeeds in providing customers with superior guest experiences. However, it still does not provide sufficient information as to why customers perceive one guest experience as having better quality than another.

Satisfiers and dissatisfiers

Satisfiers
Dissatisfiers

Finally, satisfiers and dissatisfiers illustrate specific aspects that either enhance or detract from the hospitality experience. Customers will either appreciate them or find they have a negative impact on their satisfaction level. Customers' satisfaction and perceived quality are influenced by whether their expectations of the various components making up the hospitality experience are met. These salient components can be translated into attributes and characteristics of the hospitality experience. This allows a company to focus on the particular features and characteristics that have the greatest influence on satisfying or dissatisfying guests. Continuous research by hospitality organisations needs to establish what levels will be enough to meet and satisfy the customers' expectations.

The levels of attributes, characteristics are typically context specific. In other words, levels sufficient to satisfy customers may differ across experiences. For example, the Marriott Hotel and a McDonald's franchise are housed in the same beautiful building in the centre of Brussels, a short distance away from the Grand Place. Both offer their guests the opportunity to consume hamburgers with fries on their premises. The quality of the two guest dining experiences may jointly be determined by the food quality, service quality, and the quality of the surroundings. However, each dining experience needs to conform to different levels of quality.

In an ideal world, a company designing a hospitality experience will be able to identify the attributes of the guest experience that have the greatest influence on perceived quality and satisfaction. They will set targets that the experience should meet. Customers may not always be aware of the attributes of a product that drive their perceptions of quality, but they can discern high from low-quality products, services, and experiences.

The Marriott and McDonald's share a building

To steer the organisation towards successfully meeting their customers' needs and wants, and managing the available resources for staging a hospitality experience, organisations create and manage processes to guarantee a consistent quality level. An organisation's combined processes can be regarded as Grönroos' governing system that combines and enables interaction of the available resources to stage a hospitality experience. Often, these processes are measured by internal quality targets set by the organisation. Although customers possibly perceive or experience the quality differently, in practice organisations often apply the perspective of a more internally focused definition of quality, whether the experience is conform requirements (Crosby, 1979).

Governing system

8.3 Managing processes

As the previous section mentioned, the processes associated with staging hospitality experiences need to support the achievement of quality targets. A process is generally defined as:

Process

> a specific ordering of activities across time and place, with a beginning, an end, and clearly defined inputs and outputs.

Sequence of activities

For example, a check-in process can be defined by the following sequence of activities. A customer arrives at check-in area, waits for his turn, interacts with the service employee, receives his key, and leaves for the lift. In this example, the customer arriving at the desk defines the start, and his departure for the lift defines the end of the process. The resources used as input to this process would be the labour of the service employee, the computer, the key card, the information the customer provides to the employee and the information the employee looks up in the property management system. The output of this process would be a checked-in customer with a functional key card.

Hospitality businesses often formalise processes in standard operating procedures, written descriptions detailing all the important activities of the process. They are used to ensure quality by providing consistency between processes that create hospitality experiences.

Flowcharts

We use a particular type of diagram, flowcharts, to analyse complex processes, by breaking down the process into individual steps or components. Flowcharts represent activities (also known as sub-processes or steps) in boxes, linked by arrows. The check-in example is depicted in Figure 8.1.

FIGURE 8.1 Check-in process

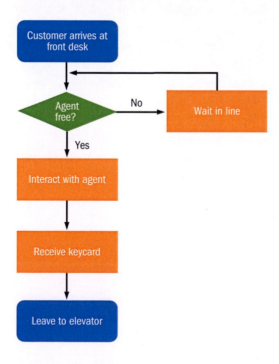

Weaknesses and inefficiencies

By examining the processes involved in staging hospitality experiences, hospitality managers can identify weaknesses and inefficiencies that lead to poor quality or higher than necessary costs. For example, in the process shown in Figure 8.1, the front desk manager might realise that customers need to wait too often before they can interact with the service agent. This could be because there are not enough service agents or because the interaction between the agent and the customer takes too long. If the latter is the case, the manager might decide to zoom in on the 'interact with agent' sub-process. This is depicted in Figure 8.2.

FIGURE 8.2   Customer-Agent interaction sub process

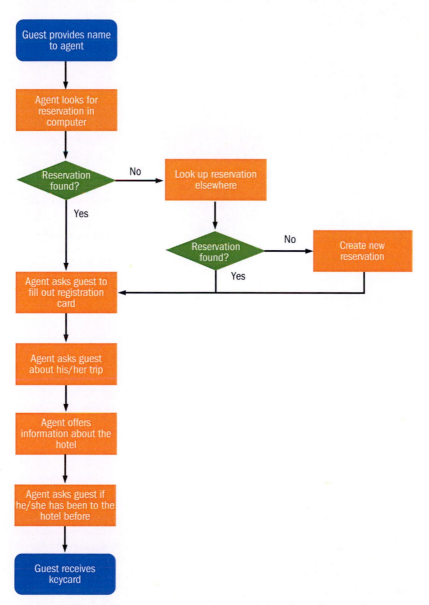

Upon careful examining the sub-process shown in Figure 8.2, the front desk might realise that it is inefficient and illogical to ask as the last question if a guest has stayed in the hotel before. If the guest has been to the hotel, he will not need extensive information about the hotel and its facilities, or need to fill out a registration form. Skipping these steps saves time in the check-in process, effectively increasing the capacity of the service without increasing the number of staff members.

FIGURE 8.3 Improved Customer-Agent interaction sub process

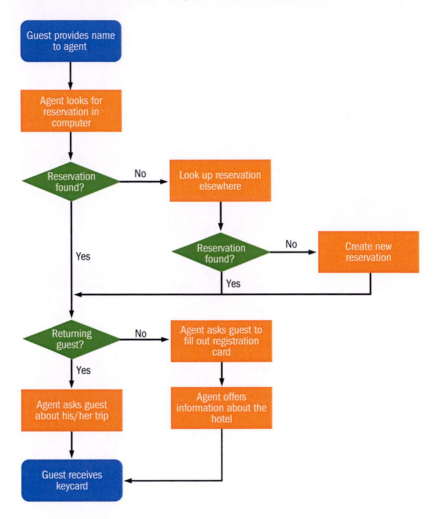

This new process not only reduces the time it takes to complete the necessary steps to check-in regular guests, the *facilitating product* (see Chapter 2), but also improves his overall experience. After studying Chapter 6, it should be evident that the *process* of staging the hospitality experience needs to be designed. Starting from the personal context (what does my guest want or expect), the social context (the scenario or *process* in which the interaction takes place) should be flexible enough to adapt the process, depending on the needs and wants of the customer. Even if a guest is in a hurry to catch his plane, a receptionist still has to cover the essentials of checking out to make sure that the payment is completed, but will most likely leave out the social talk. This contrasts with the couple who just spent a romantic weekend and are in no hurry to leave. They are happy to take the time to fill out a guest questionnaire about the hotel.

8.4 Setting quality targets

While each hospitality experience requires you to define cost and quality targets, these will differ depending on the particular hospitality experience. The design of the product, as Chapter 6 explained, as well as the intended level of interaction, hence the required number of staff, are leading indicators for determining the cost targets. Setting suitable quality targets requires firms to understand what drives customer satisfaction and translate this into measureable attribute levels that form the components that combine in the hospitality experience. Examples of these attributes could be temperature of the food served, accuracy of the reservation details on arrival, or the correct billing information on departure, as well as the room size and cleanliness. When it is impossible to measure the hospitality experience by internal quality targets, firms rely on measuring customer satisfaction with guest satisfaction surveys. This might sound logical, since it is commonly accepted 'that service quality must be defined from a customer's perspective' (Stauss & Weinlich, 1997, p. 33). Still, organisations are strongly urged to set internal targets as well, because these will let them both monitor and compare hospitality experience and design quality. The result will enable them to pro-actively adjust matters in the case of shortcomings. One aspect of guest satisfaction is related to the timeliness of the staged hospitality experience. The following sections use timeliness to define and illustrate the importance of setting quality targets. This of course can be easily substituted by any of the other attributes that make up the hospitality experience, such as cleanliness, friendliness of staff, or even the number of rings it takes an operator to answer the telephone.

Quality targets

Measureable attribute levels

Timeliness objectives
Timeliness is a quality target because hospitality experiences often involve waiting, and long waits are usually associated with customer dissatisfaction.

Waiting lines
Waiting is a common occurrence in hospitality experiences and results from temporary imbalances between supply and demand. Customers arriving to receive service often do so relatively unpredictably. Firms set their staffing levels

8

to meet an average demand, such that on average, fewer customers arrive than can be served. However, within a shorter period, possibly more customers will arrive than can be served. For example, between 9AM and 11AM McDonald's may have enough servers to handle six customers in two-minute periods. However, ten customers may arrive at once and no customers during the next two minutes. This temporary imbalance will lead to the formation of a queue.

Queues and customer satisfaction
Long waiting lines lead to customer dissatisfaction. That is common knowledge (Maister, 1985) so hospitality organisations invest lots of resources to prevent or reduce waiting lines. This is especially true for facilitating products (Grönroos, 1987) such as check-in and checkout, where interaction between the guest and service employee is necessary to acquire the guest's legally required details, but could be omitted for regular guests, or kept to a minimum for tired guests who have travelled a long way. Waiting for service causes customers to feel bored, impatient and as if they are wasting their time. Boredom in turn can lead customers to overestimate their waiting time, and be even more dissatisfied with the overall hospitality experience.

Waiting lines

● www.nytimes.com

Disney tackles major theme park problem: lines

To handle over 30 million annual visitors – many of them during this busiest time of year for the megaresort – Disney World long ago turned the art of crowd control into a science. But the putative Happiest Place on Earth has decided it must figure out how to quicken the pace even more. A cultural shift towards impatience – fed by video games and smartphones – is demanding it, park managers say. To stay relevant to the entertain-me-right-this-second generation, Disney must evolve.

And so it has spent the last year outfitting an underground, nerve centre to address that most low-tech of problems, the wait. Located under Cinderella Castle, the new centre uses video cameras, computer programs, digital park maps, and other whiz-bang tools to spot gridlock before it forms and deploy countermeasures in real time.

In a corner, employees watch flat screen televisions that depict various attractions in green, yellow, and red outlines, with the colours representing wait-time gradations. If Pirates of the Caribbean, the ride that sends people on a spirited voyage through the Spanish Main, suddenly blinks from green to yellow, the centre might respond by alerting managers to launch more boats. Another option involves dispatching Captain Jack Sparrow or Goofy or one of their pals to the queue to entertain people as they wait. 'It's about being nimble and quickly noticing that, 'Hey, let's make sure there is some relief out there for those people',' said Phil Holmes, vice-president of the Magic Kingdom, the flagship Disney World park.

The primary goal of the command centre, as stated by Disney, is to make guests happier – because to increase revenue in its $10.7 billion theme

8

park business, which includes resorts in Paris and Hong Kong, Disney needs its current customers to return more often. 'Giving our guests faster and better access to the fun,' said Thomas O. Staggs, chairman of Walt Disney Parks and Resorts, 'is at the heart of our investment in technology.'

December 27, 2010
By Brooks Barnes, adapted

Captain Jack Sparrow

The fairness of the waiting line process plays an important role in guest satisfaction (Schmitt, Dube, & Leclerc, 1992). Waiting lines are often seen as social systems with rules and procedures that need to be respected by all. A guest violating the waiting order can generate negative emotions and

Fairness

Emotions

dissatisfaction in other waiting guests if the service provider fails to prevent or rectify this violation.

Integral part

Hospitality experiences deviate somewhat from the accepted wisdom that all waiting lines are bad, as (the context for) waiting is sometimes purposely designed as part of the experience. For instance, the most popular theme park in the Netherlands, *De Efteling*, has managed to make waiting time an integral part of the hospitality experience. They stimulate people with images and impressions of the attraction, and constantly play contagious songs, raising the customers' expectancy levels, and distracting them from the negative emotions that are usually linked with waiting. Another example of functional waiting times are when restaurant guests have to wait between courses during multi-course dining experiences. These periods are part of the dining experience, and allow guests to take a break between dishes, and socialise. If these periods become too long, guests may become impatient and dissatisfied. However, attempting to minimise waiting periods would also lead to dissatisfaction, as guests may feel rushed and not ready for their next course. This means that restaurant staff should not necessarily strive for the shortest waiting time, but for the *right* waiting time. And this can vary per customer and situation.

Artificially generate waiting time

Restaurants are known to artificially generate waiting time by first directing guests to the bar before leading them to their table. The benefit is that it gives the image of a busy and therefore desirable restaurant, while spreading demand for the kitchen and increasing the average check.

Quality targets associated with waiting time

Waiting time

Hospitality organisations can set several associated metrics when managing waiting time. A very commonly used metric is average waiting time. Service providers set targets for the average time guests will wait in a particular period. This will depend on the type of hospitality experience. The target average waiting time for check-in at a five-star business hotel in Paris will be different from that of a two-star beach resort.

A limitation of average waiting time as a quality target is that it does not represent time variations. In other words, you cannot infer from an average waiting time if some guests wait an excessively long time. For example, a company might achieve its desired target average waiting time of two minutes. However, this could be because 15 guests had no wait-time at all, but five guests waited eight minutes each. Even though the target average waiting time was achieved, 25% of the guests would be very dissatisfied.

Service level

Average waiting time is therefore often used along with service level. A service level is defined as the proportion of guests that wait less than a specified duration. In the above two-minute example, 15 out of 20 guests waited under two minutes, resulting in a 75% service level. If the target service level were 90%, the firm would have failed to reach the target.

While average waiting time and service level are used most commonly, many other metrics are associated with waiting time, such as average queue length, average time spent in the process (includes waiting time and service time), and average number of customers in the process (includes numbers of customers waiting and/or receiving service). Operators are interested in average queue length since a fast queue that looks long may deter customers from joining it. Also, knowing the average queue length is useful when planning the space in which the waiting will occur. Average time spent in the process and average number of customers in the process can be useful when designing services in which waiting is part of the hospitality experience.

Managing waiting time
There are several ways to manage waiting lines in a hospitality experience. First, the hospitality organisation can manage the actual waiting time through the design of the processes involved, and by ensuring they have enough capacity to meet demand. Processes can be designed so as to be less time consuming. You can address this by adjusting the *tangible* components as well as the *intangible* attributes of the hospitality experience, as we discussed in Chapter 6. For example, the SOPs of many hotel chains call for small talk during the check-in process. Front-office agents are expected to ask guests whether they had a safe journey. While engaging in this kind of chat may lead the guests to feel more welcome, it can increase the time it takes to check-in a customer. Conversely, the technological advances in hotel property management systems and customer-relationship management systems often ensure hotels have information for guests available prior to their arrival, effectively reducing the time needed to check-in.

Technological advances

On the other hand, the service setting needs to be designed so as to accommodate for staffing levels sufficient to meet maximum demand. Service operators can then adapt to variations in demand through staffing levels. For example, hotels in Las Vegas commonly have more than 20 check-in counters, of which at most three are occupied on any given Tuesday morning. However, all are manned on Friday afternoons, the busiest time for check-in in Las Vegas.

8

When designing their waiting lines, hospitality organisations also put a lot of thought into configuration. Since customer perceptions of justice are almost as important as their perceptions of waiting, they often choose for single lines feeding multiple servers. This kind of waiting line ensures that the principle of first-in first-out is adhered to as it prevents a customer who joined the line later to be served first. However, this type of waiting line configuration does have several disadvantages. Specifically, while it may move very fast, a single line can soon seem very long, discouraging customers from joining it. Also, in situations where customers have luggage such as in hotels and airports, it can be uncomfortable to constantly have to lift a suitcase for just a few metres. The discomfort increases the customers' perceived waiting time. This dilemma shows that many decisions in designing hospitality experiences are imperfect, and need to be weighted carefully in the context of the particular experience and the overall customer journey.

Configuration

When we cannot manage actual waiting time, we can resort to managing perceived waiting time by adding distractions. This is why so many hotels have mirrors in their lobbies and elevators and Disney characters walk around the rides. Giving customers something to do while they wait, even unknowingly, reduces the perceived duration of that experience, as this story on waiting illustrates.

● www.nytimes.com

Why waiting is torture

Some years ago, executives at a Houston airport faced a troubling customer-relations issue. Passengers were lodging an inordinate number of complaints about the long waits at baggage claim. In response, the executives increased the number of baggage handlers working that shift. The plan worked. The average wait fell to eight minutes, well within industry benchmarks. But the complaints persisted.

Puzzled, the airport executives undertook a more careful, on-site analysis. They found that it took passengers a minute to walk from their arrival gates to baggage claim and seven more minutes to get their bags. Roughly 88% of their time, in other words, was spent standing around waiting for their bags.

So the airport decided on a new approach. Instead of reducing wait times, it moved the arrival gates away from the main terminal and routed bags to the outermost carousel. Passengers now had to walk six times longer to get their bags. Complaints dropped to near zero.

Paradoxically, as the Houston airport example shows, optimising a service can sometimes backfire.

August 18, 2012
By Alex Stone

8.5 Managing resources

The available resources linked to the processes of staging a hospitality experience need to support those processes in a timely, high quality and cost effective way. While managing the processes associated with staging hospi-

tality experiences is important, it will not be enough if the necessary resources are not present. Resources include the setting or context of the
staged hospitality experience, the technology used, and the people involved.

Resources

Setting/context

As we have shown in Chapter 6, the physical setting of the hospitality experience is called the servicescape and most of its features are usually established at the design stage. The servicescape includes the physical attributes of the hospitality experience environment, ranging diversely from
employees' uniforms, the colour of the wallpaper, the height of the chairs,
the type, and volume of music playing, the ambient temperature, and even
the scent of the area. All these have the potential to influence customers'
emotions, perceptions of quality, and satisfaction. For example, uplifting
music can increase guests' sense of well-being. A stained employee uniform can reduce a restaurant customer's perception of quality by communicating a sloppy image. Similarly, scratched furniture or a torn pillowcase
might lead guests to perceive the hotel as old and poorly kept. These examples also contribute to the atmosphere of the hospitality experience, relating it to the *augmented* product of Grönroos' model (1987) explained in
Chapter 2.

Servicescape

Atmosphere

Another element of the servicescape is formed by the products that facilitate the provision of the service at the core of the hospitality experience, as
we discussed in Chapter 2. According to Grönroos' model (1987), facilitating products are essential for customers to enjoy the hospitality experience.
This includes items such as napkins and salt shakers in a restaurant,
amenities in a hotel, even toilet paper. While representing a relatively small
part of the total experience, facilitating products can have a disproportion-
ate effect on perceptions of quality. For example, a malfunctioning salt shak-
er can irritate guests and ruin an otherwise excellent dinner experience.

The importance of facilitating products is crucial for large-scale events. For example, the New York City marathon, which takes place each November, is very
much a challenge to the logistics required to facilitate the overall experience.

● www.nytimes.com

Behind the scenes, a race of logistics

With more than 43,000 participants, 2.5 million spectators and a course
that stretches over 26.2 miles and five boroughs, the New York City marathon is more than a sporting event, it is a vast international spectacle. 'We
believe this is the greatest sporting event in the world for one day,' Ciaccia
said a few weeks ago. 'It's on par with the Olympics. We're putting New
York City on a platform.'

To any doubters, Ciaccia provides statistics. To get to the starting line, runners will board 12 ferries leaving from Manhattan. About 500 buses will
take runners to the start at Fort Wadsworth on Staten Island from points in
Manhattan, Brooklyn, and Long Island, New Jersey and beyond.

At the start on the Verrazano-Narrows Bridge, there will be 1,694 portable toilets, 42,000 PowerBars, 90,000 bottles of water and 563 pounds of Dunkin' Donuts coffee beans, enough to make 45,000 cups. About 500 volunteers will collect more than 10 tons of sweat suits, sleeping bags, and Snuggies, much of which will be cleaned and given to charities. The bridge must be cleared within an hour of the last runner's leaving. More than 70 United Parcel Service trucks will take the athletes' belongings to the finish line.

Along the course, 62,370 gallons of water and 32,040 gallons of Gatorade will be served in 2.3 million paper cups that can now be recycled, thanks to new technology. Another 60,000 PowerBar Gel packets will be available at Mile 18.

About 11 tons of trash will be collected at the 24 fluid stations, much of it cardboard, plastic jugs and cups. The 24 station 'captains' have more than 400 years of experience combined. Along the course, 137 bands (all vetted by New York Road Runners) will perform on dozens of stages. Runners can check their times on the 106 clocks on the course.

Among the more than 6,000 volunteers on race day are medical workers at the 38 aid stations. They will have on hand 11,410 pounds of ice, 13,475 bandages, 57,059 salt packages, and 390 tubs of Vaseline. They will have 435 cots and 30 defibrillators that, hopefully, will not be needed.

In all, 1,200 vehicles will be used during the race, including many assembled into convoys that clean the course as runners push ahead. School buses will pick up stragglers. Runners who make it to the finish will be handed one of the 52,000 medals, and possibly one of the 60,000 heat sheets and 52,000 food bags.

Jim Heim, who works with Ciaccia, said the Road Runners operations staff was 'a well-oiled machine,' in part, because it has hosted events throughout the year. But he acknowledged that 'at every event, there's something that is going to go wrong.'

November 5, 2010
By Ken Belson, adapted

In addition to its effect on customers' emotions, perceptions of quality, and satisfaction, the servicescape plays a role in the hospitality business' ability to stage experiences at a particular quality level. For example, the layout of the building influences how long it takes to bring a room service tray from the kitchen to a guest's room. The size of the plate determines how many plates a restaurant waiter can carry. These seemingly small details can play a significant role in the business' ability to meet its targets. As a result, defining realistic and logical targets is strongly related to the different layers of both the hospitality experience (see Chapter 2), and its design (see Chapter 6). For example, a long route from kitchen to restaurant severely impacts food serving temperatures or timeliness targets, and a canteen-style restaurant with fluorescent lighting will not create a romantic dinner setting. That will only lead to disappointed customers, if romance was part of the value proposition that you communicated to potential customers.

Technology

Technology has had a major impact on how businesses design and manage their processes and on their ability to meet targets. Customer interaction is an important part of the hospitality experience, and the increased use and availability of technology has allowed firms to tailor the hospitality experience to the individual needs of the customer. In addition, technology has helped companies to achieve productivity gains by allowing customers to take on an even bigger co-production role. Self-service technologies consist of technological interfaces (e.g., self-service kiosks, interactive voice recognition systems and the internet) that allow customers to produce hospitality experiences independently of service employees' involvement (Meuter, Ostrom, Roundtree, & Bitner, 2000). Examples of self-service technology are most noticeable at the airport, where airlines direct their passengers to complete the check-in procedure on terminals, drop-off their luggage at a self-service machine, and complete the security procedure with an iris scan while they scan their passport. To show that self-service does not mean *no service,* you find customer service agents on standby, ready to guide you through the procedure if and when required. But, self-service technologies can contribute to increased productivity and far more consistent quality, as well as substantial savings in staff costs.

Self-service technologies can have major advantages for customers. For example, customers no longer have to limit themselves to a restaurant's operating hours when booking a table. They can use an online reservation system to book their table any time they want. Customers also typically benefit from reduced transaction costs, increased customisation opportunities and speedier transactions. Self-service technologies also offer customers an increased sense of perceived control (Rodie & Kleine, 2000). For example, hotel guests checking in do not have to wait in line and make small talk with an inquisitive front desk employee. Instead, they can choose to use a self-service kiosk.

In addition, developments in technology, such as sophisticated and ever more accurate systems for applying revenue management and customer-relationship management allow organisations to tailor-make their product better according to individual needs and wants of their customers. Employees have swift access to customer data, based on which they can adjust the delivery or interaction of the hospitality experience. Recent developments in

Technology

Self-service technology

8

Revenue management

Customer-relationship management

technology even give customers the opportunity to personalise their physical setting, by adjusting the smell, colour of their room and playing their favourite music. These advances in technology help improve the perceived quality of the hospitality experience by positively adjusting the experience to the expectations of the customer.

People

During the hospitality experience, customers frequently interact with employees, and this interaction represents a substantial part of the overall experience. Besides tangible, carefully designed components, choosing the right people or employees is at least equally important. After all, popular wisdom advocates that an overcooked steak can be compensated for by outstanding service, but a perfectly cooked dish cannot make up for bad service.

Service quality, and the role of people in assuring it, has been the subject of extensive research over the years. Researchers have created and tested models, such as the servqual model (Parasuraman, Zeithaml, & Berry, 1985), and these have in turn been confirmed, criticised, even disputed. Some main findings can still make a difference today. Keywords such as 'aesthetics, attentiveness/helpfulness, care, communication, courtesy, flexibility, friendliness, reliability and responsiveness' (Johnston, 1995) are all examples of satisfiers or dissatisfiers important to customers that are directly influenced by the behaviour of individual hospitality employees.

Training programmes

Once again, this illustrates the importance of hiring the right staff and subsequently nurturing and developing their talents through training programmes. It goes beyond the scope of this chapter to fully explore how this can be done, but the following real-life example illustrates the importance many hospitality leaders attach to this aspect.

8

Right mentality

A general manager of a large four-star hotel in the Netherlands explained that he is always on the lookout for talent that he can recruit for his front of house departments. For example, when he goes to the supermarket, or is filling up his car at the petrol station, he frequently hands out business cards and asks people to come and work for him. His motto? 'If I see that they have the right attitude, I can train them how to do a check-in, or how to make a reservation. But doing it with the right mentality is much more difficult to develop.'

Authenticity

In the back offices of companies like Disney, at the entrance to the front-of-fice area, you often find a mirror with the text *Smile, you're on stage*. The message underlines the importance that both customers and organisations attach to friendly and welcoming staff. It explains why companies go to great lengths in training their staff to deliver service with a smile, including it in their procedures, and evaluate how well staff conform to these procedures through mystery visits. The key to 'service with a smile' is the authenticity of the friendly face. Does the employee really mean it? In today's society, where demanding customers seem to have developed highly sensitive antenna for authenticity, it can enhance a positive response to the perceived quality (Grandey, Fisk, Mattila, Jansen, & Sideman, 2005). In contrast, some hospitality experiences do not require staff to produce a smiley face. As you can image, it would not be appropriate when people offer condolences to a grieving family.

Because of their frequent interaction with customers, front-line employees are the 'eyes and ears of the organisation' and thus an important source of valuable customer information. Processes need to be put in place that enable employees to capture this information and make it available for improving and customising the experience for future visits with the technology solutions discussed earlier.

● www.businessjournal.gallup.com

How the Ritz-Carlton manages the mystique

Joanna Hanna arrived in The Ritz-Carlton after a bad flight experience. 'I had to get to a conference in New York, but my flights were delayed over and over. If I arrived seven hours later than I meant to, it'll be too soon,' she says. 'The gentleman who escorted me to my room at the Ritz-Carlton asked how my day was, and I told him, the poor guy,' says Hanna. 'He said he'd be happy to book me into the spa, or send up a masseuse, or even have a rose-petal bath drawn for me, and I'd have loved all of that. But there was no time.' So he told Hanna to wait a moment, and then he returned with a scented candle. 'I was so touched, I was speechless. It was so thoughtful and helpful, like something a friend would do,' says Hanna. 'So I told the people at the desk. And now whenever I check into a Ritz-Carlton, there's a candle waiting for me.'

Perhaps any hotel employee could figure out that a tired and frazzled guest could use a little help. But making sure that every employee notices, cares, thinks, and acts as thoughtfully as the one who served Hanna – well, that takes something special.

The Ritz-Carlton calls that something special 'The Ritz-Carlton Mystique.' It's a way of conceptualising the brand's image and the ambiance of each of the company's more than 70 worldwide locations. 'Mystique' sounds enigmatic, but it's achieved through the most straightforward of methods, extremely close attention to performance data collection and a broad educational platform to deliver the findings.

'What we get from the data is essential,' says John Timmerman, the Ritz-Carlton's vice-president of operations. 'Everything we learn we use to set strategies, and every strategy is communicated to our people. That learning environment is how we stay agile in an ever-changing world.'

Adapted

Having sufficient employees available is essential for staging efficient hospitality experiences. The continuity and consistency of hospitality experiences depend on forecasting the expected demand levels for different times. For ski resort hotels, this might mean hiring more employees on short contracts to cover for the busy winter periods. For downtown business hotels,

Overstaffing

Understaffing

this could imply adjusting staffing levels per day of the week, or even per hour of the day. In the case of *overstaffing*, which could result from over optimistic predictions of demand levels, labour costs will be too high. It could also lead to demotivated staff, since they will get bored and decide to look for a more challenging job elsewhere. The opposite case of *understaffing* could also prove to be costly. Although it might seem to be a great way to save on labour costs, eventually it will turn out to be counterproductive. Due to the significant role of customer interaction in the process of staging hospitality experiences, failure to provide adequate numbers of staff to do this well could lead to a diminished perceived quality by customers. A growing number of complaints that need rectification, plus stressed-out demotivated staff who eventually need replacing leads to far higher costs in the long run.

8.6 Costs associated with quality

No matter how you define 'quality', providing the right level of quality is crucial for any company. Providing quality service and products is expensive so hospitality organisations frequently try to save money on quality.

Types of costs

Costs

Yet, not providing quality can prove to be even more expensive. Several types of costs are associated with quality, depending on the phase of the hospitality experience in which they occur. We often refer to the different types of costs as the P-A-F model (Philip B. Crosby, 1979):
1 Prevention costs
2 Appraisal costs
3 Failure (internal and external) costs

Companies usually incur prevention costs and appraisal costs in the 'prior' (or pre-service) phase of the hospitality experience. It is done to prevent failures in the 'during' (or service) phase from occurring. The cost of these failures can extend to the 'after' (or post-service) phase, depending on the severity of the failure.

Ad 1 Prevention costs
As the name suggests, prevention costs are associated with preventing quality issues. These costs are first incurred at the design stage of the hospitality experience when potential sources of service failures are identified, and then arise regularly to maintain the conditions necessary to prevent malfunctions from happening. In practice, this is similar to setting up and maintaining a formal or informal quality system. An example of a formal quality system restaurants often use is HACCP, which stands for Hazard Analysis Critical Control Point. HACCP is meant to prevent food-borne illnesses by identifying hazards and critical points in the process of preparing food for consumption. Other well-known quality control systems are Total Quality Management, Six Sigma, and Statistical Process Control. A common characteristic of all formal quality programmes is the importance they give to employee training.

Employee training

Employee training is probably the most common form of prevention cost. Even when hospitality organisations do not use a formal quality programme, they have a thorough training programme to familiarise their new employees with their brand and standards. Companies incur the cost of training to ensure that employees provide hospitality experiences that meet specified targets. For example, new employees of Radisson graduate from the chain's 'Yes I Can!' programme and earn the 'Yes I Can!' pin.

Prevention costs can be controversial, since they are incurred away from the actual hospitality experience. Consequently, the relationship between prevention costs and reduced service failures can be difficult to establish, leading to the temptation to save on these types of costs. In periods of economic downturn and slow demand, hospitality organisations might be tempted to postpone preventive maintenance on their equipment or tangible product, in order to meet profit targets. However, this will most likely lead to more expensive service failures later on.

Ad 2 Appraisal costs

Companies incur *appraisal or detection* costs in the attempt to identify failures before guests do. Appraisal costs are associated with the inspection process. The housekeeping supervisor's check of a clean hotel room is an example of an appraisal cost. In many hotels, the supervisor checks after the housekeepers leave and before the guest enters the room to ensure that cleanliness and presentation meet all the targets and standards. Similarly, in many restaurants, the chef inspects the dishes before the waiters are allowed to take them out to the customers. During food preparation, the chef tastes the dish to ensure it meets the required quality. This is an example of a less formal and expensive, yet equally important appraisal cost.

Chef inspects

Prevention and appraisal costs are both incurred to try to prevent customers from experiencing a failure. They work best when used concurrently. In an ideal situation, if the inspection process reveals that a particular failure occurs frequently (appraisal costs), the processes associated with the hospitality experience will be revised, or redesigned to remedy this (prevention costs). However, in practice, the two processes often work independently, preventing the organisation from learning from its mistakes. A typical example occurs in housekeeping. Many hotels outsource room cleaning, meaning that an outside company employs and trains the housekeepers, and the hotel's supervisors who check the housekeepers' work have no influence over their training. Adjusting these processes to each another can therefore be a potentially complex and sometimes time-consuming process.

Ad 3a Internal failure costs

The flaws identified in the inspection process can lead to another type of cost. Internal failure costs are incurred when you identify and rectify a failure (often in the inspection process) before the guest can experience it. Internal failure costs consist of scrap costs, the cost incurred when discarding something, and rework costs, the cost of repairing something to make it fit for sale. For example, during the inspection of a cleaned room, the housekeeping supervisor may notice the bed sheets are frayed. The cost of inspecting the room is an appraisal cost. However, the additional labour cost incurred to rectify the issue (replace the bed sheets before the guest arrives) is a rework and thus internal failure cost. Similarly, when he tastes the food, the chef may notice that the fish is overcooked. Once again, additional labour costs and raw material costs will be incurred to cook another fish, a rework cost, and to throw away the first fish, a scrap cost, adding to the internal failure expenses.

Inspection

Companies often underestimate internal failure costs and this is especially true in the context of hospitality experiences where there is time pressure due to the presence and interaction of the customer in the process. Especially in hospitality firms, failures identified internally are quickly rectified, **Registered** soon forgotten, and their cost almost never registered. This leads to the unfortunate situation where the firm underestimates its internal failure costs and fails to realise that it may be better off spending more on prevention costs, instead of incurring the sum of the appraisal and internal failure costs.

Ad 3b External failure costs
External failure costs are associated with a failure experienced by the guest. They can take various tangible and intangible forms. Hotels commonly face the situation of a guest discovering that his or her television does not work. This leads to inconvenience for the guest, as maintenance needs to access the room to repair the television. If this discovery occurs later in the evening, when the maintenance crew has already left for the day, the hotel may need to further inconvenience the guest by asking them to move to another room. If the hotel is sold out, the hotel may not be able to rectify the situation. While the costs of repairing the television or offering another room to the guest may be tangible and easy to quantify, the costs of inconveniencing and/or disappointing the guests may be harder to estimate. The hotel can try to mitigate the fault by offering the disappointed guest a discount, a free dinner or even a free stay. Dissatisfied guests may vent their frustration to others, in person or by word of **Irreparable** mouse (posting negative reviews online), leading to irreparable damage to **damage** the firm's reputation and to lost sales, and that can add up to huge sums of missed revenue.

8

> ● www.nytimes.com
>
> ## Company news; Jack in the Box's worst nightmare
>
> Since the outbreak of food poisoning from hamburger sold at Jack in the Box outlets here in mid-January left two children dead, the stock of the chain's parent company, Foodmaker Inc., has dropped more than 30%. The 60 Jack in the Box restaurants in the state have been barraged by anonymous telephone callers accusing them of being baby killers. Customers are scarce. And local newspapers have carried advertisements by lawyers offering to represent poisoning victims.
>
> 'In the last 10 years, we've sold 400 million pounds of hamburger safely and without incident,' said Robert Nugent, president of Jack in the Box, the nation's fifth-largest hamburger chain, with 1,170 outlets in 13 states in the West. 'Then bang, it hits you. It's your worst, worst nightmare.'
>
> The finger pointing has been intense. The San Diego-based chain blamed its supplier, the Vons Companies of Arcadia, Calif., for supplying tainted

meat and filed a lawsuit against Vons on Thursday. The meat was contaminated at the slaughterhouse, according to Washington State health officials; Jack in the Box acknowledges that its contract did not call for Vons to test the meat.

Analysts worry whether Jack in the Box will be able to recover. Public relations specialists say the chain had acted correctly in offering to cover the medical expenses of victims, in setting up a special telephone hotline, in making a generous contribution to help find a cure for the E. coli infection and in replacing Vons and letting the public know through an advertising campaign.

February 6, 1993

Adapted

External failure costs have become increasingly important in the past ten years due to the rise of online reviews. The external failure costs stemming from word of mouse can be exponentially higher than those stemming from word of mouth since the first can reach a much broader global audience than the latter, and at a much higher speed. Although organisations cannot influence what their customers write in the review of their hospitality experience, they can influence the quality of the actual experience that they write about. It is therefore imperative that organisations spend the necessary sums of money on prevention and appraisal costs, to prevent customers becoming disappointed.

Broader global audience

Relative costs of quality

Companies are often reluctant to incur the costs necessary to prevent service failures. Prevention costs occurring during the design phase of a hospitality experience increase the investment costs. This is a time when, very often, cash is already low. Similarly, appraisal costs increase the cost of staging hospitality experiences. Organisations are too often tempted to save on prevention costs to produce a higher short-term profit. This is a mistake, as most times the cost associated with failures will be much higher, as the Jack in the Box example shows. Obviously Jack in the Box should have spent more resources on the careful selection of a supplier (prevention cost) or testing the incoming meat (prevention cost). Jack in the Box could also have chosen to test the hamburger cooking temperature (appraisal cost) and discard poorly cooked hamburgers (internal failure costs). Instead, it is now facing much higher costs, as it needs to compensate victims (external failure costs). Bad publicity generated by this failure and the ensuing reduced sales (external failure costs) are also very likely to hurt the company in the long term.

8

Setting cost targets

Hospitality organisations are faced with several types of costs. The general level of these costs is set in the design stage. Decisions made here will have the greatest financial impact in the long term. Such decisions include size (number and size of rooms, number of seats, number, and type of facilities) and service level (quality of furnishings and fixtures, approximate lev-

Types of costs

el of staffing, number of parking spaces). As we discussed before, both the tangible and intangible part of the hospitality experience influence the type of experience, and as a result determine the costs associated with staging it. When an organisation, for example, decides to use lower quality materials during the design phase, it not only leads to a different experience for customers, but also quite possibly to higher repair costs. However, often the implications and additional costs are not included in budgets, leading to unexpected expenses at a later stage. The Standard Operating Procedures also have a bearing on the total costs, as they directly affect the number of staff required. For example, waiting lines could be eliminated altogether if there were enough servers to meet peak demand. In other words, a hospitality organisation would need to hire enough staff so that, even at busiest times, there is always someone available to help a customer. It would also mean that most of the time, outside peak hours, or when demand is slow, these servers would be idle. This company would quickly go bankrupt.

Arguably, many hospitality organisations design beautiful, but financially unsustainable hospitality experiences. As the Tavern on the Green story shows, this restaurant was once regarded as highly successful, attracting many customers. Despite its success, it unfortunately had to close its doors since the revenues it was generating were not sufficient to cover its costs.

● www.centralpark.com

Tavern on the Green

Established in 1934, when it replaced the sheepfold that had once housed the sheep of Sheep Meadow, Tavern on the Green quickly became a New York City icon. The restaurant consisted of several rooms, including the well-known Crystal Room, which offered beautiful views of the adjacent garden. It was the second highest-grossing restaurant in the US owned by an independent party, having earned its revenue from over 500,000 visitors.

During its early years, Tavern on the Green was known for its spacious dance floor that offered nightly dancing to live music, surrounded by elm trees and twinkling lights. As the century progressed, the restaurant was frequented by famous artists and celebrities such as Grace Kelly and Fay Wray. John Lennon celebrated several of his birthdays at Tavern on the Green in the late 70s, and it was the restaurant of choice for opening night festivities of Broadway shows.

Despite its popularity, Tavern on the Green welcomed guests for the last time on December 31, 2009 after filing for bankruptcy. No longer the famed restaurant featured in shows such as Live with Regis and Kelly and 30 Rock, the building re-opened in October of 2010 as an information centre and gift shop.

Adapted

Tavern on the Green in Central Park, New York

8

8.7 Making quality count

It is imperative for any type of organisation to ensure they deliver what they promise to do. They can achieve this by measuring the quality of their products. A common definition of quality is conformance to specifications, and as the term implies, under this definition a product should conform to certain specifications to be considered of high quality. These specifications consist of product or experience characteristics with predefined acceptable levels. For example, Coca Cola can measure the quality of a can of its famous soft drink by measuring the ratio of Coca Cola syrup to carbonated water and comparing it to the prescribed standard. Similarly, McDonald's can measure the quality of its fries by measuring their temperature, amount of salt, and crispiness against their standards. Dominos Pizza can measure the quality of their service by timing how long it takes to deliver a pizza order after it was placed, and compare it to their 30-minute standard.

Conformance to specifications

In contrast to manufactured products, hospitality experiences cannot always be defined in terms of attributes and characteristics. Among other things, this is due to the interactions between the host and the guest, making it difficult to identify target levels for these attributes and characteristics. For example, the quality of a restaurant dinner experience may be jointly determined by food quality, service quality, and the quality of the surroundings. Each of these can in turn be determined by tangible and intangible factors. For example, the quality of the surroundings may be determined by the ambient temperature, the music volume, the scent, the colour of the decor, how full the restaurant is. Service quality may be determined by the cleanliness of the waiter's uniform and his cheerfulness. Identifying the complete set of attributes and characteristics that represent the corresponding levels of the customers' needs and wants is therefore a challenge when applying the conformance to specifications definition. Furthermore, the definition does not always account for the fact that not all attributes and characteristics of a hospitality experience have the same weight in customers' experiences. In practice, customers do not notice all the attributes or characteristics that meet their expectations. Instead, their satisfaction may be impacted by the one attribute or characteristic of their experience that deviated significantly from their expectation.

Active monitoring

Bringing the different definitions of quality together, it becomes clear that a hospitality experience can be defined, measured and managed in many different ways and requires active monitoring by the management of a hospitality organisation. While many operating decisions are made in the design stage, hospitality organisations still have a relatively broad range of options in their decision-making. The most common decision hospitality managers have to make on an almost daily basis concerns the optimal level of staffing necessary to ensure a financially sustainable yet sufficient level of service to customers. Similarly, hospitality managers need to be careful when selecting suppliers, to find those that consistently provide the highest quality product and services at the lowest cost. Finally, hospitality managers need to carefully monitor and assess the processes involved in staging hospitality experiences to identify opportunities for efficiency, quality improvement, and cost reduction. All the above implies that to stage profitable hospitality experiences, as a hospitality manager you need to be able to formulate and manage the processes associated with the hospitality experiences. You need to identify the performance measures that let you achieve the targets that you or others set in the design phase of the hospitality experience.

The unpredictable nature of hospitality experiences, explained by the involvement and interaction of customers, sets them set aside from manufactured goods. Because of the inseparability of production and consumption, hospitality managers are in direct contact with their customers and so need to be competent in different areas than their counterparts from the production industry. We will elaborate on this in the next chapter.

Summary

▶ The American Society for Quality's definition of quality leaves room for interpretation on which features and characteristics of hospitality experiences have the ability to satisfy guests.

▶ Quality can be defined and measured in terms of:
- customer satisfaction
- perceived quality
- satisfiers and dissatisfiers

▶ Measuring quality is crucial for companies in the process of monitoring preset satisfaction targets. At the same time, it is just as important for companies to receive vital information from customers on the various components that make up the hospitality experience, as this will allow them to improve their product.

▶ In the hospitality experience context, the design process arranges all relevant activities across time and place, clearly indicating the input and output of each activity, as well as the actors required. These processes are normally formalised as standard operating procedures (SOPs).

▶ Hospitality organisations set internal quality and cost targets to pro-actively adjust both the tangible and intangible components of the hospitality experience in the event of flaws or shortcomings.

▶ Resources must support the staging processes for hospitality experiences:
- the setting or context of the hospitality experience
- technology
- people

▶ Hospitality organisations incur various costs at different stages of the hospitality experience:
- prevention costs
- appraisal costs
- failure costs

8

Food for thought

As you learned in this chapter, quality lies in the eyes of the beholder, and as a result it can be defined and measured in different ways. When you look at the contents of this chapter, consider the following topics as a starting point for further discussion:

1   During the selection procedure for studying hotel management, potential students are often asked why they want to pursue a career in hospitality management. The vast majority say that they want to work with people. Hospitality organisations need to ensure that they strike the right balance when selecting their staff. What other capabilities would you look for when selecting staff?

2   Organisations do not make their own reputations; customers give it to them. Review sites, such as Tripadvisor or Zagat, are important shapers of reputation, as they make customer reviews readily available to a worldwide audience. Although companies cannot influence *what* their customers write, they can of course influence *the hospitality experience that they write about*. How can hospitality organisations actively encourage their customers to share their positive reviews? What kind of examples can you come up with?

3   Waiting time is an example of a quality target that we presented in this chapter. Can you provide three other examples of internal targets that hospitality organisations could set to measure the quality of their hospitality experience? How would you translate these targets to specific metrics?

8

9

Competencies and leadership

Xander Lub, Hans Breuker, and Lesley Tomaszewski

This final chapter focuses on the management of hospitality experiences and hospitality professionals. It reviews various ways of looking at leadership and the contextual factors that influence leadership. It serves as a basis for discussing what kind of management and leadership is required of hospitality managers and culminates in a list of the main management competencies that any hospitality leader should master.

9

The age of change

Roeland Vos is the former President of Starwood Hotels and Resorts for the Europe, Africa, and Middle East region. As of 2001, he has led the operation of nearly 250 hotels across 60 countries for over a decade. A Dutch national, he started his career with Starwood Hotels in 1982 as a Management Trainee at the Sheraton Brussels Hotel and Towers.

Starwood is a leading global, lifestyle hospitality company with nine distinct brands, including Sheraton, Le Méridien, The Luxury Collection, and St. Regis. It has a reputation for brand-building and ground-breaking innovations such as the Westin Heavenly Bed or, more recently, the inception of the Aloft brand, which shook up the mid-market segment just as W Hotels Worldwide changed the luxury lifestyle hospitality space.

For Roeland, the hotel business is the ultimate people business – and one that never stands still. There is the impact of globalisation with more 'mega-travellers' than ever before, each year going to more places around the world. The rise of the middle class will see millions of travellers from emerging markets such as China and India; Generation Y, the 20-30-year olds that grew up with travel, will make up the majority of customers in the next 5-10 years. Furthermore, connectivity is already changing everything we do today and resulting in even more travel.

Together, these global trends present huge opportunities. To make the most of them, Roeland believes that it is essential to deliver even more personalised experiences. Ultimately, people want to be treated as special and unique, across geographies, cultures and income levels. Especially in a digital world, with innovations that allow us to get closer to our guests, there is still nothing quite like the human touch.

Roeland, 'To succeed in the hotel business requires the ability to embrace change, teamwork and a forward-thinking attitude. With commonsense and passion, all this will take you a long way in an industry that promises an exciting future.'

9.1   Hospitality management as a profession

The previous eight chapters provided an overview of almost all the ingredients needed to stage a hospitality experience. We defined hospitality experiences and explored various ways they can be used to create (monetary) value both in the context of the hospitality industry and beyond its borders. We also explored a wide range of business models that are based on the staging of specific hospitality experiences, the vast array of environments in which hospitality experiences are and can be staged, and the history and future of the hospitality industry. Finally, the last three chapters established a range of specific reference points to consider in the process of designing, delivering, and supporting hospitality experiences.

Now, in this final chapter, we return to a key issue put forward in the first chapter of this book. Hospitality management is not simply a combination of two words. It refers to a specific profession. Those entering this profession need to understand all the ins and outs of the industry and what it takes to create successful hospitality experiences. They also need to be able to take the (operational) lead in the industry and make the design of the experiences come to life. In other words, hospitality managers need to be able to lead others in staging successful hospitality experiences.

Hospitality management

Specific profession

As Roeland Vos suggested at the start of this chapter, what makes a person a successful leader in the hospitality industry today is far more complex than it was 30 years ago. Earlier chapters have shown that the same applies to other industries and environments, and being able to stage appropriate hospitality experiences plays a crucial role in those contexts too. The economic environment has become increasingly competitive and guests, customers, and employees put increasing individual demands on service experiences. Hospitality has become a generic management competency and what is expected of a hospitality manager has evolved.

All this means that hospitality management, that is 'taking the lead' in staging hospitality experiences, most certainly is more than two words put together. Therefore, the remainder of this chapter focuses on exploring the specific reference points for leadership and management in a hospitality context and trying to answer the question, what does it take to excel in the hospitality management profession?

To set the stage for answering that question, the next section focuses on management and leadership in generic terms. What do those concepts actually mean? What is a leader? What does it take to 'take the lead'? What is the difference between leadership and management? Using the answers to those answers and relating them to the previous eight chapters, the final section lists ten main competencies that any hospitality leader should develop and master to be successful.

9.2   Leadership and management

The quality of leadership is a key determinant for the success or lack of success of organisations. You could argue that this is true for businesses in any industry, not just the hospitality industry. Indeed, many authors and

Quality of leadership

Leadership experts refer to leadership as a key ingredient of success. However, what exactly is meant by the word leadership? What are the attributes of a great leader and leadership? And how is leadership similar to or different from the related word 'management'?

'A business short on capital can borrow money and one with a poor location can move. But a business short on leadership has little chance of survival.'

— Warren Bennis

If you enter 'leadership' or 'management' into any internet search engine, the number of hits is staggering. A wide variety of definitions, theories, and famous quotes will appear. Arguably, this variety causes more confusion than understanding. The terms leadership and management seem to be used differently in many circumstances. They seem to refer to an almost endless collection of aspects and attributes. Both these concepts bear an interesting resemblance to the concept of hospitality. Nearly all of us often use the words hospitality, leadership, and management, attaching a specific meaning to them. Yet, it is not a given that we all attach the same meaning and distinguish between leadership and management in the same way.

Therefore, it is important to explore the relationship between leadership and management. Consequently, this section provides a brief overview of the history of leadership theories, with special emphasis on the most important current views. This is followed by a description of some key challenges that leaders face in the society and business world of today and tomorrow in a world often referred to as 'the global village'.

Leadership versus management
Leadership and management are definitely related, but they also have important distinctions. Management can be seen as representing the overall concept, whereas leadership is an aspect involved in successfully managing an organisation, a business, a process, and so on. In this context, leadership usually refers to specific activities involved in managing, such as commanding, controlling, steering and organising, aimed at influencing the people working in the organisation.

Management However, management and leadership are often used to represent two contrasting styles of being a 'leader'. As Table 9.1 illustrates, these two words convey the differences between types of leaders. Obviously, when used in this way, leadership is no longer an aspect of management, but rather a new perspective on what successful or appropriate management entails.

TABLE 9.1 Management versus leadership

Management	Leadership
Managers do things right	Leaders do the right things
Managers work in the system	Leaders work on the system
Managers think in term of improvements	Leaders think in term of change
Managers think incrementally	Leaders think radically
Managers do things by the book	Leaders write the book
Managers use power to get compliance to stated goals	Leaders get people to make goals part of their value system and way of working
Managers delegate tasks and give advice, facilitate and overview the work	Leaders are the first to take action and the one to take the risks, they are active in most tasks

Source: adapted from Mullins, 2010

Leadership theories

Over the years, many theories on leadership have emerged, especially on the differences between ineffective and effective leadership. As the example on authentic leadership illustrates, there is no undisputed answer to the question, what is effective leadership?

Authentic leadership

Effective leadership

● hbr.org

Discovering your authentic leadership

During the past 50 years, leadership scholars have conducted more than 1,000 studies in an attempt to determine the definitive styles, characteristics, or personality traits of great leaders. None of these studies has produced a clear profile of the ideal leader. Thank goodness. If scholars had produced a cookie-cutter leadership style, individuals would be forever trying to imitate it. They would make themselves into personae, not people, and others would see through them immediately.

After interviewing 125 CEOs, we believe we understand why more than 1,000 studies have not produced a profile of an ideal leader. Analysing 3,000 pages of transcripts, our team was startled to see that these people did not identify any universal characteristics, traits, skills, or styles that led to their success. Rather, their leadership emerged from their life stories. Consciously and subconsciously, they were constantly testing themselves through real-world experiences and reframing their life stories to understand who they were at their core. In doing so, they discovered the purpose of their leadership and learned that being authentic made them more effective.

Analysing 3,000 pages of transcripts, our team was startled to see you do not have to be born with specific characteristics or traits of a leader. Leadership emerges from your life story.

These findings are extremely encouraging. You do not have to be born with the specific characteristics or traits of a leader. Instead, you can discover

9

your potential right now. As an interviewee said, 'All of us have the spark of leadership in us, whether it is in business, in government, or as a nonprofit volunteer. The challenge is to understand ourselves well enough to discover where we can use our leadership gifts to serve others.'

Discovering your authentic leadership requires a commitment to developing yourself. Like musicians and athletes, you must devote yourself to a lifetime of realising your potential. Most people Kroger CEO David Dillon has seen become good leaders were self-taught. Dillon said, 'The advice I give to individuals in our company is not to expect the company to hand you a development plan. You need to take responsibility for developing yourself.'

February 2007
By Bill George, Peter Sims, Andrew N. McLean,
and Diana Mayer, adapted

Reviewing some of the theories shows that our interpretation of successful or appropriate leadership has changed over time.

Trait theory
Trait theory focuses on the personality of the leader. In the 19th century, the view emerged that leaders are born, not made. Later, from the 1940s on, this view was expanded to look at particular personalities of leaders. Based on trait theory, good leaders are assumed to possess certain important basic qualities (also called traits). This view is still widely accepted. For instance, the 'Big Five' list (Table 9.2) is often used to highlight five key traits **Big Five** to distinguish between effective and ineffective leaders. Ultimately, the logic of these theories is that successful leaders share a specific personality profile, which can be described based on specific traits.

9

TABLE 9.2 The 'Big Five' traits applied to leadership

Extraversion:	**outgoing/energetic** instead of solitary/reserved
Conscientiousness:	**efficient/organised** instead of easygoing/careless
Mental stability:	**secure/confident** instead of sensitive/nervous
Agreeableness:	**friendly/compassionate** instead of cold/unkind
Openness to experience:	**inventive/curious** instead of consistent/cautious

Source: adapted from Zhao & Seibert, 2006.

Behavioural and situational leadership theories
Behavioural and situational leadership theories do not dispute that specific qualities or traits are important for leaders. However, these theories point to the fact that qualities or traits in themselves do not indicate how a leader is supposed to act in specific, different situations. They focus on what types of behaviour are required to meet the needs of a specific situation and how to stimulate and enable employees to perform well in those circumstances.

Managerial Grid The *Managerial Grid* by Robert Blake and Jane Mouton (1964) is an influential model from this group of theorists (Figure 9.1). Blake and Mouton suggest that leaders must have concern for the job to be done and the production targets to be met (focus on task) as well as concern for the employees

FIGURE 9.1 Managerial grid

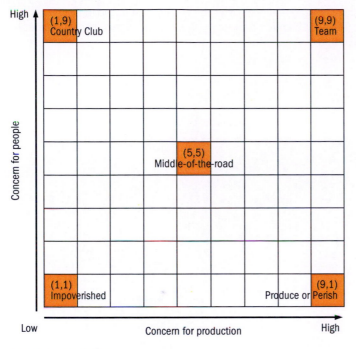

Source: Blake & Mouton (1985)

who perform the tasks related to that job (focus on people). An effective leader should always balance both aspects. If a leader neglects both, he will obviously be ineffective. If he focuses too much on the people component and neglects the task component, the organisation will lack purpose. Similarly, if he focuses on the task component without paying enough attention to the people component, the organisation will not be able to count on the commitment of its employees. Ever since Blake and Mouton introduced their model, these two dimensions of leadership, concern for task or production and for people, have played an important role in discussions about appropriate leadership.

Many discussions focus on the fact that different situations may require different behaviours from leaders. For one thing, the employee's nature and the qualities need to be taken into account. Secondly, the state of the organisation as a whole needs to be taken into account. To illustrate this, imagine two businesses. Business 1 is currently making huge profits, but staff turnover in the past year is higher than ever. Many leavers indicate that their reason for leaving was the unpleasant atmosphere in the company. Business 2 is not making any profit, but the staff is happy and almost everyone feels that their company is like a happy family. They have no plans nor desire to leave. From a leadership perspective, it is clear that the balance in concern for production and concern for people requires urgent attention in both businesses, but definitely not in the same way.

9

Situational aspects

Many other theories addressing the situational aspects of leadership have appeared over the years. The logic of most is similar to that in the model by Paul Hersey and Ken Blanchard (1988), which we first discussed in Chapter 7. To remind us, Figure 9.2 shows how four follower profiles require four different leadership behaviours.

FIGURE 9.2   Model of Hersey and Blanchard

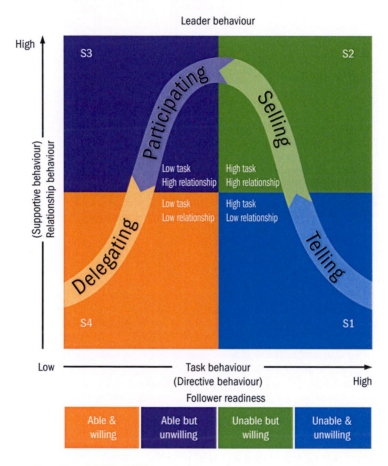

Source: Hersey & Blanchard (1988)

In Chapter 7, this model focused on types of feedback. Here, it is important to note that the same logic applies to all other aspects of leadership. According to this model, the overall style of leadership must fit the situation and the individual employee (also called follower). The choice of most appropriate style is based on the follower's level of readiness (also called the follower's maturity level). This combines two dimensions, ability and willingness. Table 9.3 shows how combining the two dimensions leads to four possible categories of employees and the appropriate style of leadership for each of them.

TABLE 9.3 Clarification of the Hersey and Blanchard (1988) model

Category of employees	Style of leadership
Unable and unwilling (or insecure)	Telling: the leader basically tells the follower what to do and how to do it
Unable but willing	Selling: the leader encourages the follower and provides him with information and direction
Able but unwilling (or insecure)	Participating: the leader takes part in the work activities, sharing decisions and responsibilities with the rest
Able and willing	Delegating: the leader transfers most responsibilities to the team, staying in the background and monitoring progress

Transactional and transformational leadership
A final example of a leadership theory worth mentioning here was first introduced by James McGregor Burns (1978), who made a distinction between two 'extreme' kinds of leadership; transactional leadership and transformational leadership.

Transactional leadership emphasises the importance of a clear hierarchy in the organisation. This type of leader interprets the relationship between himself, as leader, and his employees or followers as an exchange (transaction). The leader provides a salary and the employee offers his skills and efforts in exchange for that salary. Ultimately, this interpretation of leadership means that the leader has all the authority and provides for a specific position or role for the employee in the organisation.

Transactional leadership

Obviously, this perspective on leadership is based on the view that people are primarily externally motivated. The leader is seen as the person in command, like a general directing his troops. Using reward and punishment, based on a system of rules, is seen as an appropriate and effective motivational technique.

In contrast, transformational leadership emphasises the importance of a sense of connection between all organisation levels. This type of leader interprets the relationship between himself, as leader, and his employees or followers (note that the word employee is probably less logical here than the word follower) as based on trust and aimed at mutual development (transformation).

Transformational leadership

9

This type of leadership is based on the view that people are internally motivated. They want to perform well and develop as people, and this objective is not necessarily related directly to only providing a reward of salary in return. The leader is seen as someone with great vision and charisma, who shows new possibilities and inspires others to follow him. The leader is seen as a coach, a mentor, who treats each follower as an individual and even stimulates them to develop their own leadership abilities.

Clearly, these two styles of leadership are miles apart. They can best be considered to represent two extremes of a continuum. Positions in between, or combinations of elements, are possible and will be seen more often in real life than the two extremes. In cooperation with various others,

Continuum

Bernard Bass further built on this theory in developing the full range leadership model (see Figure 9.3). It shows a continuum shaped by two extremes, but the actual leadership styles identified on this continuum are intermediate styles, also based on combinations of elements from the two extremes.

FIGURE 9.3 Full range leadership model

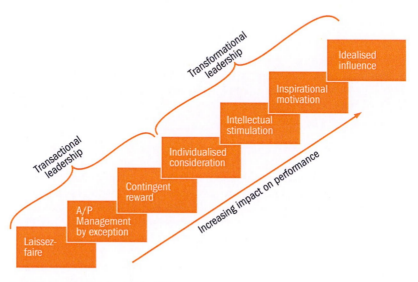

Source: Bass & Avolio (2002); Bass & Riggio (2006)

Table 9.4 provides a more detailed explanation of how the leadership styles mentioned by this model can be characterised from the perspective of both transactional leadership and transformational leadership.

TABLE 9.4 Transactional and transformational leadership styles

Transformational leadership styles	Transactional leadership styles
• Idealised influence: serves as a role model, provides vision and a sense of mission, gains respect and trust • Inspirational motivation: expresses purpose, communicates expectations, inspires by providing meaning and challenge to followers' work • Intellectual stimulation: stimulates followers' efforts of innovation and careful problem solving • Individualised consideration: pays special attention to individual needs, coaches, listens effectively	• Contingent reward: promises rewards for good performance, recognises accomplishments • Management by exception (active): actively monitors for mistakes, and takes corrective action • Management by exception (passive): intervenes only if mistakes are made • Laissez-faire: ignores responsibilities, avoids making decisions

Source: adapted from Bass & Riggio, 2006; Robbins & Judge, 2009.

Obviously, this perspective on leadership styles, based on considering transactional and transformational leadership as two archetypes, bears a close resemblance to the discussion on differences between management and leadership (Table 9.1) earlier in this section. Transactional leadership styles and the 'management style' of leading are very similar, as are transformational leadership styles and the 'leadership style' of leading.

'Management style' of leading

'Leadership style' of leading

In present day management and leadership theories and literature, these two styles of 'taking the lead' and 'leading others' lie at the core of intense discussions and extensive research. Interestingly, these discussions closely resemble the discussions on how to interpret and define hospitality, as conveyed in Chapter 1. Once again, we see heated debate with people taking up extreme positions, but, simultaneously, we can see how many people are looking for ways to make optimal use of both perspectives. Whereas some portray transactional leadership as old fashioned and outdated, others argue that it still contains valuable elements for getting things done professionally, effectively and efficiently. However, transformational leadership should not be ignored in facing the challenges of the 21st century. Personal commitment, finding meaning and fulfilment in working life, and a sense of connectedness are clearly powerful motivators in modern organisations.

9.3 Hospitality competencies

As today's business world becomes ever more complex and connected, the importance of good leadership is greater than ever before. This is true for all kinds of organisations and businesses. As the previous chapters have shown, the context shaped by the hospitality industry, and applying hospitality principles beyond the borders of this industry, is also increasingly more complex and connected. Hospitality leaders of today and tomorrow will face a number of the challenges mentioned above. Thus, they will have to make sure they apply the various elements and views of management and leadership, as discussed above, in a smart way, depending on the situation and circumstances at hand.

This final section briefly revisits some main challenges hospitality leaders are facing and their relation to management and leadership. It draws on the material discussed in previous chapters to identify ten management competencies that any hospitality leader will have to develop and master to be successful.

Main challenges

Main challenges
- *Technology*. Although the essence of staging hospitality experiences remains the same, recent technological advances are no less than revolutionary. We have come to live in a different world. The internet and social media have changed the rules of the game, in the hospitality industry as well. Reading review sites and posting and twittering about experiences have become the basis for the choices of many customers. This forces hospitality leaders to join the game. Finding ways to use technological possibilities to their advantage is clearly a main challenge facing hospitality leaders.

Technology

- *Ethical issues*. Doing business in an ethically responsible way has become a central consideration for all industries, including the hospitality industry. This is expressed through concepts like corporate social responsibility, the People-Planet-Profit model and in concrete certification

Ethical issues

schemes like Green Key and Green Globe. Some hospitality leaders will get involved because of a sincere wish to contribute to dealing with these global challenges. Others will be forced to do so by their stakeholders. Regardless, successfully dealing with ethical issues is definitely the second main challenge facing all hospitality leaders.

Cross-cultural differences

- *Cross-cultural differences*. In today's global village, hospitality organisations will have more and more relations with people from other cultures, both as customers and staff. Obviously, management and leadership by hospitality leaders will have to adapt accordingly. The following quote from Han de Windt, general manager of Le Méridien Al Khobar, illustrates this challenge:

'Having worked in eight different countries throughout my career, I can safely say that Western leadership principles should be adapted to each country's cultural practices.
In the Netherlands, we are raised with a great sense of social justice and are living in a very open and direct society. We have an opinion on every subject and want to be heard. Even in nearby Belgium our Dutch style of managing our associates needs to be adapted to a more diplomatic style, far less direct and more one-on-one talks.'

'Personally, I believe that openness to different cultures and religions, the willingness to adapt to local circumstances and the flexibility of those in a leadership position are the most important tools to succeed in hotel management.'

Generational differences

- *Generational differences*. Clearly, hospitality is experienced and created by people. This also means that staging successful hospitality experiences requires hospitality leaders to 'lead others', their staff members, and stage experiences together.

However, equally clear is that different generations have different aspirations and expectations. This is illustrated by the following excerpt from a paper dedicated to the differences in work values by various generations.

> '... managers from Boomers have a very low opinion of Generation X and Millennials. Managers from Boomers think that younger employees have no work ethic, and they are "slackers." The Boomers believe that even though younger employees still have a lot to learn and do not really take ownership, they are after recognition and promotions. The Boomers' despise this attitude. In addition, findings also suggest that the Boomers' employees do not have very high opinions of their Gen X managers. The Boomers employees think that their Gen X managers do not have the experience to manage and Xers do not respect Boomers' life experiences. Boomers also indicated that Xers lack people skills and rely on technology too much.'
> Gursoy, Maier & Chi, 2008, p. 453

Whereas the 'baby boom' generation (now in their 50s or 60s) might want security and steadiness, Generation X (now in their 30s and 40s) are looking for fair organisational policies and opportunities for professional development, and Generation Y (also called the Einstein generation; now in their 20s) want opportunities for personal development, challenges and fun. Once again, hospitality leaders will have to account for these differences and act accordingly.

Differences

● Jochems, 2011

Club Einstein – an example of bottom-up leadership

Bilderberg Hotel Group commissioned a study on generational differences among employees of their company in 2009. The results clearly indicated that particularly Generation Y had lower commitment to the organisation as well as higher intention to leave. Considering the cost (money, energy and time) of staff turnover, the hotel group decided to install a think-tank of Generation X and Y employees to address this issue. This group named itself Club Einstein and was given free rein to develop new practices and ideas that could increase commitment. The group's ideas improved the commitment of the employees and raised the quality of leadership of supervisors. For example, Club Einstein's 24 hours @ Bilderberg programme allows employees to spend a day working at another hotel in the group, in a department of their choice. The programme was very successful, and beside the commitment effect it also raised the level of personal and professional development as well as mutual learning between employees of different hotels in the group. General Managers are now visiting Club Einstein think tanks to gather new ideas!

This shows that leadership is not necessarily linked to the formal leaders in a company. Anyone with a great idea and the power to move others can demonstrate leadership.

Adapted

9

Ownership structures

- *Ownership structures*. Rapid change in ownership structures is one of the most dynamic aspects of today's hospitality industry. Especially hotels, even hotel chains, are frequently bought, sold, split up or combined into bigger conglomerates. The owners of the building(s) are less involved with everyday operations and management contracts and franchise concepts shape the context in which hospitality leaders operate. To be successful, hospitality leaders will have to build and maintain fruitful relationships with all parties involved. Stakeholder management has clearly become a main challenge.

Stakeholder management

Keys to stakeholder management are trust, openness and mutual respect

As a General Manager, you not only deal with associates, guests, suppliers, head office, but also with owners. In most cases our hotel company is not the owner of the hotel nor do we rent the building, but rather we run the hotel for the owner's account. This means that the owner carries the biggest risk of a downturn in business.

Therefore, key in the relations to an owner is trust, openness and mutual respect. Trust from an owner that we do the best to run his property, openness from our side to keep him informed how business is going and how the forecasts are developing. Mutual respect as we appreciate each other's knowledge and expertise.

It is essential to develop the trust to get the freedom to run the operation without too much interference of the owner. We inform owners in quarterly meetings about the results, answer their questions and discuss major projects. The management contract determines which information has to be given and which decisions need the owner's approval, but it can help to go beyond that and keep them informed about anything that might be of interest. This openness helps in getting their buy-in for any changes/projects when needed.

The most gratifying operator-owner relation is one where the owner is convinced that our hotel company is the best partner to work with and this leads to the development of new hotel projects together. That is what we are aiming for!

Kurt Renold, Area Manager Starwood Hotels, the Netherlands

Developing and mastering the right competencies

Competencies

Competencies are best defined as the knowledge, skills, and abilities/attitude that people must develop and master to be able to perform their tasks in the best possible way (Boytazis, 1982). The logic behind the competency-based approach is that individuals need to develop and master specific combinations of competencies (knowledge, skills and abilities/attitudes) to perform tasks and take on responsibilities. They cannot rely simply on their natural ability and intelligence to perform any task at hand (McClelland, 1973).

Many organisations in the hospitality industry use the competency-based approach to development to help employees improve their performance and, ultimately, increase the productivity and efficiency of the organisation (Burgoyne 1993; Hoffman, 1999).

Developing my competencies

Since graduating I've just spent my first six months on the job, and last week I had my first performance appraisal. I was kind of nervous, but in the end I had a very nice chat with my supervisor. In preparation for the appraisal interview my supervisor and I both filled out a competency scan about me. During our conversation we discussed the results. Looking at my competencies made it clear what I can develop further in my current job and how I personally can

develop further not only in my area of expertise but as a person altogether.

We decided that I could get more responsibility in areas of my work that I'm proficient in, and in which areas I need support and coaching to further develop myself.

Jack, 22 years old, Food & Beverage supervisor,
Bilderberg Hotels

Many regard developing competencies through coursework, internships, trainings and coaching as a prerequisite for success on the job market and a successful career.

Probably the best way to conclude the discussion on staging and managing successful hospitality experiences, as presented in this book, is to identify and elaborate on the crucial competencies you have to develop and master to be able to 'take the lead'.

- *Competency 1: Creating value through hospitality/staging hospitality experiences*
Of all hospitality competencies, this one immediately sets the stage. It refers directly to developing and mastering a hospitality mind-set to create

Mind-set

value. A hospitality mind-set requires you to interact with all stakeholders, not just customers, in a positive and emotionally engaging way in order to create the (welcoming) atmosphere (Kerfoot, 2009) that lies at the core of staging hospitality experiences. This requires you to develop a certain type of personality (friendliness, empathy, leadership, hospitality, and responsibility), along with the motivation and self-knowledge to further develop your hospitality mind-set. This mind-set allows you to set up and maintain authentic relationships with others, while accounting for the rules and norms that apply to the situation at hand.

Staging hospitality experiences

Thinking and behaving based on a hospitality mind-set means conducting business from the perspective of someone who experiences hospitality, for example a customer. It implies really getting to know the people you will be conducting business with and basing decisions on how to serve them in a way that truly adds value for them. This means ensuring that all stakeholders have positive interactions with your organisation which, again, means taking their expectations, needs and characteristics into account.

Obviously, you cannot have a hospitality mind-set without knowing and understanding the practices and cultures of hospitality companies worldwide or being aware of relevant trends and developments both in and outside the industry. Furthermore, creating added value refers to all stakeholders, including staff, management, owners and other relevant parties.

Today's hospitality leader is a true global citizen, culturally sensitive and aware of his responsibilities and the consequences of his daily choices for people everywhere.

- *Competency 2: Developing vision based on changes and trends in the external environment and developing relationships/networks/chains*

Vision

Besides a hospitality mind-set, having a clear vision is equally important. Hospitality leadership requires insight into the impact that the complexities of the external environment has on your organisation. Understanding that, ultimately, the market belongs to the consumer is crucial. The ability to apply existing hospitality concepts to new contexts and develop new concepts based on this understanding is a requirement for success.

In today's global village, the market place and distribution channels are changing and becoming more cross-cultural than ever before. This implies the need for being able to use solid knowledge of cross-cultural issues to analyse trends and make changes that will support your organisation and your stakeholders. It also implies the ability to conduct research and propose changes based upon thorough trend analysis, not on fads.

- *Competency 3: Analysing policy issues, translating them into policy goals and alternatives, and preparing decision-making*

Planning

Proper and solid scenario planning is important to the future of any business in or outside the hospitality industry. In an ever-changing and increasingly interconnected environment, the ability to position your organisation according to transparent decision-making processes that account for the impact on all relevant stakeholders is crucial to success and survival.

- *Competency 4: Applying HRM to organisational strategy*

It goes without saying that appropriate human resources management is crucial to any business model for staging hospitality experiences. The hospitality industry and applying hospitality principles are built upon creating the right interaction between hosts and guests. This not only applies to the relation between hospitality provider and paying customer, but also to the relation between a hospitality business or manager and its or his employees. Hospitality leaders apply HRM based on the awareness that hospitality staff are both host and guest – host to their customers, guest to their organisation. Ultimately, the objective of any HRM decision by hospitality leaders is to help staff thrive in both roles. Only then can you ensure that employee behaviour truly contributes to creating added value by staging hospitality experiences.

Human resources

- *Competency 5: Designing, managing, and improving organisational processes*

Staging hospitality experiences can only be successful in creating added value if this is supported and facilitated by appropriate organisational processes and systems. Hospitality leaders need to design, manage and improve these processes and systems. The functioning of existing processes and systems needs to be monitored and reshaped where required. A full understanding and application of quality and operations management principles and techniques is crucial to doing this.

Processes and systems

- *Competency 6: Analysing financial and legal aspects as well as the internal processes and external environment of an organisation*

Having full insight into critical environmental factors that influence the functioning of your organisation is essential. Decisions by hospitality leaders need to be based on information collected from various sources (management information, quality standards, financial constraints and regulations) and then processing this information into something meaningful for your specific organisation and stakeholders.

Financial constraints and regulations

- *Competency 7: Developing, implementing, and evaluating a process of change*

In the hospitality setting, hospitality leaders work in an ever-changing complex world that is certainly more international and multicultural than it was five years ago, and probably more so than many other settings. Hospitality leaders need to simultaneously develop new hospitality concepts and apply existing concepts to new contexts. This makes a full understanding and application of change management principles essential to success. It implies not only the ability to base decisions on the interests of all stakeholders, but also the ability to involve all stakeholders in change processes and manage any conflicting interests that may arise along the way.

Change management

- *Competency 8: Initiating and creating entrepreneurial hospitality concepts, products, and services*

It goes without saying that developing new hospitality concepts and applying existing concepts to new contexts needs to be based on a full understanding of how to design and implement the staging of new hospitality experiences. Hospitality leaders need to take the lead in this on-going process of partial or complete modifications to the organisation's portfolio. Entrepreneurial concepts, services, and products should be based on a

Design and implement

9

thorough understanding of the ever-changing market, opportunities and avenues to maximise long-term profitability.

- *Competency 9: Communicating effectively*

Obviously, mastering the previous eight competencies would be impossible without the ability to communicate effectively. Hospitality leaders must be able to build relationships with various types of people with various roles and responsibilities, inside and beyond the borders of their own organisation. They need to create networks of relationships on three levels: the individual, the intra-organisational, and the inter-organisational levels. Ultimately, creating and maintaining these relationships is crucial to the hospitality leader's personal, professional and business success.

Create networks of relationships

- *Competency 10: Self-reflection*

As with any other type of leader, finally, the success of any hospitality leader depends on his ability to be self-reflective and to develop and adapt himself accordingly. Obviously, the willingness to reflect on one's own actions and to learn from them actions and associated results is important to the development of any professional. However, in the context of people-oriented industries like the hospitality industry, this competency is especially crucial.

Develop and adapt

This concludes the discussion on the hospitality leader's main competencies. It highlights, once again that in an industry context founded on adding value through staging hospitality experiences, thus through interaction between people, living up to expectations is the key to success. The authors and editors sincerely hope this book will help you do so.

9

Summary

▶ Hospitality management is far more than a combination of two words. It is a profession.
Leadership and management are related but different concepts.

▶ Over the years, many theories on leadership have emerged, such as:
- trait theory
- behavioural and situational leadership theories
- transactional and transformational leadership

▶ Some main challenges facing hospitality leaders are:
- technological advances
- ethical issues
- cross-cultural differences
- generational differences
- changing ownership structures

▶ Competencies are a combination of:
- knowledge
- skills
- abilities/attitudes

▶ The most important competencies that hospitality managers/leaders need to master are:
- creating value through hospitality/staging hospitality experiences
- developing a vision based on changes and trends in the external environment and developing relationships/networks/chains
- analysing policy issues, translating them into policy goals and alternatives, and preparing decision-making
- applying HRM related to organisational strategy
- designing, managing, and improving organisational processes
- analysing financial and legal aspects as well as internal processes and external environment of an organisation
- developing, implementing, and evaluating a process of change
- initiating and creating entrepreneurial concepts, products, and services
- effective communication
- self-reflection

9

Food for thought

This chapter discussed the concepts of management and leadership in relation to hospitality management and taking the lead in staging successful hospitality experiences. It established the ten most important competencies that any hospitality manager/leader should develop and master. The following questions, challenges and topics could serve as interesting starting points for further discussion:

1 What is the difference between management and leadership?

2 How have leadership theories developed over time? What do you think are the most important characteristics of a hospitality manager, also according to the content of the previous eight chapters?

3 As the authors and editors of this book, we would like you to take on one last key challenge. Assess how well you master the ten hospitality competencies. Which aspects, knowledge, skills and abilities/attitudes do you need to develop further?

9

References

Chapter 1

Brotherton, B. (1999). Towards a definitive view of the nature of hospitality and hospitality management. *International Journal of Contemporary Hospitality Management, 11(4),* 165-173.

Brotherton, B. & Wood, R. (2000). Hospitality and hospitality management. In C. Lashley & A. Morrison (Eds.), *In search of hospitality: Theoretical perspectives and debates.* Oxford: Butterworth-Heinemann.

Kerr, J. (2007). 'Welcome the coming and speed the parting guest': hospitality in twelfth-century England. *Journal of Medieval History, 33,* 130-146.

KPI Hospitality Service (2009). An Introduction to Mystery Guest Reports

Lashley, C. (2000). Towards a theoretical understanding. In C. Lashley & A. Morrison (Eds.), *In search of hospitality: Theoretical perspectives and debates.* Oxford: Butterworth-Heinemann.

Lashley, C. (2008). Studying Hospitality: Insights from Social Sciences. *Scandinavian Journal of Hospitality and Tourism 8(1),* 69-84.

Lashley, C., Lynch, P. & Morrison, A., Eds. (2007). *Hospitality: A Social Lens.* Oxford: Elsevier.

Morrison, A. & O'Gorman, K. (2006). Hospitality studies: Liberating the power of the mind. Paper presented, *CAUTHE 2006,* Melbourne.

O'Connor, D. (2005). Towards a new interpretation of 'hospitality'. *International Journal of Contemporary Hospitality Management, 17(3),* 267-271.

O'Gorman, K. (2009). Origins of the commercial hospitality industry: from the fanciful to factual. *International Journal of Contemporary Hospitality Management, 21(7),* 777-790.

Pine, J. & Gilmore, J. (1999). *The Experience Economy: Work Is Theatre & Every Business a Stage.* Boston: Harvard Business School Press.

Slattery, P. (2002). Finding the Hospitality Industry. *Journal of Hospitality, Leisure, Sport and Tourism Education, 1(1),* 19-28.

Chapter 2

Barsky, J. (2013). How Guests Select Hotels Around the World – Global Results Retrieved 27 May, 2013, from http://corp.marketmetrix.com/how-guests-select-hotels-around-the-world-global-results/

Brotherton, B., & Mooney, S. (1992). Yield management – progress and prospects. *International Journal of Hospitality Management, 11(1),* 23-32.

Collins, M., & Parsa, H. (2006). Pricing strategies to maximize revenues in the lodging industry. *International Journal of Hospitality Management, 25(1),* 91-107.

Cross, R. (1997). *Revenue Management: hard-core tactics for market domination.* New York: Broadway Books.

Gilmore, J., & Pine, J. (2002). Differentiating hospitality operations via experiences: why selling services is not enough. *The Cornell Hotel and Restaurant Administration Quarterly, 43(3),* 87-96.

Grönroos, C. (1987). Developing the service offering – A Source of Competitive Advantage. In C. Surprenant (Ed.), *Add Value to Your Service* (pp. 81-85). Chicago: American Marketing Association.

Kohler, T., Matzler, K., & Füller, J. (2009). Avatar-based innovation: Using virtual worlds for real-world innovation. *Technovation, 29*(6–7), 395-407.

Kotler, P., Bowen, J., & Makens, J. (2003). *Marketing for hospitality and tourism* (Third ed.). Upper Saddle River, New Jersey: Pearson Education Inc.

Ng, I. (2008). *The Pricing and Revenue Management of Services: a strategic approach* (Vol. 36). Abingdon: Routledge.

Normann, R. (1984). *Service Management: Strategy and Leadership in Service Businesses*. New York, NY: John Wiley & Sons.

Piercy, N., Cravens, D., & Lane, N. (2010). Thinking strategically about pricing decisions. *Journal of Business Strategy, 31*(5), 38-48.

Pine, J.. & Gilmore, J. (1999). *The Experience Economy: Work Is Theatre & Every Business a Stage*. Boston: Harvard Business School Press.

Porter, M. (1985). *Competitive Advantage: Creating and sustaining superior performance*. New York: The Free Press.

Prahalad, C., & Ramaswamy, V. (2004). Co-creating unique value with customers. *Strategy & Leadership, 32*(3), 4-9.

Shoemaker, S., & Mattila, A. (2009). Pricing in services. In V. R. Rao (Ed.), *Handbook of Pricing Research in Marketing* (pp. 535-565). Cheltenham, UK: Edward Elgar Publishing Limited.

Weatherford, L., & Bodily, S. (1992). A Taxonomy and Research Overview of Perishable-Asset Revenue Management: Yield Management, Overbooking, and Pricing. *Operations Research, 40*(5), 831-844.

Chapter 3

Accor (2007). *Reaching for the impossible, 1967-2007*. Paris: Le cherche midi.

Bhaduri, Sayoni, 'Budget means business', *Express Hospitality*, 18/10/2012. http://www.expresshospitality.com/columns/623-budget-means-business (acc. 07/12/2012).

Ferdinand and Wesner, 'The International Events Environment', in Nicole Ferdinand and Paul J. Kitchin, *Events Management. An International Approach*. London: Sage: 2012. 23-47.

Hensens, Wouter, *Hotel Rating through Guest Feedback*. PhD. Thesis. Port Elisabeth: Nelson Mandela Metropolitan University, 2010.

Lattin, Gerald W., *The Lodging and Food Service Industry*. Lansing: American Hotel & Lodging Association, 1998 and 2005.

Pine, J. & Gilmore, J. (1999). *The Experience Economy: Work Is Theatre & Every Business a Stage*. Boston: Harvard Business School Press.

Reic, Irma, 'The Development of the Corporate Events Sector', in Nicole Ferdinand and Paul J. Kitchin, *Events Management. An International Approach*. London: Sage: 2012. 267-296.

Rushmore, Stephen. *Hotel Investments Handbook*. Mineola: HVS, 2004.

Schlosser, Eric. *Fast Food Nation. What the All-American Meal Is Doing to the World*. London: Penguin, 2001)

Spang, Rebecca L., *The Invention of the Restaurant*. Cambridge: Harvard University Press, 2000.

Wit, B. de, & Meyer, R. (2010). *Strategy, process, content, context, an international perspective* (4th ed.). Andover: South-Western Cengage Learning.

Chapter 4

Gunnarsson, J., & Blohm, O. (2003) *Hostmanship. The art of making people feel welcome*. Stockholm: Dialogos Förlag.

Mandelbaum, A. (1990), Transl. The Odyssey of Homer

Pine, J. & Gilmore, J. (1999). *The Experience Economy: Work Is Theatre & Every Business a Stage*. Boston: Harvard Business School Press.

Slattery, P. (2002). Finding the Hospitality Industry. *Journal of Hospitality, Leisure, Sport and Tourism Education,* 1(1), 19-28.

Chapter 5

Ackoff, R, & Emery, F. (1972). *On Purposeful Systems: An Interdisciplinary Analysis of Individual and Social Behavior as a System of Purposeful Events*. Chicago: Aldine-Atherton.

Bergman, A., Karlsson, J.C., & Axelsson, J. (2010). Truth claims and explanatory claims – An ontological typology of futures studies, *Futures, 42*(8) 857-865.

Boswijk, A., Peelen, E., & Olthof, S. (2012). *Economy van Experiences*. Amsterdam: Pearson Benelux B.V.

Cline. R.S. (2005). *The Hotel Organization of the Future: Capitalizing on Change is Prelude to Success*. Retrieved from http://www.hotel-online.com/Trends/Andersen/future.html.

Gansky, L. (2010). *The Mesh, Why the Future of Business is Sharing*. New York, NY: Portfolio Penguin.

Godin, S. (1999). *Permission Marketing: turning strangers into friends, and friends into customers*. New York: Simon & Schuster.

Howe, N. & Strauss, W. (1991). *Generations: The History of America's Future, 1584 to 2069*. New York, NY: Harper Perennial.

Howe, N. & Strauss, W. (2007). The next 20 years: how customer and workforce attitudes will evolve, *Harvard Business Review, 85*(7), 41-52.

Matthewman, J. (2011). *The Rise of the Global Nomad: How to Manage the New Professional in Order to Gain Recovery and Maximize Future Growth*. London: Kogan Page.

Nino Caceres, L., Rijnders, R., Lub, X.D. (2012). *Horeca Future Moments. Trends report for the Dutch hospitality industry*. Zoetermeer: Bedrijfschap Horeca & Catering.

Osterwalder, A. & Pigneur P. (2010). *Business Model Generation, A Handbook for Visionaries, Game Changers and Challengers*. Amsterdam: Modderman.

Raymond, M. (2010). *The Trend Forecasters Handbook*. London: Laurence King.

Shirky, C. (2008). *Here Comes Everybody: How Change Happens when People Come Together*. London: Penguin.

Stickdorn, M. & Schneider, J. (2011). *This is Service Design Thinking: Basics, Tools, Cases*. Amsterdam: BIS.

Zaltman, G (2003). *How customers think, Essential insights into the mind of the market*. Boston: Harvard Business School.

Chapter 6

Aaker, D.A. (1991). *Managing brand equity: Capitalising on the value of a brand name*. New York: Free Press.

Beck, U. (1992). *Risk society: Towards a new modernity* (Vol. 17). SAGE Publications Limited.

Brady, M.K., & Cronin Jr, J. J. (2001). Some new thoughts on conceptualizing perceived service quality: a hierarchical approach. *The Journal of Marketing,* 34-49.

Bitner, M.J. (1992). Servicescapes: the impact of physical surroundings on customers and employees. *The Journal of Marketing,* 57-71.

Bitner, M.J., Booms, B. H., & Mohr, L. A. (1994). Critical service encounters: the employee's viewpoint. *The Journal of Marketing,* 95-106.

Customer Service Institute of Australia (2011). *Creating a deliberate signature service experience*. Retrieved from http://www.csia.com.au/ ?page_id=467.

Falk, J.J.H., & Dierking, L. D. (1992). *The museum experience*. Howells House

Grove, S.J., & Fisk, R.P. (1983). The dramaturgy of services exchange: an analytical framework for services marketing. *Emerging perspectives on services marketing,* 45-9.

Kapferer, J.N. (1997). *Strategic brand management: creating and sustaining brand equity long term,* 2. Auflage. London.

Kotler, P., & Armstrong, G. (2004). *Principles of marketing*, 10th International Edition. London.

Mowen, J.C., & Minor, M. (1998). *Consumer behavior*. NJ: Englewood Cliffs.

Parasuraman, A., Zeithaml, V.A., & Berry, L. L. (1985). A conceptual model of service quality and its implications for future research. *The Journal of Marketing*, 41-50.

Pine, B. J., & Gilmore, J.H. (1999). *The experience economy: work is theatre & every business a stage*. Boston: Harvard Business Press.

Schechner, R. (1988). *Performance theory*. Routledge.

Stickdorn, M., & Schneider, J. (2010). *This is service design thinking: Basics–tools–cases*. Amsterdam: BIS Publishers.

Stuart, F.I., & Tax, S. (2004). Toward an integrative approach to designing service experiences: lessons learned from the theatre. *Journal of Operations Management*, 22(6), 609-627.

Veblen, T., & Almy, C. (1899). *The theory of the leisure class: An economic study in the evolution of institutions*. Macmillan & Company Limited.

Wilson, A., Zeithaml, V. A., Bitner, M. J. and Gremler, D. D. (2008), *Services Marketing: Integrating Customer Focus Across the Firm (1st European Edition)*. New York: McGraw-Hill.

Chapter 7

Blanchard, K., Fowler, S., & Hawkins, L. (2005). *Self Leadership & the One minute manager*. New York, NY: William Morrow.

Brady, M.K., & Cronin Jr., J.J. (2001). Some New Thoughts on Conceptualizing Perceived Service Quality: A Hierarchical Approach, *The Journal of Marketing*, 65(3), 34-49

Brunner-Sperdin, A. & Peters, M. (2008). What influences guests' emotions ? The case of high-quality hotels, *International Journal of Tourism Research*, 11(2), 171–183.

Chiang, C.F. & Jang, S.S. (2008). An Expectancy Theory model for hotel employees. *International Journal of Hospitality Management* 27, 313–322.

Kapferer, J.N. (1998). *Strategic Brand Management, 2nd edition*. New York, NY: Kogan Page.

Kusluvan, S., Kusluvan, Z., Ilhan, I., & Buyruk, L. (2010). The Human Dimension A Review of Human Resources Management Issues in the Tourism and Hospitality Industry. *Cornell Hospitality Quarterly, 51*(2), 171-214.

Luft, J. & Ingham, H. (1955). The Johari window, a graphic model of interpersonal awareness. *Proceedings of the western training laboratory in group development*. Los Angeles, CA: UCLA.

Mehrabian, A. (1981). *Silent messages: Implicit communication of emotions and attitudes (2nd ed.)*. Belmont, CA: Wadsworth.

Mohsin, A., McIntosh, A. & Cave, J. (2005). Expectations of the service experience offered by restaurants and cafes in Hamilton. *Journal of Hospitality and Tourism Management, 12* (2), 108-116.

Oxford Dictionaries (2013). *Oxford Dictionary of English*. Oxford: Oxford University.

Schnapper, M. (1975). Nonverbal Communication and the Intercultural Encounter. In J.E. Jones & V.W. Pfeiffer (Eds.), *Annual Handbook for Group Facilitator* (pp. 155-159). La Jolla, CA: University Associates.

Solomon, M.R., Suprenant, C., Czepiel, J.A., & Gutman, E.G. (1985). A role theory perspective on dyadic interactions: The service encounter. *Journal of Marketing, 49*(1), 99-111.

Schulz von Thun, F. (1981). *Miteinander reden 1. Störungen und Klärungen. Allgemeine Psychologie der Kommunikation*. Berlin: Rowohlt.

Schulz von Thun, F. (2010). *Hoe bedoelt u ?* Groningen: Noordhoff Uitgevers.

Spencer, L. & Spencer, S. (1993). *Competence at Work: Models for superior performance*. New York: John Wiley & Sons Inc.

Vroom, V.H. (1964). *Work and Motivation*. New York, NY: Wiley.

Watzlawick, P. (2011). *Pragmatics of Human Communication*. New York, NY: WW Norton & Co.

Winsted, K.F. (2003). Service Behaviors and Customer Satisfaction. In S. Kusluvan (Ed.), *Managing employee attitudes and behaviors in the tourism and hospitality industry* (pp. 201-209). New York, NY: Nova Science.

Chapter 8

Anderson, C.K. (2012). The Impact of Social Media on Lodging Performance *Cornell Hospitality Report* (Vol. 12). Ithaca: Cornell University.

Bugg Holloway, B., & Beatty, S.E. (2008). Satisfiers and Dissatisfiers in the Online Environment A Critical Incident Assessment. *Journal of Service Research, 10*(4), 347-364.

Cronin Jr, J.J., Brady, M.K., & Hult, G.T.M. (2000). Assessing the effects of quality, value, and customer satisfaction on consumer behavioral intentions in service environments. *Journal of Retailing, 76*(2), 193-218.

Crosby, P.B. (1979). *Quality is free: The art of making quality certain*. New York: McGraw-Hill.

Grandey, A.A., Fisk, G.M., Mattila, A.S., Jansen, K.J., & Sideman, L.A. (2005). Is 'service with a smile' enough ? Authenticity of positive displays during service encounters. *Organizational Behavior and Human Decision Processes, 96*(1), 38-55.

Grönroos, C. (1987). Developing the service offering – A Source of Competitive Advantage. In C. Surprenant (Ed.), *Add Value to Your Service* (pp. 81-85). Chicago: American Marketing Association.

Grönroos, C. (2001). The perceived service quality concept – a mistake ? *Managing Service Quality, 11*(3), 150-152.

Johnston, R. (1995). The determinants of service quality: satisfiers and dissatisfiers. *International Journal of Service Industry Management, 6*(5), 53-71.

Litvin, S.W., Goldsmith, R.E., & Pan, B. (2008). Electronic word-of-mouth in hospitality and tourism management. *Tourism Management, 29*(3), 458-468.

Maister, D.H. (1985). The psychology of waiting lines. In M.R. Solomon, J.A. Czepiel & C.F. Surprenant (Eds.), *The service encounter: managing employee/customer interaction in service businesses*. Lexington, MA: Lexington Books.

Meuter, M.L., Ostrom, A.L., Roundtree, R.I., & Bitner, M.J. (2000). Self-service technologies: understanding customer satisfaction with technology-based service encounters. *The Journal of Marketing, 64*(3), 50-64.

Parasuraman, A., Zeithaml, V.A., & Berry, L.L. (1985). A conceptual model of service quality and its implications for future research. *The Journal of Marketing*, 41-50.

Rodie, A., & Kleine, S. (2000). Customer Participation in Services Production and Delivery. In T.A. Swartz & D. Iacobucci (Eds.), *Handbook of Services Marketing & Management* (pp. 111-127). Thousand Oaks, CA: Sage Publications, Inc.

Schmitt, B.H., Dube, L., & Leclerc, F. (1992). Intrusions into waiting lines: does the queue constitute a social system ? *Journal of Personality and Social Psychology, 63*(5), 806-815.

Shea, L., Enghagen, L., & Khullar, A. (2004). Internet Diffusion of an E-Complaint. *Journal of Travel & Tourism Marketing, 17*(2-3), 145-165.

Stauss, B., & Weinlich, B. (1997). Process-oriented measurement of service quality: Applying the sequential incident technique. *European Journal of Marketing, 31*(1), 33-55.

Chapter 9

Avolio, B.J. & Bass, B.M. (2002). *Developing Potential Across a Full Range of Leadership. Cases on Transactional and Transformational Leadership,* London, UK: Lawrence Erlbaum.

Bass, B.M. & Riggio, R.E. (2006). *Transformational Leadership* (2nd Ed.), London, UK: Lawrence Erlbaum.

Blake, R., & Mouton, J. (1985). *The Management Grid*. Austin, TX: Scientific Methods.

Burns, J.M. (1978). *Leadership*. New York, NY: Harper & Row.

Boyatzis, R.E. (1982). *The Competent Manager: A Model for Effective Performance*. New York, NY, Wiley.

Burgoyne, J.G. (1993). 'The Competence Movement: Issues, Stakeholders and Prospects', *Personnel Review*, 22(6), 6 – 13.

Eisner, S.P. (2005). 'Managing Generation Y', *SAM Advanced Management Journal*, 8(2), 4-15.

Gursoy, D., Maier, T. A., & Chi, C. G. (2008). Generational differences: An examination of work values and generational gaps in the hospitality workforce. *International Journal of Hospitality Management*, 27(3), 448-458.

Hersey, P., & Blanchard, K. (1988). *Management of organizational behavior: Utilizing human resources* (5th ed.). Englewood Cliffs, NJ: Prentice Hall.

Hoffmann, T. (1999) 'The meanings of competency', *Journal of European Industrial Training*, 23(6), 275 – 286.

Jochems, A. (2011). 'Je eigen hotel door de ogen van een collega [Your own hotel through the eyes of a colleague]', *Horeca Info*, Vol. 4, pp. 4-6.

McClelland, D.C. (1973). 'Testing for competence rather than for intelligence.' *American Psychologist*, 28(1), 1-14.

Mullins, L.J. (2010). *Management and Organisational Behavior*. 9th Edition. Englewood Cliffs, NJ: Prentice Hall.

Robbins, S.R., Judge, T.A. (2009). *Organizational Behavior* (13th Ed.). Upper Saddle River, NJ: Pearson/Prentice-Hall.

Zhao, H. & Seibert, S.E. (2006). 'The Big Five Personality Dimensions and Entrepreneurial Status: A Meta-Analytical Review', *Journal of Applied Psychology*, 91(2), 259-271.

Acknowledgments

p. 12	Imageselect, Wassenaar
p. 14	Shutterstock, New York
p. 15	Wentworth Mansion (inkoop 100,- USD)
p. 10, 16	iStock, Calgary
p. 18	iStock, Calgary
p. 20	iStock, Calgary
p. 21	iStock, Calgary
p. 24	iStock, Calgary
p. 29	iStock, Calgary
p. 10, 31	iStock, Calgary
p. 40	iStock, Calgary
p. 44	iStock, Calgary
p. 38, 51	iStock, Calgary
p. 38, 54	Imageselect, Wassenaar
p. 68	iStock, Calgary
p. 75	iStock, Calgary
p. 66, 78	Corbis/Hollandse Hoogte, Amsterdam
p. 80	iStock, Calgary
p. 83	Imageselect, Wassenaar
p. 84	Corbis/Hollandse Hoogte, Amsterdam
p. 86	iStock, Calgary
p. 88	iStock, Calgary
p. 91	iStock, Calgary
p. 100	iStock, Calgary
p. 107	www.booking.com
p. 107	www.booking.com
p. 109	Imageselect, Wassenaar
p. 98, 110	Imageselect, Wassenaar
p. 98, 110	Imageselect, Wassenaar
p. 112	iStock, Calgary
p. 117	iStock, Calgary
p. 122, 124	Corbis/Hollandse Hoogte, Amsterdam
p. 130	Corbis/Hollandse Hoogte, Amsterdam
p. 122, 132	iStock, Calgary
p. 134	www.thegreenhousehotel.co.uk
p. 142	www.moxyhotels.com
p. 149	Corbis/Hollandse Hoogte, Amsterdam
p. 154	Photodisc
p. 156	www.citizenm.com
p. 154, 167	Corbis/Hollandse Hoogte, Amsterdam
p. 171	www.newyork.com
p. 171	www.trendland.com
p. 188, 190	Imageselect, Wassenaar

p. 193	iStock, Calgary
p. 201	Corbis/Hollandse Hoogte, Amsterdam
p. 188, 206	Imageselect, Wassenaar
p. 214, 216	Corbis/Hollandse Hoogte, Amsterdam
p. 214, 219	iStock, Calgary
p. 220	Imageselect, Wassenaar
p. 221	iStock, Calgary
p. 225	Marriott Hotels of Brussels
p. 230	iStock, Calgary
p. 231	Imageselect, Wassenaar
p. 234	iStock, Calgary
p. 236	iStock, Calgary
p. 245	Imageselect, Wassenaar
p. 250, 252	Polaris Images/Hollandse Hoogte, Amsterdam
p. 250, 262	iStock, Calgary
p. 265	iStock, Calgary

About the editors and authors

The following editors and authors have contributed to this book:

▶ **Rob Blomme, PhD**
Professor
Research Centre
Hotelschool The Hague
The Hague, The Netherlands

▶ **Jeroen Bosman, MSc**
Senior Lecturer
Hotelschool The Hague
The Hague, The Netherlands

▶ **Hans Breuker, MA**
Senior Lecturer
Hospitality Business School
Saxion University of Applied Sciences
Deventer, The Netherlands

▶ **Michael N. Chibili, MSc, MA**
Senior Lecturer
Stenden Hotel Management School
Stenden University of Applied Sciences
Leeuwarden, The Netherlands

▶ **John Hornby, BCom, CPT, MBSI**
Senior Lecturer & Researcher
Research Unit in Service Studies
Stenden Hotel Management School
Stenden University of Applied Sciences
Leeuwarden, The Netherlands

▶ **Stan Josephi, MPhil**
Senior Lecturer
Academy of Hotel Management
Breda University of Applied Sciences
Breda, The Netherlands

▶ **Alinda Kokkinou, PhD**
Senior Lecturer & Graduation
    Coordinator
Avans School of International Studies
Avans University of Applied Sciences
Breda, The Netherlands

▶ **Annemieke de Korte, MSc**
Senior Lecturer
Hotelschool The Hague
The Hague, The Netherlands

▶ **Xander Lub, PhD**
Research Programme Manager
    Hospitality
Hospitality Business School
Saxion University of Applied Sciences
Deventer, The Netherlands

▶ **Frans Melissen, PhD**
Senior Lecturer & Manager of
    Research
Academy of Hotel Management
Breda University of Applied Sciences
Breda, The Netherlands

▶ **Rob Nierse, MSc**
Trainer & Senior Lecturer
Hotelschool The Hague
The Hague, The Netherlands

▶ **Jeroen Oskam, PhD**
Programme Manager
European Tourism Futures
    Institute (ETFI)
Stenden University of Applied
    Sciences
Leeuwarden, The Netherlands

► **Monique van Prooijen-Lander, MSc**
Senior Lecturer & Portfolio Manager
Hotelschool The Hague
The Hague, The Netherlands

► **Jean-Pierre van der Rest, PhD**
Professor & Director
Research Centre
Hotelschool The Hague
The Hague, The Netherlands

► **Bert Smit, MSc**
Senior Lecturer
Academy of Hotel Management
Breda University of Applied Sciences
Breda, The Netherlands

► **Lesley Tomaszewski, PhD**
Senior Lecturer
Hospitality Business School
Saxion University of Applied Sciences
Deventer, The Netherlands

► **Rolf van der Veer, MSc**
Trainer & Senior Lecturer
Hotelschool The Hague
The Hague, The Netherlands

► **Tjeerd Zandberg, MSc**
Lecturer & Researcher
Hotel Management School & European
 Tourism Futures Institute (ETFI)
Stenden University of Applied
 Sciences
Leeuwarden, The Netherlands

Index